7

VALE OF LAUGHTER

THE AUTHOR AND RALPH LYNN IN 1932

BEN TRAVERS

Vale of Laughter

An Autobiography

LONDON
GEOFFREY BLES
1957

Printed in Great Britain by
Wyman & Sons Ltd Fakenham
for the publishers
Geoffrey Bles Ltd
52 Doughty Street London WC1

First published in 1957

What is he buzzing in my ears?
"Now that I come to die,
"Do I view the world as a vale of tears?"
Ah, reverend sir, not I.

ROBERT BROWNING

ACKNOWLEDGEMENTS

The author wishes to express his thanks to Messrs. John Lane the Bodley Head Ltd., for permission to quote the two extracts from *The Fram* and *The Sub-Contractor* by Stephen Leacock. He also wishes to thank Messrs. Robert Hale Ltd., for permission to quote an extract from the foreword to *Yours Indubitably* by Robertson Hare. The original caricature of John Lane by Max Beerbohm is the property of Sir Allen Lane who has kindly lent it for reproduction in this book,

CONTENTS

I.   BEN THUMB   1

II.   PINERO IN MALACCA   25

III.   BURLINGTON ARCADIA   49

IV.   PILOT IRVING   74

V.   "QUITE EXTRAORDINARY PEOPLE"   97

VI.   ALDWYCH ENTRÉE   118

VII.   ALDWYCH HEYDAY   143

VIII.   THE SECOND AMBITION   172

IX.   THE GOLDFISH   197

X.   REMAINDER BISCUIT   224

     INDEX   245

ILLUSTRATIONS

The Author and Ralph Lynn in 1932   *Frontispiece*

facing page

John Lane. A caricature by Max Beerbohm	52
Stephen Leacock	68
The Cuckoo air torpedo	84
The Author in a box-kite trainer	84
The standard Aldwych victimisation scene	148
"Death"—a *Thark* scene	164
The Author with Tom Walls and Ralph Lynn on location	164
Chapman's catch at Brisbane, 1928	180
Sydney Cricket Ground, 1928	180
Scene from *Banana Ridge*	196
The Australian Cricket Team, 1930	196

CHAPTER I

Ben Thumb

"Yoᴜ'ʟʟ finish on the gallers," said Mr. Gulliver. He put the stick back into his desk and slammed down the lid. I call it a stick, but it was a strange implement like an outsized paper-knife, tapering to a thin flat end for the mere slapping down of minor offences, but with a great round thick solid end for the punishment of real wickedness. I had just had the thick end.

Mr. Gulliver delivered his awful Dickensian prophecy on my untidy blond head and I crept back to my humble place in the form, an insignificant, woefully grubby Eton-collared creature, uncommonly little for the age of ten. I remember sniffing back the tears as I went, in order to show the rest of the form that these were a propitiatory sop to Mr. Gulliver and not in any way to be attributed to the pain of the beating.

There was no uniformity of type among assistant prep-school masters in the 1890's. The Abbey School, Beckenham, boasted several unique and formidable specimens on its staff but Mr. Gulliver towered above the lot. I wonder how old he really was at that time and really how large? A red waistcoat with brass buttons spread at its base to embrace his notable paunch. He sported that popular feature of his time, the moustache luxuriant, and this he had a habit of twirling with both hands simultaneously with the sweeping action of one swimming. His rapid, if slightly provincial, voice was thunderous. His breath would whistle through his great nostrils like a steam exhaust. His eyes were swords.

I

To me he quite genuinely filled the role of the earthly and visible representation of that God of Wrath whom our infant minds were so incessantly impelled to observe and fear. It was the rule of fear, based on religious precept, which in those days at school—and in many cases at home—formed the basis of a child's upbringing. It was fear and fear alone which had brought me that beating. For what had been my crime?

This—we did sums; and when we had done what always seemed a grievously large number of these sums Mr. Gulliver read out the answers and we had to put R or W against each particular sum in our exercise books. The results were not questioned; it was left to our honour to report whether we'd got the sums right or wrong. Mr. Gulliver was wont to read out the answers rather too quickly for my convenience, and, that morning, getting characteristically a little behindhand and muddled in my R-and-W marking, I had, quite inadvertently and in my eagerness to catch up, slipped in an R where a W should have been. Some devilish intuition prompted Mr. Gulliver to forgo his credulous custom and to inspect our books. Now, sixty years later, I recall most vividly the agony of that moment when he discovered my fallacious R. His face came slowly round into mine. His green eyes pierced me with accusation. The huge moustache bristled down upon me and the great hairy nostrils whistled condemnation. I tried to gibber some honest explanation but the panic of the culprit unmasked must have been only too clear. I suppose I realised the utter hopelessness of trying to assert the real truth and sticking to it. I shrank back from that awful Kitchener moustache and my quivering lips found themselves somehow blurting out the pitiable false admission, "Oh, s-s-sir; the temptation was too great."

Such cowardly surrender to intimidation seems contemptible even in a frightened ten-year-old. But I have never really got

2

much better in this respect. My reason for capitulating to Mr. Gulliver was probably much the same reason as that which, throughout my professional career, has instructed my immediate acceptance of modification—and even downright rejection—of my work, with the implication that anyone else knows better than I do. Indeed, my reason for beginning with Mr. Gulliver, his terrifying beating and even more terrifying (if momentarily less important) forecast of my finish, is that the incident supplies a perfect example of that inability to assert myself, which has been my most marked characteristic throughout the whole of my sensitive seventy years.

Of course I heartily forgive Mr. Gulliver—well, I could scarcely blame him, could I? He has, needless to say, been long since borne to the tomb, escorted thither, I understand, by Messrs. Haig & Haig. I also forgive Harrowing, who alone of the form treated my self-confessed chicanery to a sneer of contempt. Harrowing later, I believe, became a pretty big pot somewhere in the north of England. I seem even to remember hearing that he had received a knighthood. I expect so.

I think the main cause of my being so lacking in self-assertion, at any rate during my boyhood, was my size. I have said I was uncommonly little. I was, in fact, tiny. On my first afternoon at the Abbey School the boys gathered round me in the playground and hooted with laughter. About five years later, when I was taken to Charterhouse to sit for my entrance exam by the second master of the Abbey, "Pickle" Ellis, I remember taking anxious stock of the other candidates from the other schools to see whether, by some heaven-sent boon, any one of them was nearly as small as I. None was. They were all towering; many of them a good deal taller than "Pickle" Ellis. Even when I left Charterhouse after a normal span of four years, I honestly believe I was still

3

the smallest boy there. I put on a few saving inches when I was nineteen and twenty; and although I have always been a short man I have been spared the tribulation of going through life as the midget I was in my schooldays. Indeed, when I finished growing I had the satisfaction of knowing that I was well above the average height in some countries, such as Japan and Wales. And, in any case, in my old age I have long ceased to worry about it. But, my goodness, all through my boyhood how bitterly conscious I was of my littleness. And in those cruel days I was seldom given the chance to forget it.

This physical peculiarity and other peculiarities which will emerge have made me, all through my life, extremely sensitive to criticism. But to none more keenly than to self-criticism. The self-criticism which has caused to be destroyed unproffered about seventy per cent of all I have ever written comes defensively into action at this point. I have examined dozens and dozens of reminiscences of childhoods of elderly autobiographers. Many of them have been illustrated with reproductions of tintypes of fathers or, worse, grandfathers, their faces obscured by jungle and their legs by corrugations; of mothers with their overworked bosoms firmly encased in the final satin and decorated with a long-service locket. The text of such passages in such autobiographies is, in my experience, duller than anything in modern literature, always excepting, of course, handbooks telling one how to do or make anything. I have, therefore, decided, so far as my childhood is concerned, to try to confine myself to those experiences which really influenced the formation of my queer character or which seem to provide a comment on the same. But a detailed description of my home life at Bromley, Kent, and at Caterham, Surrey, at the turn of the century, no. And anyone who saw Queen Victoria's Diamond Jubilee will not need me to tell him or her about it. Anybody who did not see it will not want me to.

Nevertheless, occasional extraneous incidents crop up in the memory and will not be denied. Many others still living must have seen W. G. Grace make a century; but the one he made for me tended to corroborate the legend that he so enjoyed batting that he preferred to go on batting. When I was watching him he appeared to be caught at short leg when he had made about fifteen, and Brockwell, the Surrey professional, threw the ball up delightedly. But the Old Man turned on Brockwell, flourishing his bat as though to fell him, while the umpires looked on, awestruck and mute. Grace then continued his innings. Ranji was at the other end. He made a hundred too. I saw one of the two matches featuring both W. G. and that promising beginner, Jack Hobbs. I also saw the most famous of all innings in the most classic of all Test Matches, G. L. Jessop's 104 against Australia at the Oval in 1902, with the astonishing spectacle of staid and frugal citizens sending their boater hats sailing like boomerangs into the blue.

If my encounter with Mr. Gulliver brought to light a permanently weak spot in my nature another of a different kind became lamentably established round about the same period. My mother took me to stay at a small hotel at Martin Mill, near St. Margaret's Bay. It was not the summer holiday season; I had had flu and wanted a short rest cure or something; and we were the only visitors except for a mysterious Italian gentleman and one or two of his stooges. He was engaged in some fantastic attempts to communicate with another stooge who was stationed in the South Foreland Lightship. So I can claim to have witnessed the earliest successful experiments by Marconi in wireless telegraphy. He was well disposed to me and quite ready to be cordial and explanatory, and most boys would have revelled in the experience. So it seems a

B 5

pity that it should have happened to one who was totally lacking the right sort of intelligence to appreciate or, candidly, to bother in the least about, what the eager little Italian gentleman was up to.

But all through my life I have remained absolutely devoid of the slightest knowledge of or interest in any sort or kind of applied science or practical mechanics. I once, late in life, learnt how to deal with a fuse; but I have long forgotten what one does, and now, if a fuse occurs in my cottage, I have to light a candle and telephone for the man. I can't even change an electric light bulb without qualms of suspense and strange contortions of countenance. I am incapable of undertaking elementary household repairs, such as altering whatever it is that regulates the temperature of a frigidaire, or that thermostat thing which heats up the water in the cupboard tank. If adjustments are needed the man has to come, and even if the man tells me what to do another time I forget what he says almost instantaneously. The inner workings of such things as cars, bicycles, lawn-mowers and ball-cocks in lavatory cisterns are beyond my ken. The last time I tried to remove something which was stopping up the pipe of the kitchen sink I flooded the whole ground floor of my cottage. Any attempt on my part to do any sort of repair work to a clock or a radio set, a gramophone or a camera always results in complete wreckage. Minor and familiar objects in everyday use by other people become impractical directly I try to use them. Nobody has ever invented a fountain-pen which will not saturate my fingers with ink; nor have I ever been able to operate any type of cigarette lighter. In the 1914–18 war I achieved and deserved a reputation as a pilot of aeroplanes and after the war I was awarded the Air Force Cross for my services. But I was never able to grasp more than the barest rudiments of the principle of the internal combustion engine. I dare say I could have forced myself to learn; the trouble was that I simply didn't want to—the thing bored me. All that section of my mentality which should be applied to practical knowledge has been permanently sealed off into a derelict depository of pessimistic laziness.

Let me hastily add that I am glad to be like this. It has saved me a vast amount of objectionable labour. It has meant that those associated with me have never looked to me to mend things and would much rather I didn't try to. It has also meant the casual but welcome employment of a large number of the men. Perhaps, like my lack of self-assertion, the whole trouble can be traced to my childhood; perhaps my littleness and timidity created in me a chronic fear of taking the initiative. But this seems a far-fetched explanation and I think I have always simply been one of those individuals who are not meant by nature to do clever things beneath the floor-boards of rooms or the bonnets of cars.

I have said that religion played a great part in my early education, and this was generally true of any small boy of my time. When he went to a prep school they took him and doused him with what was referred to comprehensively as "scripture". There was a great deal of religion, too, in my home life; and while I am eternally grateful for this, it is interesting nowadays to recall the tremendous importance which was attached to the Old Testament as a guide to infant morality. Special emphasis was placed on the stories of the more drastic judgments of the Almighty on some of the refractory characters of Hebrew lore. *Line Upon Line,* a children's book of the period (I believe it is still in circulation) had a place in every self-respecting nursery. It related some of the Old Testament incidents in the form of a series of cautionary verses and certainly pulled no punches in emphasising what the God of Wrath had in store for the unruly. I recall a typical extract:

When children in their wicked play
   Mocked old Elisha so,
And bade the prophet go his way—
   'Go up, thou baldhead, go'—
God quickly stopped their wanton sport
   And sent two raging bears,
Who tore them limb from limb apart,
   'Mid blood and groans and tears.

But my mother, though meticulous in her piety and devotions, was full of loving-kindness and understanding. She also loved to dissolve into tears of laughter at the smallest excuse, and anybody who can do this is naturally endearing. No, the favourite haunt of the God of Wrath was this Abbey School, Beckenham, where we were encouraged to imagine him as a stern and rather irritable Almighty, glaring into our everyday lapses from rectitude and fairly itching to administer vengeance. The effect this had on our infant minds may be illustrated by one of my regular and secret observances. Every night at my bedside in my little cubicle I used to kneel and repeat the word "perhaps" hundreds of times—"perhaps, perhaps, perhaps, perhaps"—catching my breath in my haste. This was done in order to qualify the number of lies I might have told in the course of the day and thus to foil the impending punishment which was being cooked up for me by the God of Wrath, who, it must be admitted, was always conveniently dilatory in taking action.

Today, I believe, religious teaching and observance at schools are run on reasonable and necessary lines. The Sunday programme at the Abbey School sixty years ago seems almost incredible now. We had, of course, to don our Eton suits and top-hats and in them to go to both morning and evening services at the local parish church. We had also to learn by heart both the collect and either the epistle or gospel

appointed for that particular Sunday and to be able to repeat
them to the headmaster in the course of the day. A pretty
sharp punishment awaited anybody who was uncertain of his
lines. But this by no means completed the spiritual schedule
of the day of rest. Immediately after we had dragged our
melancholy boots back from morning church the headmaster
recapitulated the sermon, giving us notes on the same; and
during the afternoon each boy had to write out his own version
of this invariably obscure and dreary discourse.

Boys at public schools had their full whack of religious
observance of Sundays too. The result was that a large number of young men, once their liberty was gained, cut free from
religion with a whoop of delight. On me, in my littleness and
susceptibility, that preposterous Abbey School curriculum
made a deep and lasting impression. My belief has by now,
it is true, assumed a form of assured optimism, but that has
been the combined results of the passage of time and of
introspection, encouraged by my devotion to the works of
Robert Browning. And, in any case, it owed much more to
the influences of home than to those of school. Nevertheless, I
feel that the Abbey School's tough insistence on "scripture"
can, in my case at any rate, claim some results. And I dare say
that, according to their lights, the old fire-eating scholastic
apostles of wrath were sincere in their desire to pitchfork
righteousness into the bosoms of the Victorian young. Only
—rather after the manner of the modern journalist who works
on the principle that bad news is news—they were inclined to
concentrate on the terrors attending the Fall rather than on
the blessings of the Redemption.

I left Charterhouse in 1904 by mutual consent.

I had distinguished myself at nothing; but if I never got into
the Upper School I never got into any real disgrace. All the
masters I came across disliked me intensely, with the exception

of Leonard Huxley, father of Aldous and Julian Huxley, who was a saint among schoolmasters. By way of a belated justification of Mr. Gulliver I cheated freely whenever I had the chance and struggled through my Latin and Greek lessons with the aid of cribs. This was the universal practice, but the cribs were apt to let you down, being hard to memorise and extravagantly flowery in phraseology. I remember an incident in the Middle Fourth at Charterhouse, presided over by Charlie Weekes, the original housemaster of Weekites. A boy named Cuffe, of Hodgsonites, was attempting to translate Latin prose into English and making singularly heavy weather of it. At last, however, he reached a word he knew: "Inquit". "Inquit, sir," he translated ingratiatingly, "quoth he." "Oh, did he indeed?" replied Charlie Weekes. "Bring me your crib, and you shall see the headmaster tomorrow morning."

Those were the days when it was the custom at Charterhouse to rag any master who lent himself to the treatment. I was too timid to take part in the ragging myself but I always lent keen moral support to others more adventurous. Incredible liberties were taken in Noon's mathematical hours and in the form-rooms of those unfortunate Frenchmen whom the tradition of their time appointed to teach their native language to British schoolboys. I can recall many outrageous scenes, but memory dwells most fondly on some of the simpler examples of insubordination. I still revere the boy who, having nothing whatever to do with the class in progress, which was being taken at the moment by M. Petilleau, marched boldly into the room, seized the blackboard duster, blew his nose in it and marched out again. I like, too, the boy who smashed a beaker in Ozzy Slater's stinks form. "Who did that?" "I'm afraid I did, sir." "How did you manage to do that?" "Well, like this, sir," and another beaker crashed to the floor· Or Hancock, of Robinites, as a new boy and anxious, no doubt, to establish his reputation; when, in the maths form of

C. O. Tuckey (well known in lawn-tennis circles) he interrupted some very long-winded and chop-licking exposition of
a problem from Tuckey by rising to his feet with the brief but
sweeping comment, "Balls."

So I cribbed and cheated my time away and also was always
ready to lend a hand in any bullying that might be going on.
I was too small to do any active bullying but I was active
enough in standing by and shouting the odds. I was, I
suppose, just like any other normally insignificant boy of that
time, except, of course, for my height. But what had happened to the God of Wrath? Oh, he was still there, though
growing less imminently menacing. I was deeply penitent
for my sins, but I made not the slightest effort to reform; and
soon, when I became further involved with the problems and
practices of puberty, I was convinced that, though I still said
my prayers every night, God must have become absolutely
fed up with me. My only hope was that I might be able to
do a lot of good later in life, which might go towards balancing
things up a bit. I quite definitely formed the opinion that I
was an outstanding specimen of iniquity and that my case
called for special consideration and dispensation from on high.
I dare say there are many who, like me, heard at that age the
voice of conscience reporting this melancholy state of affairs.
I dare say there are some who, like me, hear its echoes still.

So I left school. What next? What was to be done with
me? For the pursuit of what occupation did I show zeal?
Obviously I didn't possess any qualifications but I might at
least show zeal. But what for? Did I know anything about
anything?

Yes. I was intensely interested in two subjects and had a
really exceptional knowledge of them both. Well, come
along; this sounds more hopeful. Ah, but the knowledge was
purely superficial and not technical. Never mind—if my

knowledge and enthusiasm were so remarkable, technique could perhaps be acquired.

No, that only applied to one of the subjects. The other was merely a hobby. What hobby?

Just as later on, during the wars, some schoolboys (whom I personally always found rather repellent) were infallibly expert in spotting types of aircraft and specifying their individual features, without of course being able to fly them, so I, without being able to play it very well, knew absolutely all there was to know about cricket.

If my intense love of the game had been increased by my experiences at Charterhouse, intense it must have been. I was too little for my moderate ability to be taken seriously. Moreover, my house was at low ebb during my time and, as always happens, the draw for house matches pitted us against the strongest side in the school. I fielded in one house match while G. T. Branston and C. A. L. Payne made respectively 199 and 214 in a first-wicket stand. Branston afterwards played for Nottinghamshire and Payne for Middlesex. Next year, the Weekite captain, a slaughterer named E. L. Firth, made over 300 against us and Martin Kemp-Welch, who commanded the 7th Queen's in the first war, made over 100. I was a good field; and so I should have been with all that practice. In the first of these two house matches one of the opposing side was C. V. L. Hooman, and in the second I was caught off H. A. Gilbert. Though F. L. Fane and E. G. Wynyard both played for England, Hooman was probably the best batsman Charterhouse ever produced until Peter May came along; and Gilbert certainly remains the best bowler. He was picked for England against Australia once but was left out on the morning of the Test Match.

Although nothing was less likely than that I should become a first-class cricketer myself I knew all there was to know about the performances of those who were. And when, in my summer holidays, I wasn't watching cricket I used to spend most of my time playing test matches with my brother on the lawn. So great was our enthusiasm that we would studiously imitate the idiosyncrasies and batting stances and bowling actions of each player in turn. And when, a few years ago, I played similar test matches on the lawn of my Somerset garden with a nine-year-old friend and grew rather exasperated as he kept driving my spinners into the ditch and he would say, "Sorry, I say; but what can you expect? After all, I am Hutton"; then the exasperation became whelmed in a sudden glow of affectionate memory of the days when I myself was Tom Hayward and Victor Trumper. I suppose that the encouragement and employment of such puerile pretence (and I still joined in and pretended quite earnestly that I was Keith Miller) seems preposterous and even reprehensible in the eyes of the Welfare State youth-mentor of the present day. But imagination is the spark which fires a child's enchantments; and any pinch-lipped materialists who ridicule such make-believe and cause a child to feel babyish and shame-faced ought to be shown what a millstone is really like and told to think it over.

Why, not only in childhood but all through life imagination is the refreshment of the soul. For some curious psychological reason we are ashamed to admit it; but do not you indulge in daydreams like I do in moments of relaxation, when trying to get to sleep or during a walk—not that I ever go for a walk if I can help it? Do you not play for England at Lord's or the lead in an all-star Shakespearian show at a command performance, or introduce a budget, or lead for the defence in a sensational murder trial (preferably with a Society lady in the dock) or conduct the London Philharmonia Orchestra, or preach the funeral oration over some illustrious corpse in Westminster Abbey, or clean up a poker game against an expert gang of international crooks, or follow Ambition along whatever radiant path she happens to beckon? I always have done so and do so still. I expect we all do; and that is why *The Secret Life of Walter Mitty* is just about the greatest short story ever written.

And the other subject? The Stage to be sure. Just as I knew my cricket matches and my cricketers so I knew my plays and my actors and actresses; their histories, their personalities, their potentialities.

In those days the stage-door was the portal of a great Mystery. From it emerged shadowy figures belonging to the Mystery, mysterious still in the gas-light as the waiting hansom jingled them away into the further mystery of their private lives; great ghosts and minor ghosts. What ecstasy beyond compare to penetrate the Mystery and share with them the inner secrets which lay beyond the portal. And the unspeakable joy of participating (with marked success) in the exploits and rewards of their calling. Couldn't I—extrinsic expert as I already was—couldn't I go on the stage?

Unqualified? But I could soon qualify, couldn't I? My poor parents, how gently and smilingly they disapproved. No doubt they recognised my yearnings as a normal process of adolescence, since every boy and girl has at one time or another wanted to go on the stage. And like so many of them I suspected that mine was an unique genius which would quickly find recognised and regular employment in the West End without too much bother about any tedious and unnecessary training.

Oh, of course, I was quite willing to do anything that was adjudged advisable about getting to know the ropes; but the trouble was that in 1904 the stage was not only, as now, a hazardous profession; there were social and moral objections too. It was true that Irving had transformed the profession into one which a member of the genteel class could adopt without serious loss of prestige, and the Hawtreys and Maudes and Vanbrughs and many others of impeccably patrician background had availed themselves of this early feature of the social revolution.   But——

In my case the ambition was quite a genuine one and I still think that I might have become a successful character-actor when once some well-qualified taskmaster had corrected my notion that I had nothing much to learn.   So I expect that, at first, I received my parents' amiable rebuff with the moody and injured obstinacy peculiar to youths at the spotty and pebbles-in-the-dust-kicking stage.   Because you will be glad to hear that one day my father lost his toleration of my exigent mumbles and disclosed in a memorable exclamation his real objections to them: "To be an actor—just think of it —and marry a ballet girl who kicks up her legs."

This does not mean that my father was uncommonly narrow-minded or puritanical.   He was simply giving graphic expression to the average family man's conjecture of stage life.   He didn't know what went on there, any more than he knew the details of what went on in the harem of an Oriental potentate.   Simply the stage was a branch of contemporary life which was alleged to contain snares and pitfalls from which it was his duty to protect his progeny.

Nor did the average family man presume that every one of the musical-comedy ladies whom he so eagerly studied through his sixpennyworth of hired opera glasses must necessarily be for sale or rent; he harboured a strong suspicion that she was but he didn't presume it.   But actresses were a female race apart and an actress was a young woman whose choice of profession disqualified her from being a desirable wife for the son of a man of my father's class; just as being a parlourmaid or a barmaid would have disqualified her.   And the son, if he were allowed to try to explore the same unknown country while still groping about amid the fallibilities of adolescence,

15

would fall headlong into the clutches of one of the kickers-up-of-legs who were admittedly the most attractive of the whole conglomeration.

In justice to my father this, in my case, might well have happened. Not only was I normally susceptible; I was so infernally conscientious. While half of me was being continuously pestered by the claims of physical development and imaginative raptures of their fulfilment, the other half was haunted by the conviction that these yearnings were sinful and was vainly trying to harness them to justification. And, since my upbringing had taught me that the only justification was to be found in marriage, it is quite likely I would have fallen flat for the first chorus girl pathetic enough to appeal to my conscience and alluring enough to give dispensation to that persistent and problematical other half. The old Abbey "scripture" training was still bearing fruit. I yearned for marriage partly because I wanted to go to heaven and partly because I wanted to go to bed. I must say this still seems to me to be a pretty reasonable point of view.

Although my father and mother regarded the stage, as a profession, with the suspicion proper to their traditions, they used to enjoy going to the theatre and did nothing to discourage my delight in it. From the age of about nine I was taken year after year to Drury Lane pantomime in the Dan Leno and Herbert Campbell days. Leno was the outstanding low comedian of his day. He was the protagonist of the "little man in adversity" line of business, in which later on Charles Chaplin attained unsurpassed and unsurpassable pre-eminence. Herbert Campbell was his accessory, the massive, stentorian, street-corner-commentator type—a sort of Bud Flanagan of his day, with the bonhomie but lacking the benignity of Bud Flanagan. The book of the words of the panto was always obtainable of the attendant, price one shilling, and every year, a day or two after seeing the show I was word-perfect. The comedians took some licence with the script in the knockabout scenes, but the printed version was in rhymed couplets throughout. Custom has staled this procedure. In any pantomime I have seen in recent years the rhymed couplet seems to have become the exclusive perquisite of the good fairy. But they maintained the classic formula at Old Drury and even Dan Leno and Herbert Campbell had to observe it for the most part. I recall a sample fragment:

Princess (Miss Decima Moore): Who are these people?

Widow Twankey (Mr. Dan Leno): I'm this young man's mother.

Abanazer (Mr. Herbert Campbell): And I'm this young man's mother's husband's brother.

Princess: Thank you, good woman, for your kind attention.

Widow Twankey: Don't mention it.

Abanazer: It's nothing much to mention.

Bromley was only a short journey on the London, Chatham and Dover Railway (or was it the South Eastern?) to the Crystal Palace, a heaven of awesome Victorian bliss, fed by long corridors of paradise full of tactful statuary, crestfallen palm-trees, portentous echoes and a curious pervading smell which I have never encountered since and which to my memory suggests a vast consecrated urinal. Once, but only once (I dare say my dear mother found it a little vulgar) we were taken to the Crystal Palace pantomime, which, while a pale reflection of the coruscation of Drury Lane, was rich in material for the budding actor. For weeks on end my sister and I would perform, in the drawing-room after tea, the rather dispassionate introductory love scene:

17

Fatima (discovered alone): O Selim! Selim's where?
                (*Enter Selim.*)

Selim: Here in your arms.
Fatima: Oh, Selim; I've such dreadful news to tell,
         My father is so poor.
Selim: I know that well.
         I too am poor; so being equals there,
         To claim my pretty Fatima I dare.
Fatima: Alas my Selim, that is not his plan.
         He wants to marry me to some rich man,
         Who'll pay his debts and set him free
         From poverty.
Selim: No, no; this must not be.
         You love me, Fatima?
Fatima: You know I do.
Selim: I care for naught if I am loved by you.

The final chorus, in a spirit of grateful abandon, glossed over the creditable observance paid to rhyming:

> Bluebeard, our pantomime, is nearly o'er;
> Selim to Fatima is joined once more:
> Good-bye, but don't forget to come again
> And see Bluebeard, our Crystal Palace pantomime.

On one of our visits to the Crystal Palace I saw Blondin. He walked along a wire which was stretched across the inside of the roof, duly pausing half-way to halt his little stove and cook his habitual omelet. I suppose there have since been wirewalkers more accomplished and far more spectacular than Blondin, but I am glad I saw him. He was one of those great protagonists whose names, in my lifetime, Tradition has crowned as the predominant personality in his own particular line. Irving, W. G. Grace, Captain Webb, John Roberts, Crippen—names leap to the mind.

It was during the Christmas holidays of 1897 that I was taken to see my first straight play, *One Summer's Day*, by H. V. Esmond, at the Comedy Theatre. Charles Hawtrey, then in his early forties, played the lead and opposite him, in an ingénue part was an enchantress named Eva Moore, sister of the Decima Moore who was the inquisitive princess at Drury Lane. The little boy who sat nail-biting in an intensity of admiration and delight at that matinée was to have his own first play produced by that same Charles Hawtrey a quarter of a century later. And a few years later still that same Eva Moore, admirably cast for some gracious maternal part in one of my films, was to be told quite truthfully that her youthful loveliness had awakened the first perplexing instinct of the beast in my nature.

There is a tendency to discount the enthusiasm of old gentlemen for the plays and players and playwrights of their youth. "You were at the impressionable age, remember." But what is sometimes overlooked is that the theatre-going public was at its impressionable age. The stage play was not, as it has now become, a representation of life. It was a dramatisation of life. It had to be, if it were to satisfy the aims and demands of the public in seeking entertainment. Nobody would pay twopence at a box-office to see a mere representation of life. People wanted to be elevated from the experiences and transactions of the humdrum daily routine by the colourful excitements of exaggeration. And while, in this respect, Pinero and his school catered for the sophisticated, the melodramas satisfied the good old bourgeois appetite for the starkly sensational. Their merit lay in the fact that the absurdities of situation and dialogue, far from presenting encumbrance or embarrassment, were designedly used to provide the whole structure and animation of the show.

One of the theatres I was taken to during my school holidays was the Lyceum in 1901—I was fifteen years old by then,

Here William Gillette was portraying Sherlock Holmes. The play is chiefly remembered now in connection with the appearance of Charles Chaplin as the Buttons. None of the audience then could have conceived the idea that that perky little Buttons was to become the greatest figure in the entertainment history of this century. "Billy," said Mr. Holmes, "you're a good boy, Billy." "Yessir. Thank you, sir," said Billy—I remember it was the curtain line of one of the acts. Not even Mr. Sherlock Holmes ever delivered himself of a shrewder judgment; but I was not primarily concerned with Billy, though I thought he was jolly good. For I and the rest of the audience were being borne upwards to the pinnacle of excitement, the scene in the Stepney Gas Chamber.

Holmes stands surrounded by Moriarty's evil gang. Escape, he is told, is impossible. "There are so many means of escape," he replies, "that I find it difficult to choose which to employ. On the whole, however, I think this may prove the most effective." So saying, he seizes a chair and smashes it down on the oil-lamp which provides the Gas Chamber's sole illumination. The scene is plunged into darkness, through which gleams one tiny pin-point of light up-stage. "Follow him by the light of his cigar," cries one of the thugs. Then another thug manages somehow (I forget how and I doubt whether any of the audience noticed) to light the whole place up again. Mr. Holmes stands by the open door, the key of which he has secured during the black-out. The thugs crouch before him baffled and he surveys them with an air of commanding and almost leisurely imperturbability. "Gentlemen," he announces, "I left my cigar upon the window-sill. Good evening." He bows courteously and departs. Curtain.

This is a good example of the old melodramatic method. The thugs are within handy distance and could easily spring on Mr. Holmes and detain him. But the public of those days was not going to worry about questions of reality or likelihood so long as it were given its full measure of suspense. So the baffled thugs remain stricken in their respective attitudes of bafflement. One of them, I remember, nearly over-balanced. As for Mr. Holmes, he positively dallied in order to emphasise the scorn and superiority of deliberation in peril. He did not even save a quite appreciable quota of his valuable time by saying "Gentlemen". "Gentle men," said he. Splendid old melodrama.

Splendid old Theatre and its protagonists. I look back on them now with just the same enthusiasm as I looked on them as a boy. I can remember and analyse many of those absurdities and exaggerations which made them such glorious fun for me and such refreshment for the jolly unsophisticated public of their day and I would not have had them different. "When reds and blues were indeed red and blue"—I am thankful to have known those days.

I never seem to go to a modern play in which, at one point or other, the husband does not say to the wife or the wife say to the husband, "I wish you wouldn't try to dramatise the thing." And the boy who sat quivering with excitement in his pit seat nearly sixty years ago writhes gently in his stall and murmurs to himself, "I wish you would."

But away with thoughts of the theatre and back once more to the problem of my future. What was to be done with me? Soon, if rather half-heartedly, the inevitable decision was reached. There was only one answer in a case like mine. I should go into business.

Go into business. This was another of those comprehensive, indefinite terms common to the period. The course universally adopted by or forced upon young men who left school in a general condition of inadaptability for anything in particular was to go into business. There was, of course, here and there a case of some competent and eager young man, sparkling with commercial aptitude and loud with fore-knowledge, who dashed into business and graduated almost immediately as someone in the City. But more common were the louts of scholastic non-success and prospective non-promise who, after spending a few months of post-educational mooning, drifted *faute de mieux* into business. I was one of these. Except that I was still far too little to be described as a lout.

An opening for me could be found in the venerable and venerated firm of Joseph Travers & Sons Ltd., of which my father was by now a director. But still he hesitated and temporised, uneasy perhaps about my capability even to go into business. Once more he showed, in this respect, a sagacity about me which I have only appreciated in retrospect. Then someone—my mother perhaps—thought it might be a good idea if I learnt German before I went into business. I don't think anybody ever stopped to reason why it might be a good idea. Perhaps it was considered unlikely that business and I were made for each other. If I went to Dresden for six months to learn German I might become inspired by some unsuspected design for making a respectable career. Anyhow, my father welcomed the suggestion that I should go to Dresden and shortly afterwards I was being seasick in a Hook of Holland steamboat.

Why Dresden? Because Dresden was where my sister had just been finished. This period of history was the peak-hour of the Continental finishing establishments for the daughters of British respectability. These establishments housed ten or twelve of them at a time in some appropriately cultural resort. There their social life was regulated in a manner which was a sort of moral hangover from the Victorian code of maidenly refinement. They were escorted in huddled parties to the more innocuous productions at the Opera House. Florid and carefully scrutinised native Turveydrops extolled, for pauper fees, their excruciating exercises at the music-stand and the easel.

My sister, having finished being finished at Dresden, was now back home and had reached the stage of being courted by the Caterham curate and accompanying him on the piano while he sang "Down the Vale" in the drawing-room after dinner. So it was easy to get references about suitable accommodation for me during my sojourn in Dresden. The name recommended, that of Mr. Virgin and his sisters, the Misses Virgin, must have been almost a reference in itself. But I fear the sojourn was not spent in learning German or even in trying to. My mind was still almost entirely occupied by my ambition for the theatre. I had yielded to my parents' decision about it philosophically enough. But I still fostered the ambition in my imagination, just as one of Saki's little boys fosters a forbidden pet animal and fondles it in wanton delicious secrecy.

And Dresden was a perfect cosseting-place for the ambition. The atmosphere of stolid, accepted, unspectacular romance was ideal for indolence and daydreams. The reason why I never made any real effort to learn German was because I discovered that pursuits which could be classified as education were highly enjoyable—a thing which had never occurred to me as being possible. Duty became pleasure. It had never been so before. It was not, for several years, to be so again. But in Dresden I went the rounds of duty eagerly. I lingered in the picture galleries and doffed my little bowler hat in the special sanctuary allotted to the Sistine Madonna. But my one continuous, concentrated delight was in the Opera House.

In the Opera House itself. It was not that I had any real appreciation of the operas, of one of the leading orchestras of Europe under von Schüch, or of the sweeping magnificence of the Brünhilde of von Wittich. I sat through interminable performances of *The Ring* and pretended, even to myself, that I was immensely edified. I saw and heard Richard Strauss conduct the first performance of his *Symphony Domestika* and didn't allow myself to tell myself that I'd rather have had five minutes of Lionel Monckton. No, to me the appeal was the appeal made by the place itself. And why? Because it was the appeal of Theatre. The whole atmosphere and setting, the discreetly garish lighting, the plush opulence of the auditorium and foyer, thrilled me with the realisation that here was Entertainment in its most grandiose form. Theatre *in excelsis*.

The leading performers did not contribute much to this valuation. And from the little that I have seen of opera singers at work ever since I have formed the conclusion that even in the few cases when they can act they disdain to try to, preferring to devote all their attention to the vociferous side of the job. They are further handicapped, as were my Dresden singers, by developing the most extraordinary shapes, which are mercilessly exposed by costume designers. In the case of tenors it seems an invariable rule that the bigger their tummies the tighter their trunks. But in Dresden I found only encouragement in the obvious shortcomings of the performers considered purely as actors. I exposed them to myself by frequent demonstrations to myself of my own greatly superior, and indeed quite brilliant, conceptions of how these things should be done.

The limited periods of actual drama contained in the Wagnerian operas became material for my secret rehearsal in my little bedroom at Mr. Virgin's. I treated myself to a masterly performance of Beckmesser's inept rendering of the *Preislied*. I lay on the floor at the foot of my bed and sprang suddenly to consciousness, a Tannhaüser flung back into the reality of the thraldom of Venus from his disturbing dream of the echoes of church bells. *"Zu viel zu viel! O das ich nün erwachte!"* Selim was on his way up.

CHAPTER II

Pinero in Malacca

THERE is no record of the rank or duties allotted to young Travers in the army of William of Normandy; but he was important enough to get his name included among those of the Conqueror's henchmen on the Roll of Battle Abbey. All that is certain about him is that he survived Hastings and that he then decided or was commanded to remain and settle in this country. And I am very glad that he did or was.

His progeny, so far as study of my family tree can determine, seem to have conformed to a decent, unspectacular and modestly patrician standard throughout the subsequent centuries. None of them until my great-grandfather appeared on the scene achieved eminence in any field. One of them appears to have had the ambition to do so, but he was executed for high treason and his successors evidently decided to revert to the doldrums of unadventurous propriety. Shakespeare, in *Henry IV*, Part 2, named one of his characters Travers, but found no more exalted job for him than that of retainer to the Earl of Northumberland; so it would seem that whoever the Travers was that Shakespeare knew must have suggested to the poet's mind a somewhat unpretentious type of individual.

For the past eight generations the eldest son of the eldest son of my branch of the family has been christened Benjamin. The fourth of these Benjamins was my great-grandfather. He had an exceedingly successful career and eventually became Sergeant-Surgeon to Queen Victoria and President of the Royal College of Surgeons, where a copy of his bust still stands at the foot of the main staircase. (I possess the sculptor's original.) He made a large fortune, every penny of which he spent on horses—not on racehorses but on the fashionable glories of equipage. This extravagance must, however, have been an elaborate hobby; for he was of so retiring a disposition that he firmly declined the baronetcy proffered by grateful Majesty to her Sergeant for never performing an operation on her.

He must have inherited, as my father inherited and I strongly inherit, an instinctive tendency to self-effacement. In my case it takes the form of a sort of chronic deep-seated shyness. Throughout the whole of my life I have experienced occasions of delight and success in other people's company, but I have never been able to rid myself of a compelling intuitive desire to avoid it. I have been and still am and always will be like a little boy standing at the water's edge and unable to summon the courage to jump in, who later revels with such enjoyment and confidence that he can't be persuaded to come out. Only in my case the initial timidity is so compelling that I have often lacked the resolution to take the first plunge. This is odd, because I have always had the reputation of being a genial and acceptable little man and, indeed, quite an entertaining one; for I have, in my time, enjoyed considerable success as an after-dinner speaker. And I don't have to force or assume spontaneity and ease; once in the water I am full of animation and enjoyment. It is just that I shrink from the idea of getting in.

Moreover, I always suffered from a feeling of quite genuine surprise and embarrassment when people told me they had heard of me professionally and made reference to my plays or films. I appeared pleased and affable and forthcoming and chuckled the right sort of chuckle when they quoted, incorrectly, their favourite lines; and I readily told the elderly ladies what sort of a man Tom Walls really was, and the middle-aged gentlemen my latest information about Winifred Shotter. But this was only an amiable form of bluff; I was afflicted all the time by this queer feeling of shy reluctance— a sort of timidity of my own self-consciousness. I still suffer from it in my old age. I never go into one of my clubs without feeling it. I suppose that is why I so seldom go into one of my clubs.

This has nothing to do with modesty. On the contrary, I dare say it is a sensitive and frustrating form of egotism. Nor do I think that mine is at all an uncommon case. I suspect that a large number of the most sociable people I know are not essentially social.

The real *I* has, in fact, always been the grown-up edition of the Dresden seventeen-year-older, genuine and happy only in his own hopes and reflections and intimidated by everybody including himself. But in those days, at any rate, I did have some reason to feel shy as I was still so constantly aware of my accursed littleness. The psalmist complains to his Maker of certain dreadful characters who persist in following him about saying, "Aha. Aha." I felt that in my case the psalmist had provided a perfect illustration of public-school society in general. And when I found myself in the British society of Dresden, consisting mainly of hordes of adolescent misses and their female finishers, I could not escape the conviction that my size and personality were made the pet subjects of their intimate dormitory giggles.

I challenged this misgiving by falling desperately in love with the leading and least abashed giggler of all Miss Gilderdale's coterie. And though her conversation consisted almost entirely of references to some objectionable young friend of hers at home, who was remarkably tall and handsome and had just got into the Harrow eleven, I managed to get myself photographed with her by some obliging third party. Somewhere I still have a pathetic faded snapshot, showing me standing beside her in the snow and raising myself on the tips of my toes in a vain effort to assume the proportions of an adequate suitor.

I might have recovered a bit of prestige with the Miss Gilderdale girls and with myself had I known that within the next two or three months I was going to be standing in the streets of Tokio, watching a regiment being marched away to the Russo-Japanese war; or hanging breathlessly to the wooden railings in the Cave of the Winds at Niagara; or witnessing my father being approached by a confident and jocular pimp in the heated flamboyance of Coney Island. ("Good heavens above, let's get out of this place.") But such experiences were indeed to form part of the next brief, kaleidoscopic chapter of my history. My father was being sent by the firm to visit various branches and agencies abroad. In a characteristic impulse of generosity he made up his mind to take me with him. By this I don't mean to imply that I think he wished he hadn't. My father was a very impulsive man, but all his impulses were generous, especially where his children were concerned.

It would be hard to imagine a more entrancing prelude to the daunting prospect of going into business. I do not, however, propose to offer any description of this round trip to a generation which can get to any part of the world in twenty-four hours and which, moreover, has become so sated with geography that it adjusts its visits to the pictures so as to avoid the travelogue. The tour was of great subsequent value to my imagination, but not of great immediate value to my self-assurance. At seventeen I was obviously the wrong gender for the sociabilities of ocean liners. It was all a wonderful dream, the report of which is still contained in an old dusty diary whose precocities are better left where they are.

The dream ended. I found myself one morning in stark

and gloomy reality, sitting in a stopping train to the City on the London, Brighton and South Coast Railway; creeping, in fact, like snail unwillingly to business.

At 119 Cannon Street in the City of London stand the premises of Messrs. Joseph Travers & Sons Ltd., wholesale grocers. Centuries old, the firm has survived unscathed the tides of markets and the vicissitudes of manners; even as its building survived, practically unscathed, the bombs which wrecked Cannon Street Station on the other side of the road. Stately premises, in which as you pass through the heavy swinging doors from outside you are confronted by a wide hospitable staircase which winds up from the busy but un-hurried activities of the spacious sale-room. Proud premises, dignifying the pursuance of wholesale grocery in an atmosphere which still seems graced by the ghosts of silk-hatted, snuff-blown old brokers from the Mincing Lane of the last century and of prosperous, whiskered retail grocers, poring with deferential sagacity over the displayed samples of spices and currants. The murmur of voices which accompanies rather than breaks the silence of the sale-room puts one in mind of those subdued echoes of information and comment which inhabit a cathedral in out-of-service hours. And, just as the clang of a clumsily handled door or the racket of a cleaner's fallen broom brings a jerk to the enshrined senses of the cathedral visitor, so in the sanctuary of that sale-room one's ears may suddenly be assailed by the occasional strident, if justifiable, sibilations of some enraptured tea-taster.

The whole place still remains through the years, to my great personal pride and admiration, a lasting and successful monu-ment of the long-lost charm and courtesy of Commerce.

When I joined the firm at the end of the year 1904 it had been a limited liability company for about a quarter of a century, but the family interest in it was still active and remains so to-day. My younger brother was not only the present Chairman but, at the time of his death in 1956, was serving his allotted term of three years as Chairman of the London Chamber of Commerce. His career shows how capricious is heredity; for he showed an immediate and exceptional capacity as a business man, for which role I never possessed the smallest inkling of intelligence nor the inclination to acquire it. I suppose he inherited all my share of my father's business sense as well as his own and a bit extra and, God bless him, he was welcome to it.

At the time I write about my father had recently been elected to the Board of Directors, to which he must have brought a refreshing breath of middle-aged vigour. And of tonsorial refinement. Beards, beards decorated the board-room then. Mr. J. Innes Rogers, the Chairman, had the beard of one of those patriarchs who figure in Victorian engravings depicting some of the more dramatic incidents of the Old Testament. Mr. J. Lindsay Travers had been brought up in Australia and had brought half the bush home with him. Mr. Wilkinson had one of those wire beards. Mr. Stableforth was not actually chin-bearded but cherished whiskers which sprouted diagonally from his cheeks, as from those of an impassioned cat.

The Board, steeped as it was in tradition to the very inkpots, showed in my case a reformed sense of democratic discrimination. For on my joining the firm I was cast for the meanest office-boy's job in the whole extensive catalogue of office-boys. "Let him start at the bottom." "An excellent principle." "Learn the business in detail." "Work his way up."

For the first stage I worked my way not up but rather along. I had to proceed every morning along various City streets into the mudsplashed recesses of the Borough and Whitechapel, carrying documents to warehouses. At these warehouses some extremely vulgar and abrupt gentry did something to

the documents and then handed them back to me to return
to the place whence I came. This process was known as
tea-clearing. I had no more idea what it was all about then
than I have now and vice versa. And it seems that I didn't
proceed to the warehouses and hand over the documents and
bring them back again very well. I was conscientious, goodness knows. I never dallied. I often ran. But after I had
done about six months of it I was transferred. To another
superior job? No. What really happened I was never told,
but my imagination has always pictured the scene at the
Board meeting at which the decision about my immediate
future was discussed and settled.

"Travers," said the Chairman ominously to my father.
"This son of yours. Mullins has failed to furnish me with any
very glowing reports of his tea-clearing."

Mr. Wilkinson spread his hands. "If a lad cannot tea-clear
what can he do?" he asked rhetorically.

"Why, what does Mullins say about the boy, Chairman?"
inquired my father.

"Nay, nay," replied the latter reprovingly. "Heaven—if
I may venture to mention Heaven in the board-room—forbid
that I should stoop to so undignified a procedure as to pump
Mullins. But the fact remains——"

A critical silence followed. Then Mr. Stableforth ventured
a comment, shaking his head throughout it. "I shrink with
horror from the thought that the name of Travers should
become dishonoured in our midst. Even," he added, "in
tea-clearing circles."

"Especially," put in Mr. Wilkinson briskly, "in tea-clearing
circles."

"Nay, stay," exclaimed the Chairman excitedly. "I believe
I have conceived a solution."

He grasped both arms of his chair and swung his heavy
stomach watch-chain in the direction of the Secretary.

"Which, pray," he demanded, "is the Colonial branch of this firm which is situated farthest from these headquarters?"

The Secretary dithered. "Well, sir—if I may venture—on the spur of the moment, sir, I should presume Singapore. But if I may be allowed to verify my——"

"Singapore—that'll do," cried the Chairman triumphantly. He expelled a breath of satisfaction so vigorous that it whirled his whole beard into a can-can of triumph. "Singapore, eh? So be it—Singapore."

At that period in the history of the Colonial Empire Singapore was regarded as an appropriate grave for the superior type of white man. Thither even an occasional woman went forth from England, to face the dual ordeal of marriage and the Malayan climate, with a smile of courageous determination in the manner of one taking leave of home to go and minister to a leper colony. Male candidates for jobs in Singapore had to possess two essential qualities. To be a gentleman was a recognised attribute in those days; so they had to be gentlemanly and they had to be healthy. For though, of course, nobody could be expected to remain healthy for long in that death-trap it was felt that he could at least remain a gentleman.

They were sent out for a primary spell of five years. Their directors at home, few of whom had ever been farther east than the Norfolk Broads, always gave them a few parting words of semi-jocular advice and encouragement but shook hands with them in a very final sort of way, as they bade them good-bye and wished them jolly good luck.

On his arrival in Singapore the novice received further and more practical advice from his local boss. There were three cardinal don'ts. Never venture out of doors in the daytime, even if it were to cross the road to the post office, without wearing your topee. Never fail to take some sort of violent physical exercise in the brief interval between office hours and sundown. Never (here the local boss's voice deepened an octave in intensity) never have any sort of social intercourse, however refined, with a young woman suspected of being Eurasian. The contemplation of any unrefined form of intercourse with an Eurasian girl heaven forbid. This was all right so far as purely native girls were concerned. Indeed, a good many people seemed to think that this was what native girls were principally for. But there was a universal theory that every Eurasian girl's sole ambition was to exercise some Delilah-like allurement over the young Englishman with the intention of beguiling him into marriage.

One eminent old merchant steered clear of the climatic death-trap long enough to retire home with a large fortune. His son succeeded him in the Singapore business. The son married an Eurasian girl. He was not only sacked from his job but completely cut off and obliterated from the parental memory. I knew a young fellow, an assistant in the Singapore branch of a prominent firm, who was suspected of having a mild love affair with an Eurasian. Cabled messages flashed between his local manager and the head office and he was homeward bound on a liner within the week. Today marriages between European and Chinese girls are quite common events. Such a marriage was unheard of then; never the twain were known to meet at the altar. But even if they had it wouldn't have been looked upon as so disastrous as a meeting between the one and the one-half.

I was unfortunate in my boss—a pallid, contumelious young Lerpudian with gold-rimmed glasses and a settled manner of sneering self-sufficiency. He studiously disdained everybody else in his office and as studiously ignored any society outside it. He had discovered and married an elderly arty Englishwoman who had been a medical missionary and had written a play in blank verse called *The Travail of his Soul*. This excursion on her part into the realms of my own true and lasting interests brought me a certain preliminary respect for the lady, deplorable as, on examination, *The Travail of his Soul* proved to be. But the husband was not long in forming his own opinion of the latest specimen that had been foisted upon him by the London headquarters. And finding my very presence an offence he consigned me to Malacca. "You may as well do nothing in Malacca as in Singapore," he remarked coldly.

No doubt he was justified. I was ignorant of the first rudiments of business and although in the Singapore office I was only given the simplest jobs on hand I always made the most sickening hash of them. I remember having to start a new ledger recording the shipments of pineapples. It doesn't sound very difficult, but by the time I had completed the first page of the ledger the whole thing was in such a ghastly mess that I decided to tear the page out and start all over again. Apparently it was a dire offence to mutilate a ledger in this way, as I dare say those who enjoy a knowledge of commercial ethics will agree; but to me it seemed to be a reasonable enough measure in the interests of neat and practicable ledger-keeping. I only mention the incident as evidence of my business capabilities.

One member of the staff of the Singapore office shuffles again noisily up the wooden stairs in his wooden shoes at the smallest prompting of memory. Mr. Hood Seck was an old Chinese employed by the firm to collect the sums of money falling due from the various local retailers. My morning greeting to him and his reply never varied:

"Good morning, Mr. Hood Seck. How are you this morning?"

"I am very sick."

"Oh, dear. What's the matter with you?"

"Womit. And parting minutely."

34

I never discovered what were the exact implications of this distressing and persistent form of malady. But they did not prevent Mr. Hood Seck from appropriating a large proportion of the money he was paid by the retailers and hoodwinking the firm's book-keeper in the process. Needless to add that, owing I suppose to some temporary shortage of staff, I was in charge of the books at the time. And when eventually I cottoned on to Mr. Hood Seck's little game and visited his private house with a policeman, some obscure agency had already tipped him the ominous wink and the expedient pill conveyed him to his ancestors just as retribution hammered at his door.

I remember Montero too. Montero was the office-boy and his written application for a day's leave of absence may be quoted as a good example of typical Eurasian Malapropism:

"Sir. I write to ask please leave away from today's office business in order to get a nurse for my mother who is expecting a burst."

Malacca proved my manager right in his estimate. It was the best place in the world in which to do nothing. It was the capital of Lotus-land. But tucked away among the buildings on its dreamy sea-front was, surprisingly, a small public library. In this, even more surprisingly, I discovered an old uniform set of the plays of A. W. Pinero. I fell upon them with the rapturous excitement of Ben Gunn lighting upon the treasure of Captain Flint. Work? Business? With such reading on hand who could be guilty of so unworthy a consideration as trying to do business? Especially in Malacca.

They were not merely plays to read. Each one of them was a guide-book to the technique of stagecraft. I studied them as such, counting and noting the number of speeches and the method of plot and character development. I discovered for myself the real secret of Pinero's mastery, namely his attention in every line and in every scene to the importance of climax.

My ambition was suddenly switched to another department in the realm of the theatre. My genius as an actor should be sacrificed. My gifts as interpreter would have to yield to my gifts as a creator. I would be a dramatist.

I suppose that those books containing Pinero's plays are all back permanently on the quiet library shelves everywhere. Stagey old museum pieces they may appear today. But the present-day playwright still relies, for many of his most successful effects, on the rules laid down and illustrated by that great old master craftsman. Over twenty years after my months of happy browsing in Malacca I was elected a member of the Dramatists' Club, of which Pinero was still President. I told him of my experience, adding truthfully that I had learnt more from him than from all other playwrights put together. I then made bold to ask him which of his plays was his own favourite. He put his face close to mine, as deaf people do when imparting a confidence, and said, "My boy, the one that made the most money."

In addition to reading the plays of Pinero and occasionally selling a case of canned salmon to a Chinese grocer who probably never paid for it, I went in for a certain amount of exercise in Malacca. For I had taken the three vital don'ts very seriously. So wearing my topee and avoiding the very sight of an Eurasian girl I played cricket and golf with the handful of local government officials and occasional visiting planters. I was always a bad golfer, violently erratic and so self-conscious as to be prone to black-outs of confidence at important moments. Indeed, my golf was always a direct confutation of the statement so often used by defending counsel in criminal cases that no man suddenly becomes very base.

But the golf-course at Malacca suited my game, as it handi-capped the correct and skilful player in favour of the mere brutal slogger. Unlike most golf-courses it was not a grass course; it was a sand course. On the so-called greens the sand was trodden down by a band of hired natives to a somewhat lower though by no means smoother surface than the fairways. There was no need for bunkers, as the course itself was one large bunker; but half-way down the middle of the first fairway was an abandoned Hindu temple. The local rule stated that it was legitimate to go through as well as round or over this hazard.

Another unusual local rule established a player's handicap. A new member on joining played a trial round against Mackenzie. Mackenzie was a government schoolmaster of very dour aspect; and any domineering superiority which he exercised over his small native pupils was nothing compared with that which he exercised over his fellow civil servants, Dr. Knaggs or Mr. Firmstone; or over any half-inebriated planter who engaged him on the links. So, after your trial round, Mackenzie told you what your handicap was; and there was no appeal against this until subsequent form modified his estimate. I played well in my trial round and, receiving a few strokes, managed to halve my match with Mackenzie. This shook Mackenzie pretty badly and as my final putt bounced confi-dently over a number of footprints into the hole he impressively announced, "Your hundicup's foor." It has always been a gratification to me in golfing circles to be able to say, "No, I never play nowadays but I was moderately useful earlier on. At one time I was a four-handicap man." I don't add that after my next round against Mackenzie my handicap went in one bound up to sixteen.

I have visited Malacca again quite recently. It has changed comparatively little during the last fifty years. I don't believe that even the mooted new film studios and prodigious electric power-station will, if they materialise, alter the character of the place. I hope not, for ever since I first knew it I have always had a special devotion for a town so dedicated to lethargy that the very waves seem to lap its tranquil sands in slow motion.

I found many of the same old streets with the same old shops with the same old smells. The same old customs too. On my return visit I was a guest at a dinner-party given by a Chinese millionaire on the twenty-course scale favoured by his venerated ancestors. Chinese cooking is superb when applied to civilised ingredients and a lot of Europeans have developed a partiality for Chinese food as well. Personally I find this absolutely filthy. At the banquet in question I managed to shove most of my share between myself and the edge of the table with my chopsticks. I was then careful to spread it about the floor among the feet of other guests by deft footwork of my own, lest my host should afterwards regard me as an ingrate or his staff should despise me as an untidy eater. A course of pigeons promised a welcome relief from the bits of bat and snake which had preceded it; but the host rather spoiled it for me by a demonstration of real Chinese epicurism. He begged the heads of the pigeons from his guests and munched them up, one by one, complete with eyes and beak. He washed each head down with a draught of neat brandy which he drank like beer from a long tumbler.

In contrast to Malacca other Malayan centres have developed enormously. Today I would guess that the Spotted Dog in Kuala Lumpur covers an area larger than any other club in the world, and although it is still fronted by a good broad padang, the teeming city, featuring every style of architecture known to man, crowds it on all sides and spreads its tentacles miles into the surrounding countryside. When I went to spend a night at Ipoh in 1907 it possessed only one small rest-house which was full up; so I had to go to a Chinese hotel, where the manager and his staff doped my dinner soup and peacefully robbed me of all my money while I reposed. The one European police officer in the district seemed incapable of taking any action beyond rating the hotel manager for not having left me enough to pay for a couple of stengah whisky sodas. On my last visit to the country a friend told me that Ipoh had developed quite as much as Kuala Lumpur in every way. So I decided to give Ipoh a miss.

My banishment to Malacca by the boss was not a long-term sentence. I put in long spells of residence in Singapore as well. During one of these I decided to try out a small hotel which had just been opened down on the coast some miles from the office. My rickshaw-puller, O Chye Lah, was unbeaten on the road and would undoubtedly have won an Olympic marathon if he had been allowed to tow his rickshaw over the course; and he enthusiastically agreed to trundle me to and fro. So I was one of the four original residents of the Sea View Hotel. It was then a superior shack standing in a grove of coco-nut palms through which a narrow track branched off the one coastwise road. It had half a dozen bedrooms, a combined bar and billiard-room and a stout Eurasian manager who cheated left-handed at snooker. To-day, with its long exotically decorated lounge running parallel to the sea and linking its two raucous ballrooms, it looks more like an importation from an ultra-ambitious American film studio than any other interior I have ever seen.

This serves as a spur-of-the-moment example of the outward visible change which has taken place in Singapore over fifty years. But there have been many more vital changes than the mere modernisation of its buildings. Chief of them is the emancipation of the native and almost as important has been the mancipation of the mosquito. Western science has seeped into the whole life system. When I left Singapore in 1908 there were two privately owned cars and two motor fire-engines in the whole island. Nowadays if any of the unfortunate individuals who have to deal with Western city traffic problems wants a real busman's holiday let him spend a morning in Raffles Place. The native population is not slow to sample the fruits of progress. The evening Mohammedan call to the faithful is now not only delivered by amplifier but is further expedited by the employment of a gramophone record.

In my time the night life was congested into the Malay Street quarter. Here, amid a memorable stench, hundreds of gaudily painted Japanese prostitutes swarmed in the doorway verandas of their wooden houses and screamed, against the uproar of the adjacent shooting-galleries, their unvarying falsetto appeal, "Come inside, come inside, come inside." The only less undignified port of call was an excessively dull dance-hall known as the Tingle-Tangle, whose patrons were recruited chiefly from the docks. There is no red-light district in Singapore now; though, no doubt, as in similar cases of reformation, it has been superseded rather than abolished. Meanwhile palatial picture houses display all the latest exuberances of sound, size and colour hot from Hollywood and often in advance of London. Incidentally, it tends to shock and rather to grieve the old-timer to find that these picture houses are so emphatically air-conditioned that it is advisable to take along a pullover to watch the pictures in.

And indeed on my return visits nowadays to this opulent and delightful city, when I find myself being driven in the unceasing stream of traffic, featuring the latest garish make of American car which appeals most strongly to the wealthy Chinese, through streets resplendent by night with the most up-to-the-minute neon-lighted patent-medicine advertisements; then I sometimes incredulously recall the vision of the sinewy, sweating back of O Chye Lah, as he loped along through the unfrequented outskirts of the town to Tanjong Katong between his shafts, with myself behind him, sitting with my topee on my head and my tiffin basket between my feet.

Or as I am being wafted in a smooth, silent electric lift to the sky-scraping top of some restaurant or club or business premises, my memory turns, a little wistfully perhaps, back to my own ramshackle, punkah-cooled office and up the wooden stairs, to await the clatter of Mr. Hood Seck's footfall and the doleful report of his perennial and mysterious disorder.

My mother died suddenly in 1908 and since my sister had married and my brother was still at school it seemed only circumspect that I should return to England and keep my father company at home. The manager of the Singapore branch agreed to this arrangement with an unprecedented exhibition of sympathy and goodwill.

So it was back to 119 Cannon Street. I was at first given a nondescript appointment as a sort of private non-secretary to the Chairman. I think they wanted to find out whether reports of my incompetence hadn't really been exaggerated. They did and they hadn't been. So then I was put into dried fruit. This was literally true, because I spent the next year or so with my hands plunging aimlessly into sample cases of currants and my shoes wading in a blend of sultanas and sawdust. In order nominally to gain experience but really because I was so heartily sick of my own monotonous inefficiency I served a term in a dried-fruit broker's office. I found this meant meandering around, carrying under both arms heavy packets containing samples of sultanas. This was worse than ever and I got into the habit of giving a good many of the sample packets to policemen on point duty. The policemen soon became about the only people in the City who had any use for me.

Nevertheless, I was quite happy; happier, perhaps, than I deserved to be, considering the bone-laziness and lack of ability I showed in my so-called working hours. For one thing there was no longer reason for all this despondency about my height. I had added several belated inches to my stature since I first set out for Singapore. I was now at least as tall as hundreds of other rather shortish men in the City and fairly towered over several of the Greek dried-fruit merchants.

And my prolonged spells of foot-slogging up and down the City streets were not without enjoyment. My arms may have been full of sample packets of futile sultanas but my head was full of vague, intriguing ideals and aspirations of authorship. I used to tell my father about them and he was always lavish with indulgence and encouragement. It might be thought that he was searching for any solution, however improbable, to the problem of my permanent career; but the truth is that he really thought I had capabilities and in his affection was eager to persuade himself that I had been bestowed with talents as a writer to compensate for my being such a fool at business.

The trouble now was that, like so many authors with budding ability, I lacked application. I spent so much time trying to make up my mind what to write that I never got down to writing anything. So far, all that the application had achieved had been part-authorship of a topical revue which had been successfully produced for the benefit of the easily-pleased British community in a Singapore mess. I had also sent home from Malacca a short story (written, like the revue on office paper and in office hours) which my mother had sent to her friend Stanley Weyman, the fashionable historical novelist of that period, for his opinion. Weyman sent it back without comment on my literary promise but counselling me, in writing fiction, to discover a plot and stick to it. This good advice he expressed in rather graphic style: "The story; the story; the story——" and my father, who had thought my effort a good deal better than it really was, said that Stanley Weyman was "a pedantic ass". But perhaps my father was a trifle prejudiced. It had always been hinted to me that Weyman had wanted to marry my mother, but had wanted too late or too long.

42

When I said I never wrote anything, what I meant was I never finished anything. On many a night Pinero and I would sit down together and consider our confident, provocative opening of Act I. But application was a bore or I hit on a better idea next day or something. My waste-paper basket began to receive the first trickle of what throughout my later years was to become a constant flow of reams and reams and reams of repudiation.

I read plays by the dozen. During luncheon intervals in the City I often paid a quick visit to the bookshop of Jones & Evans in Queen Street near St. Paul's. Here a venerable and grandiloquent wiseacre named Mr. Tait supplied me with the latest volumes of published plays for a good deal more than I could afford. He was assisted by a young assiduous and incontestible Scotsman, who was destined to rise to an eminence in his trade as great as that of Mr. Wilson of Bumpus's; being, in fact, Mr. Wilson himself.

Every Saturday afternoon, except, of course, in the cricket season, found me escaping hurriedly from the conglomeration of currants and sultanas as from a hive of angry bees, and dashing off to get a good seat in the pit at a matinée. In those days the theatre was governed by the feudal system. Certain actor-managers staked their claims to certain theatres and stayed there for years on end: Beerbohm Tree at His Majesty's, Cyril Maude at the Haymarket, George Alexander at the St. James's, Bourchier at the Garrick, Oscar Asche at the Adelphi, Seymour Hicks at the Vaudeville. Generally speaking they maintained the same supporting cast in each case, and at that time it was an accepted custom for an actor-manager's wife to be his leading lady; at any rate on the stage. Appearing in available but less permanent occupation were several additional actor managers, Lewis Waller, H. B. Irving, Fred Terry and others.

H. B. Irving intrigued and stimulated me above all the

others. He and his brother Laurence, who in his short career gave one astonishing and renowned performance in a play called *Typhoon*, always had to endure disparaging comparisons with their father—reasonably enough I dare say. H. B.'s somewhat bizarre personality and methods might be derided nowadays, but he was my favourite figure in those romantic larger-than-life days of the drama. In impassioned moments his voice would rise and seem to lose itself in a sort of vibrant ecstasy; and in his more sinister parts his characteristic movements and the deliberate menace in the timing of his lines and looks were, to me at any rate, enthralling. He was not the most popular of actors with the general public but he was the man for me. I saw the classic Hamlet of Forbes Robertson and found it statuesque and machine-made in comparison to the vital Hamlet of H. B. Perhaps I was prejudiced in favour of my stage hero; but I still think I was a good judge.

My original stage hero, Charles Hawtrey, was generally to be seen at one theatre or another and had many successes, on which, as I afterwards learnt, the bookmakers were the first to congratulate him. He and Seymour Hicks both used a comedy technique which sounds very old-fashioned now but was effective and strangely convincing then. They took the audience quite openly into their confidence, as though the stalls contained their own, often rather guilty, consciences. They were a great contrast—Hicks full of ebullience and flummery; Hawtrey, portly, quiet and whimsical, whispering some awful self-confession to the front, with grave eyes slowly pursuing his line of thought. He held all the gifts of comedy in the palm of his hand and manipulated them gracefully and fondly like a master conjurer.

It was dating from this period that the technique of another leading actor, Gerald du Maurier, began to exert that influence which was to revolutionise the theatre. I have mentioned the transformation from applied and intentional dramatisation to the delineation of natural speech and behaviour; for this, so far as acting went, du Maurier was solely, almost unwittingly perhaps, responsible. Unfortunately his methods and ability for reflecting reality were so supreme that their very ease disguised their proficiency. Youthful aspirants regarded them as anybody's gifts for the asking. Ever since then to this day the over-indulgence in that much abused quality known as restraint and a great deal of mannered ease and inaudibility must be attributed to du Maurier's blameless and paramount genius.

While du Maurier was revolutionising acting John Galsworthy, with, I surmise, far greater perception and ambition, was diverting the course of dramatic authorship. His earlier efforts, *The Silver Box, Strife* and *Justice*, patronised almost exclusively by the intellegentsia of the period, were laying the foundations on which were to be built all our present-day lounge halls in Sussex houses and living-rooms in flats in Chelsea. *Justice* was first produced, together with Shaw's *Misalliance* and Granville Barker's *The Madras House*, in a repertory experiment by Charles Frohman at the Duke of York's Theatre in 1910. It is an interesting commentary on the conservative attitude of the public towards the Theatre in those days that the season was rescued from disaster by a revival of *Trelawny of the Wells*. To blazes with this modernistic stuff. People wanted their plays and acting in the good old tradition.

I was one of those people, of course. And quite candidly and unashamedly I still am. I still cherish those matinée pit days of my young manhood as the best days the Theatre has known in my lifetime. But for an old man to be didactic and argumentative with the younger generations about the respective merits of past and present is a futile occupation which often only results in both parties becoming infuriated.

There is, however, one fashionable form of West End

entertainment which robs me entirely of self-restraint, though my wrath is chiefly in defence of a cherished memory. When I see some of the miserable arch-satirical little revues perpetrated and performed by untrained whimsies and accepted by the stalls public of to-day with an air of chortling, parental, you-must-make-allowances indulgence—("Of course they can't act, poor dears; and the leading girl's top notes are really terrible, but it's all so *fresh*")—then am I liable to become a conspicuous nuisance to quite a large area of the stalls. And this is not so much because of the precocious incompetence of the company and its material as in protest against the desecration of the memory of Harry Pelissier and the Follies.

But the greater the pleasure I found in the theatre and in my hesitant ambitions to contribute thereto the more futile became the demoralising job of peddling sultanas. Apart from anything else it left me no time to look for some more congenial form of employment and I wouldn't have known how to set about looking for this in any case. But suddenly deliverance arrived on the scene in the somewhat illogical form of a chartered accountant.

He was, however, miscast as a chartered accountant, for he was a gay and versatile Irishman named O. F. Odell. I had known him well in Singapore where he used to come into our office and undertake the process known as doing the books; and he had first won my affection by making light of my enormity in connection with the pineapple ledger. Odell was now back in London and through him, on some fortuitous evening in the West End, I met W. Teignmouth Shore.

Shore was a well-established free-lance journalist. He will be remembered as editor of some of the Hodge *Famous Trials*; and he bore a remarkable likeness to the accepted image of Pickwick. He proved to be the ideal consultant. He listened with keen and sympathetic attention to a recital of my

46

despondencies and vague aspirations, which was, in itself, an act of charity. But he didn't stop there. So many people would have contented themselves with a "Too bad. Cheer up. Something'll turn up one of these days", and ended the discussion by turning an inquiring glance towards the bar. This practical little man trotted off home and sat down and wrote a letter of introduction which was to change the whole course of my existence.

Whenever I recall the merry, good-natured, Pickwickian personality of Teignmouth Shore I grow sentimental. And why not indeed?

Within a week or two of his writing that letter I was working in John Lane's trade department in Brewer Street, on a course of preliminary instruction before being received into the sanctum of the Bodley Head. In 1911 the Bodley Head, Vigo Street, was the headquarters of the most individual and progressive publishing house in the country. I suddenly experienced one of those transitions so blissful that the struggle against incredulity and misgiving is all part of the bliss.

I joined what was then the proprietary firm of John Lane a few days before my twenty-fifth birthday. Twenty-five years of late Victorian boyhood and Edwardian young manhood—if my memory tries to catalogue the personalities and topics of those twenty-five years an odd potpourri comes tumbling to my mind in random reminiscence, regardless of values or selection or chronology:

An Australian lady named Miss Annie Luker diving in flaming sackcloth into a small tank from the roof of the old London Aquarium:

The London Hippodrome when it was indeed a hippodrome, half theatre and half circus and its resident clown Marceline:

And Dreyfus and German bands and bloomers and Sandow and halfpenny buns:

47

And white kid gloves with evening dress for gentlemen and Phil May and bottled ether:

Peter the Painter and the Sydney Street siege, with a view of the Home Secretary, Mr. Winston Churchill, taking cover:

And Gibson girls and the "By the Way" column in the *Globe* and *The Honeysuckle and the Bee* and Cinquevalli:

A contrivance by which cartridges were exploded in order to make soda water—they were known as sparklets and were a variation of Mr. Sherlock Holmes's gazogene:

And the Hon. John Collier's annual problem picture at the Royal Academy and Chappell's Ballad Concerts and W. W. Jacobs and early telephones with little handles which impatient old male subscribers whirred like infuriated organ-grinders:

And Gaby Deslys and George R. Sims and Sousa's Band and balloons and the Dartmoor Shepherd:

And what the contemporary Press always described as the mercurial career of F. E. Smith:

And the more gradual progress of two personal favourites of mine in whom I took a particular and almost proprietary interest, Charles V. France and Andrew Sandham.

So I was twenty-five; far removed from any hopes of worldly prosperity but full of new enthusiasm and happiness. Although Singapore was left behind it had, as I realise now, bestowed upon me another boon along with my consoling inches. For in Singapore my companions of my own age took a very philosophical view of being condemned to their life sentence with one foot in the white man's grave. They were all hard up and many of them extremely ill-behaved. But they gave me a share of their one eternally valuable possession. They gave me a sense of fun. I wonder what I've done with it.

CHAPTER III

Burlington Arcadia

LATE one evening the massive figure of G. K. Chesterton stood outside the locked door of the Bodley Head in Vigo Street. Clad in his habitual flowing cape he must have completely overspread the narrow pavement. One can picture him, puzzled rather than annoyed by the obstinacy of the door-handle and searching in quick peering movements of the pince-nez beneath his vast tilted canopy of a hat to find the bell.

As it happened, Mr. Harris, the accountant, was in a little room on the first floor, seated on an office stool and muttering over figures. Hearing the bell, he descended, unlocked the front door and confronted the formidable visitor. Chesterton carried a black Gladstone bag and from this he had already removed a set of proofs. As the door opened he offered this to Mr. Harris.

"I have brought my corrected proofs," he said in that near-falsetto tone which always seemed to emanate surprisingly from so gargantuan a frame. "But I seem to have done so rather late in the day."

"Oh, yes, sir," replied Mr. Harris, a rueful type of individual with an unkempt sandy beard and spaniel eyes. "The office staff have all gone long ago. I'm just the accountant, you see. But if you care to leave the proofs with me I'll see they're handed to the right quarter."

Chesterton presented him with the proofs. "Thank you very much," he said. "I am greatly obliged to you for your

49

courtesy. In fact, I would like to give a practical demonstration of my gratitude." He drew a bottle from the Gladstone bag as he spoke. "Will you join me in a glass of port?"

"Oh, thank you very much, sir," said Harris, "but I'm afraid I can't do that. The fact is I'm a teetotaler."

"Good heavens," exclaimed Chesterton, the unnatural falsetto rising to a top note of horror. "Give me back my proofs."

In the course of my three years with the Bodley Head most of the active literary celebrities of the period passed through the narrow outer office to and from John Lane's little private room, before my eyes uplifted in privileged curiosity. But the thumping personality of Chesterton looms up before any other when I look back to those Bodley Head days. He wasn't a frequent visitor and I myself only met him once or twice; but if I couldn't call myself an acquaintance of his I was, like many others, an eager devotee. He differed in a characteristic way from other celebrated wits who had preceded him, the Whistlers and Wildes and W. S. Gilberts. They produced comment and repartee in brilliant and often caustic flashes of inspiration. Chesterton always appeared to me to be like a large and leisurely and genial cook who kept the whimsical point of view and the quaint simile always on the simmer and ready to bubble over at the appropriate moment.

Once, during a conversation with him, a friend of mine made use of the adjective "good" in a loose colloquial way—so-and-so was a good authority or such-and-such was a good policy. Chesterton disagreed, but expressed his disagreement with his customary moderation. "Good? A word so freely used to mean such different things. If a man shoots his mother-in-law he is not necessarily a good man. But nobody can deny that he is a good shot."

I once heard him speak in a debate on a favourite topic of

his, the party system. His opponent was a young Irish peer who was gifted with the gab but who clouded the issue by a rambling diatribe on the parliamentary procedures in various European countries. Chesterton protested meekly. "I am sorry to have made a foolish mistake; but when I was invited to discuss the party system I am afraid I assumed this to mean the party system in vogue in this country. After all, when a man says to you 'Let's all go down the Strand', you do not leap to the conclusion that he means the strand of the Euphrates."

The predominant leviathan gathers his cloak around him and squeezes his way out of sight to make room for other interesting visitors. But, first, what of the man they came to visit?

John Lane was probably the most enterprising man in the history of publishing. But his enterprise had none of the spirit of adventure which one associates with enterprise in any physical sense. If taking a risk gave him a certain glee it was not because success would bring him a personal satisfaction, but rather the satisfaction that something which he knew to be good should receive its just reward. His soft voice and slow smile gave little evidence of his spirit of wild enthusiasm and impulse in the discovery and exploitation of talent and innovation. His head reader, Frederic Chapman, used to say that Lane had a sixth sense which enabled him to discern merit in a derelict manuscript or in some original and revolutionary project without himself ever reading a page or investigating a detail. He hated detail. The whole of his career as a publisher was one continuous flair.

He was short and jaunty with a neat grey beard which looked as though it ought to have been worn above a ruff. He had a perceptible west-country burr and a weakness of the eyes which tended to make them weep as he talked to you. This mild affliction only lent kindliness to his expression but many of his authors must have accused him of shedding crocodile tears and I certainly don't blame them. For Lane's extraordinary gift for unearthing talent was counterbalanced and in many cases brought almost immediately to naught, so far as commercial results were concerned, by the rapacity of his business methods. Most writers had to fend for themselves in those days, and in any case the very mention of a literary agent sent Lane hopping with indignation. I think that authors of first novels received a pretty good hiding from most of the other publishers, but John Lane remunerated them with scorpions.

But I don't think this was due to inherent meanness or to the desire to get more than his fair share of any ample returns. As I have said, his objective seemed to be to win for any fledgling talent the public esteem which he thought it deserved, and he seemed to expect the possessor of the talent to be of the same mind. The result was that some authors—H. G. Wells had been one of them and Arnold Bennett another— once Lane had brought their proficiency to light, had had no hesitation, nor, I suspect, the smallest qualm of conscience in breaking with him. All the same, there was something in Lane's nature which inhibited feud or rancour. He was a Quaker, but apart from any moral principles, his pacifist outlook regarded disputes and squabbles as waste of time. During my years with him I met both Wells and Bennett in his company, and he burred at them and blinked his moist eyes at them in the most benign manner, though neither of them responded with any marked cordiality. Indeed, Bennett, who was one of my fellow guests at a luncheon-party at Lane's house, only uttered one sentence throughout the meal, being obviously offended by the loquacity of some confident foreign gentleman who was another of the guests. The conversation turned to an anonymous article which had been published that morning in the *Daily Telegraph* and there was

JOHN LANE
A caricature by Max Beerbohm

some speculation as to who had written it. Mrs. Lane, an
exuberant American hostess, thought this a good opportunity
for wooing her disgruntled guest of honour. "Perhaps *you*
wrote it, Mr. Bennett," she said ingratiatingly. Bennett, in
that remarkable voice of his which put one in mind of the
sound of tyres on the road when somebody has suddenly
jammed on the brake, made reply. "I don't even *read* the
Daily Telegraph," he said and relapsed into silence.

By the time I joined the Bodley Head in 1911 the flair had
been in operation for some twenty years. Some of its early
products, such as the *Yellow Book* and Oscar Wilde's *Salome*,
with illustrations by Aubrey Beardsley, had stirred the placid
waters of the literary world of the nineties into a maelstrom of
delicious consternation. When the Wilde scandal broke in
1895 one of Lane's office-boys figured in the charges. This,
added to the fact that the name of John Lane was so eminently
associated with the more aesthetic and erotic elements in
current art and literature, might have ruined him as a publisher.
But beneath all the flair and resourcefulness, Lane preserved an
inherent spirit of Quaker innocence. Knowing him as I did
later on, I am convinced that the whole thing suddenly came
upon him as a completely unsuspected and horrifying revelation. It is true that, both at the time and for many years to
come, he was maligned for having found it essential to fulfil
an urgent business mission in America during the turmoil of
the scandal. But I do not believe that he was guided by an
instinct of self-preservation from the scorn and ridicule of his
rivals and critics. If he were cowardly, he were cowardly
of his own distress; and his innate repugnance of antagonism
also no doubt encouraged him on his way to the shipping
office.

But you could always find a reasonable and generally a
worthy motive for anything John Lane did, however egregious.

E

It is an interesting comment on his character to add that you always wanted to. It is an even more interesting comment to add that whether you wanted to or not he would always have expected you to.

The Bodley Head premises were—and remain—unique in being almost the only section of Albany ever to have been appropriated by commerce. How Lane had originally managed to effect this act of refined spoliation I don't know; but I suppose some impressionable authority had been successfully subjected to the burr and the pathetic eye-moisture at the critical moment; and a set of ground-floor and first-floor chambers were duly adapted and partitioned and metamorphasised into various office rooms of incredibly impracticable shape, size and proportion. In the course of time the staff doubled and redoubled, but it never occurred to Lane to consider any modifications, and by the time I found my way into it the whole place was like an intellectual rabbit warren. The outer office, now the show-room of a pleasant and decorative bookshop, had to provide desk space for four assistants, a lady typist and an office-boy. There were also the odd slabs of table and counter here and there for the odd piles of volumes and proofs and scripts; while considerable space was devoted to the bookshelves which occupied every available inch of wall from floor to ceiling, to say nothing of the contingent ladders and a chair or two for any visitor who might be kept waiting on the way to see Mr. Lane or to be shown into the converted corridor which served as a private office for his manager. Even so, passage room through the outer office had to be left, even for a caller of Chestertonian proportions. But to me the whole hugger-mugger squash and inconvenience seemed part of my newly-found intimacy with happiness. It seemed as though the less room there was to move about in the more closely was I embraced by the buoyant spirit of delight I had at last found in my working hours. I loved every moment of it.

Lane had a dim, bottle-glass windowed little room, tucked in beside our main office. It was always cluttered up with piles of books and of manuscripts humbly and hopefully awaiting the awakening of the sixth sense. But Lane did not apply this only to literature; he was also a collector of unheralded but potential masterpieces of nineteenth-century portraiture, specimens of which invariably occupied any of the seating space and, propped up against the available furniture, most of the floor space of his room. Quite important personages had often to conduct their interviews with him standing in the doorway.

The rooms above our office and the manager's corridor were a part of somebody else's chambers, but up a narrow flight of wooden stairs there was, to one side, a cramped first-floor section of the warren. This consisted of three rooms, one of them the cashier's, from which Mr. Harris descended to wreck G. K. Chesterton's faith in the gratitude of man. Another was occupied by a guarded and virginal lady of middle age, who held the recondite post of private secretary to Mr. Lane and used to get me to roll her umbrella. The third was in the possession of a hearty and rather beery Cockney who had fourteen children but what he did during office hours I cannot now remember.

At one time or other I did every technical job there is to be done in a publisher's office, from gumming press cuttings into an album upwards. During my last year with Lane, in the summer of 1914, I even took over the manager's duties while he was on his holiday and put in a fortnight as his understudy in the corridor. But when I picture myself back there it is generally at my little table squashed into the window, bent on some routine work of devising advertisements or tinkering with proofs and goggling at any arrival worth the goggling.

William J. Locke was a tall, thin, familiar figure. I don't

know whether his novels are read nowadays but he was then one of the most popular novelists in the country and easily Lane's best seller. Perhaps in Locke's case shrewdness tortured Lane into an unwonted generosity in making terms; perhaps Locke's sense of rectitude prevailed. If this was reflected in his manners it was probably so, for he was, I think, the most courteous man I have ever known. In any case, he stuck to Lane, and there was a legend current in the office that Lane paid the whole of the Bodley Head expenses out of what he made out of Locke, which considering the salaries Lane paid was not unlikely.

Locke's urbanity was an exception to the general rule. The artistic temperament was a fashionable propensity and was freely exploited by those who possessed it and adopted by many who did not. William Watson, the poet, was one of the genuine possessors. Shortly before I joined the staff, the Bodley Head had been the scene of one of his more dramatic displays of the temperament. Some unrevealed offence in connection with the publication or reception of one of his poems had been attributed by Watson to negligence on the part of Lane. He called to protest, swinging in from Vigo Street and taking up an intimidating stance in the midst of the outer office—a Titan of a poet in size and aspect. I can imagine Frank Baker, the bespectacled office-boy, rising from his stool with his air of take-'em-for-granted impassivity which never varied in the reception of any visitor from Thomas Hardy to a printer's tout. But Watson ignored Frank Baker and remained for a moment or two, erect and quivering. Then his eagle eye fastened on one of the chairs in which the less urgent visitors were wont to await their summons. He took a step towards the chair, seized it and raised it aloft. Then crash— fragments of chair flew in various directions in the midst of the already congested office. And Watson strode out again without having uttered a word.

The incident has always endeared Watson to me. There was a general popular theory in those days that if a man were a poet he was liable to be more or less lunatic, and he gloriously vindicated this ironical allegation. He seems to have been a man of violently contrasting moods and emotions, which affected even his appearance. His handsome face, when clean shaven, was the face of the fervent visionary, the sublimity of whose *Ode in May* so enraptured the anthologists, and even of the sentimental lyrist whose April, April laughs her girlish laughter more enduringly still. But during a certain period—perhaps more than one—Watson wore a moustache, which, in outward appearance at any rate, changed his personality into that of the typical and relentless chair-breaker. His poetical mood seemed to vary accordingly. His spasm of vindictive doggerel called *The Woman with the Serpent's Tongue* and generally supposed to be directed against Mrs. Asquith, as she then was, if it were utterly unworthy even of the moustached Watson, proved at least the genuine irrepressibility of this strange character.

One morning when Frank Baker, who treated Mr. Lane with the same unawed assurance with which he treated everyone else, was in the little room next door, trying to get it into something like order and making the most outspoken comments on the utter jumble he always found it in, another poet arrived in the outer office. I jumped to my feet and edged my way through the furniture to receive him with an alert "bags-I" enthusiasm. His entrance had none of the Watsonian impetuosity; he seemed to drift from Vigo Street into the Bodley Head as though from one portion of a dream to another. Nor, apart from his somnambulism, did he bear the appearance of a poet. He had a pallid sturdiness and looked like a bewildered edition of Napoleon Bonaparte. I recognised him at once, and his being a poet was a secondary consideration with me. To me his importance was as a great man of the theatre. He had written a succession of plays which had caused him to be hailed as the greatest blank verse dramatist since Shakespeare. He was Stephen Phillips.

I don't remember now what he had called about; I don't think he himself remembered at the time. But I do remember the enraptured interest with which I gazed on the creator of those dramas which I was so fond of spouting to myself in the vainglorious bedroom moments in which, despite the wonder and delight of my present occupation, I still exhibited my true métier. At Her Majesty's Theatre Beerbohm Tree had found in those Phillips dramas rich material for the gigantic pro-digalities of production and setting so dear to his heart and to the heart of the public; while the mellifluous empurpled periods rolled delectably from the tongue. In the latest production, *Nero*, a speech describing the character of Poppeia had been originally allotted to the slave, Acte, played by Dorothea Baird; but the concluding lines so appealed to Tree that he removed them from their setting and appropriated them for his own Nero. They may be quoted as typical of the Stephen Phillips euphony:

> Yet fairer none has come into this world,
> Nor wandered with more witchery through the air,
> Since she who drew the dreaming keels of Greece
> After her over the Ionian foam.

Alas, poor Phillips—forgotten I suppose today; at any rate never produced and seldom mentioned. But I have never lost, nor wish to lose, the glow of enthusiasm with which I popped up from my desk that morning to salute him. He outlived his popularity for a few years before he passed, still no doubt somnambulating inquiringly, into the beyond. It was always an open secret that he sought even greater inspiration from Bacchus than from Calliope. He left five pounds and a lasting memory of the pleasure he had given me and many others.

The works of many contemporary poets, major and minor —Watson, Richard le Gallienne, Ernest Dowson, John Davidson, Stephen Phillips, A.E., Alice Meynell, Margaret L. Woods and others, bore the imprint of the Bodley Head. Lascelles Abercrombie joined the fold at about the time of my admission and quickly demonstrated his claim to inclusion in the artistic temperament brigade. He said he wanted to sit up all night and work but had nowhere to go; so Lane rather hesitatingly lent him the key of the Brewer Street trade premises. Abercrombie duly went along there but did not fulfil his intention of working all night. He departed before dawn, leaving the door wide open. He is alleged to have replied to Lane's subsequent protest by saying that in the unlikely event of any chance marauder electing to steal books, he would certainly have drawn the line at any books published by Lane. But perhaps this is somebody's invention; though I cannot help feeling that if Abercrombie didn't say it this was only because he didn't think of it.

But although there was always a strong mutual attraction between Lane and the poets the flair had a wide range. It hovered over the whole wide field of literary effort spotting the seeds of talent and originality. For two successive years while I was with him he selected and published simultaneously four discoveries, in the form of the first novels of four authors, none of whom achieved, or, I fear, deserved any remarkable distinction. Lane spent quite preposterous sums in advertising these quartettes, not only as a bait to entice any hesitant creators of embryonic best sellers, but also in order to publicise himself as the champion of the novice. *Punch* regarded the enterprise as a promising target for derision and published a striking lampoon of the advertisement on both occasions, thereby doubling its value and setting Lane chortling with satisfaction. But the result, needless to add, was a constant flow of mistaken ambition from further candidates for discovery.

During part of my second summer at the Bodley Head London groaned and reeked with one of those rare and prodigious heat-waves which drive the statisticians to consult past records. I don't suppose I should remember this had it not coincided with the arrival, on a visit to this country, of Stephen Leacock. A year or so previously the *Spectator*, in a moment of exceptional but commendable levity, had published a contribution, written in an original and spontaneous vein of humour and called *My Financial Career*. Lane had pounced on this article, discovered its author to be Professor of Political Economy at McGill University and dashed off a cable to Canada, offering to publish this and a collection of similar articles in book form.

By the time of his visit *Literary Lapses* and *Nonsense Novels* were on the market and, without creating any immediate or sensational success with the general public, had that quality which makes an unconventional author, particularly a humorist, appreciated and boosted by a gradual epidemic of appreciation. He was a great favourite with us at the office even before he arrived and he did not disappoint us. Unlike other authors he treated us in the outer office with a ready and jolly sociability, standing and sucking his pipe and rallying us with his impressions of London. His exterior was rugged and bear-like and he seemed to think that if nature had endowed him with a crop of errant hair and a ginger moustache it was nature's job to look after them. He had a rough and ready vigour and obstinacy both of opinion and in his actions too; for he didn't walk the streets so much as stalk through them with an air of purposeful and scrutinising challenge.

But this energy was ill-suited to a heat-wave. So was his

get-up. He wore the coarse serge suit and cumbersome brown boots typical, at that time, of the Dominions on tour in England. On about the third morning of his visit he came lunging into the office from one of his stalking tours in the blazing sun outside. I think I have never seen a man in a state of such dilapidation from heat. The sweat poured from his face and had long reduced his stiff white collar to pulp. He stood mopping himself vainly with a red handkerchief, then swung round at me in an outburst of ferocious denunciation.

"Listen," he said. "I have just been around to your Piccadilly Circus; and stuck up there I see a notice 'Gentlemen —Hot and Cold Lavatories'. What shape should a man be in to need a hot lavatory?"

Leacock loved his own jokes. When he was promenading what available floor space he could find, puffing clouds of smoke and caricaturing his own emphatic opinions, his final confident glance used to come to rest on me, as though he thought I were the most receptive member of the party to share the grin with. I did not really get him to myself during that visit, but next year Lane took me to New York where he had a branch office. Leacock was in New York at the time and seemed to welcome my company on some of his stalking expeditions. He was a dogmatic man; he not only held strong convictions but was always ready to crack you over the head with them. Not that my head offered him much of a target; I was merely his pliant and delighted disciple. But I remember on one of our striding outings making some trivial and as I thought rather amusing comment on the manners of the New York police. This naturally led to our discussing the burning topic of Home Rule for Ireland, on which Leacock held such emphatic views that he caused an obstruction of the sidewalk traffic while he stood and upbraided the iniquity of the Conservative party in opposing the proposed surrender to John

Redmond. With characteristic abasement and no little embarrassment at the scene we were creating, I agreed to grant Home Rule to Ireland immediately and we proceeded on our way. Humour was always uppermost in Leacock's mind and I often got the impression that he was trenchant and intolerant in his assertions and denunciations chiefly because he got so much pleasure out of ending it all in a chuckle.

I saw him only once again after our New York meeting but we kept up a random correspondence over the years. Some of the extracts from his letters bear the characteristic Leacock touch. When I was flying in the first war, in 1916, part of one of his letters read:

"I am posting you my new book (*Further Foolishness*). Take it up in the air with you ... Then you might perhaps send me a testimonial saying the higher you got up the funnier the book seemed."

And of my own first novel:

"It is awfully good and I quite agree about the dramatisability (that's a hell of a word, isn't it?)"

Or, in reply to a letter in which I extolled an article he had written in appreciation of O. Henry:

"Talking of O. Henry I met in N' York the other day a man who had known him and he told me that O. Henry
(a) drank *all* the time, not part of it but *all* of it,
(b) couldn't live with his wife,
(c) probably took the money from the bank at Austin, for which he went, as you know, to jail for 3 years.
But I don't care if he did. He was a great writer and a fine man."

Leacock was unique among authors I have ever known, both in his personality and his work, with his practical and devastating perception of the funny side of life. He was brusque and opinionated and untidy—a sort of laughing swashbuckler of literature. But anybody who still treasures his *Sunshine Sketches of a Little Town* will know what sort of a heart he really had.

In direct contrast to Lane's tendency to be parsimonious in the terms he inflicted on the tenderfoot novelist, was his insistence that every book he published, whatever its size, shape or content, should be turned out in the best possible style. Either in private libraries, where these still exist, or in the remainder shelves of Charing Cross Road veteran Bodley Head publications can be identified at a glance by the portly elegance of their format and finish. And when the flair suddenly animated him with the idea of publishing a series of English translations of the works of Anatole France, its habitual counsellors of economy were, for once, thrown to the winds. He produced a sumptuous edition of demi-octavo volumes at seven and sixpence each. I don't suppose that, even in those days, better first-hand value for money was ever offered to the book world.[1]

Frederic Chapman was the editor of the series with J. Lewis May as his consultant and between them they showed remarkable discrimination in choosing their team of translators. My memory dwells fondly on Chapman and it would be ungrateful and negligent if it didn't. For he not only contributed to my personal happiness and enthusiasm in my Bodley Head days, but he typified the gentle, delicate, erudite bibliophile of his time. He used to do all his reading at home but he

---

[1] This opinion does not seem to be shared by the book-collectors of today. On April 10th, 1956 ten of these volumes were sold at Sotheby's for a total sum of £1.

would drift into the office several times a week, large and slow and peering and congenial, looking as though he had sat up all night in his clothes, which he quite likely had; for it was a hard and fast rule that no submission, however abortive in aspect, should be rejected until Chapman had read it. When, as sometimes happened, I was deputed for a second opinion which I then learnt, to my dismay, was in direct opposition to his, he was never hasty or disdainful or condescending. He received and overruled any such contrary views with a quiet consideration and respect which made a lasting impression on me. For my own ambitions were still being preserved and cherished in a state of dormant optimism. It must, I told myself, show that one possessed pretty exceptional gifts if a man of such culture and penetration took such godfatherly interest in telling one how wrong one was.

The series of Anatole France translations, published at regular intervals over a few years, appealed only to a limited number of discriminating readers, but the general public had by this time become aware of the author as one who must be sufficiently eminent in his own country to warrant this systematic attention in ours; and his decision to pay a visit to London was treated as an event of national importance. I think I am right in saying that Lane instigated the visit, though in the result it didn't matter much whether he did or not, because he certainly forestalled and appropriated all the kudos for it.

The reception of Anatole France at the Bodley Head was a ceremony attended by unprecedented fuss and ill-rehearsed dislocation. Lane decided at the last moment that a space should be cleared in the outer office, through which he himself would proceed in order to greet the master, while we members of the staff were instructed to fall in behind him as a strangely assorted guard of honour. This meant that a good deal of the furniture had to be pushed to one side and the place was nearing a state of complete chaos when the great man made his rather puzzled appearance. Lane duly advanced and burred his address of homage but this was quite unintelligible to Anatole France, who had no English; while the dignity of the scene was further discounted by an audible commentary on the general course of the proceedings from Frank Baker in the background.

My impression of Anatole France throughout that visit was that from the first he struggled nobly to disguise his regret for having made it. He seemed to be steeling himself patiently and politely to endure an ordeal of unutterable boredom. I imagined the relief with which he would find himself back in his villa, in his dressing-gown and skull-cap, rubbing his great nose along the pages of some obscure codex of apocryphal lore and abstractedly accepting the methodical ministrations of his elderly female companion. This lady accompanied him to London and followed doggedly in his shadow wherever he went. We, in the outer office, speculated eagerly on whether she was his wife, mistress, secretary or housekeeper. Her homely appearance and mute docility seemed essentially to suggest the last. The only certainty was that, whatever her functions, she wasn't his interpreter.

For the last night of Anatole France's visit Lane organised a dinner which assumed the proportions of a sort of literary state banquet. It was held at the Savoy Hotel and all authors who, in Lane's estimation, qualified for the honour were invited to come and pay at least a sufficient amount of tribute to the master to cover the cost of their meal. A few of the leading lights found they had previous engagements—some of them perhaps harboured a protracted if entirely one-sided antipathy to Lane—but it was a fairly representative gathering, being one of those ostentatious, "among-those-present" occasions, which most of the leading novelists and biographers of the day found it essential to attend in their own interests, quite apart from those of M. France.

Having negotiated the primary arrangements and issued his list of distinguished starters, Lane, as usual, declined to be bothered with detail; and a girl named Margaret Roberts and I were made responsible for the joint and appalling job of arranging the seating plan for the various members of the congregation. If only the accommodation had been in the form of a head table with a shoal of small satellite tables it wouldn't have been so bad; but the skeleton plan showed a head table with two or three grim parallel branches, and we were instructed to observe the rites of precedence in our allocations. To be called upon to rank, in order of precedence, an imposing muster of contemporary authors of both sexes and of divers ages seemed a novel, indeed unique exercise, and I remember my feeling of gleeful self-satisfaction at the thought that I, of all people, had been appointed to perform it. From the start it was obviously bound to be a task calling for a blend of diplomacy and determination; and, moreover, entirely unrewarding, since the individuals who were allotted the best seats would have considered themselves insulted if they hadn't been, and a large number of those who found themselves in secondary side-table seats would consider themselves insulted because they did. Add to which, Lane was certain to get belated, spur-of-the-moment notions about promotions and relegations he thought advisable or judicious, and would mess up the whole completed plan, probably after it had gone to press. Which, of course, he did.

When Margaret Roberts came to lend me a hand I discovered that there was an additional hazard which, in my innocence, I had never anticipated. She was not actually on the staff of the Bodley Head but did occasional secretarial work for Mr. and Mrs. Lane in their house at Lancaster Gate Terrace; and she seemed to have a remarkable knowledge of the private and domestic circumstances of the prospective diners. It appeared that in some of the homes of the literary clans rivalry ranged beyond the confines of the study. My allocations had to undergo a severe overhaul, having here and there failed to observe a tactful segregation of husbands, lovers, wives, mistresses, ex-wives, ex-mistresses, discarded spouses and co-respondents. Fortunately Miss Roberts proved as dexterous as she was well-informed and thanks to her adjustments the ceremony passed off in what was from my apprehensive point of view an atmosphere of sedate anticlimax. Anatole France, inspired alike by the assurance that the end of his visit was in sight and by the plump and motionless proximity of his vegetative lady, rose and delivered a long and animated oration. I remember only his opening line, but perhaps that is because it was the only one I understood: "*Je ne sais pas que je ne rêve.*" Nor at any time were the proceedings sub-jected to any outward manifestations of mutual abhorrence or challenge on the part of his British votaries. But I don't mind betting that, as the company took their seats, the Savoy waiters overheard some pretty tart asides on the subject of precedence.

I never lost my first feeling of almost incredulous jubilation at being at the Bodley Head. But this was due, in part, to the Bodley Head being where it was. I can still feel the exhilaration with which I would step out of the office into Burlington Gardens and walk across Bond Street into Albe-marle Street to spend my luncheon hour at the Public Schools Club, of which I was an original member. It always delighted me to realise that it was all part and parcel of my job to be situated here, in the heart of the West End, with all the delectable air of expansive Edwardian luxury which still clung to it; to know that I belonged to it and that it belonged to me.

I dare say some people may consider it incongruous that anybody should have been animated in this way by the sur-roundings when one views them today. Perhaps only those of my own generation (and sentimentalists at that) will appreciate my youthful exuberance. The Albany itself and Burlington House are over forty years older but still present much of their sedate tranquillity to the pandemonium of a modernised Piccadilly, like two very old members blinking in stolid abstraction through their club windows at the extraordinary procedures of a changed world. Burlington Arcade, too, with its gay little shops tinkling with allurement as of old, still fills my nostrils with the nostalgic redolence of patchouli. Even Bond Street still seems to possess a portion of the spirit of my sumptuous days. Then the motor car and the electric carriage had only recently arrived to challenge the brougham and the hansom cab for the right of way of a Bond Street which now surges with towering motor buses vying with tradesmen's vans and infiltrating private cars, the whole conglomerate stream being dammed into traffic blocks organised by relays of infatuated policemen. Yet still, still, Bond Street suggests to my mind a pre-eminently aristocratic dowager (opposite number to the two old club members) preserving her spirit of dignity and nursing her poor worn-out old complexion in a charabanc-load of trippers. Its wares—pictures, jewellery, hats, scent—are now, as then, among the most exquisite and exorbitant that London has to offer. But the pavements which today are pervaded by a fleeting succession of noses, being poked into shop windows and whipped away again ("Hurry up, Jennifer, or we'll miss the bus") were then a privileged parade-ground, where the hobble-skirted ladies of fashion, escorted by bespatted and buckskin-gloved attendant nuts, lingered in appreciative bemusement.

What a glorious and uplifting contrast it all was to the grim and greasy surroundings of Billingsgate. In the City everyone I had ever met had been elbowing his way through the day in the hustling contentions of trade. Here the whole of my working hours were spent in a realm of elegant hedonism.

STEPHEN LEACOCK

To this day my memories of the City are encompassed by an impenetrable greenish murk; my memories of my three years with John Lane in Vigo Street are never out of the sunlight.

The Bond Street I knew then was the Bond Street where, only a few years earlier, the pony driven by A. E. Matthews had shied, throwing that promising young actor from his gig, which necessitated his carrying his broken arm in a sling when he appeared as the midshipman son of Aubrey Smith and Ellen Terry in J. M. Barrie's *Alice-sit-by-the-Fire*: the Bond Street which had been the beat on which a young Metropolitan policeman named Tom Walls enjoyed his preliminary experience of night duty. And when I say enjoyed, I mean enjoyed.

Party politics (Liberal versus Conservative) were the subject of discussion and controversy to a far greater extent than ever before or since. They automatically cropped up as the natural and preliminary topic of conversation at every social function, at every dinner-table, in every railway carriage, in every barber's shop. Only some momentous event such as the sinking of the *Titanic*, or some really abnormal freak of the weather, or some outstanding atrocity on the part of the suffragettes could temporarily supplant the rival policies of Free Trade and Tariff Reform or the question of Home Rule for Ireland as the universal, anticipated ingredients of conversation.

At the Bodley Head political opinions were fairly equally divided, though the town traveller, a fiery little Glaswegian who used to pop in daily and appropriate some of our precious space in the outer office, was a particularly rampant and virulent champion of Liberalism. One of our junior members even had the bravado to declare himself a Socialist. This was going pretty far and he used to be regarded by myself and my fellows with the horrified pity of tolerant minds for a voluntary outlaw. Lane himself was a bigoted Liberal. He used to

F   69

pour patronising scorn on my inherited Conservatism, implying that it was a proof that my intelligence had not properly
matured and hinting that this was a great disappointment to
him as he found me in other respects a fairly desirable appren-
tice. But in politics, as in other matters, he refrained from
discussing details and I soon formed the opinion that, although
I knew next to nothing about the issues involved, Lane
himself knew absolutely nothing at all.

Although he never lost an opportunity of showing off his
fervour for the Liberal cause (particularly in Liberal company)
Lane was not the man to let political bias interfere with a good
bargain. No Conservative writer of the day was a better
marksman than H. H. Munro. Without ever going out of
his way to lug a political allusion into his beautifully polished
Morning Post stories he could release an occasional arrow of
satire at the Asquith government and its ministers which would
wring a yelp of indignant pain from such Liberals as Mr.
Crockett, the town traveller. But Lane, puckering his beard
in forbearance, appreciated "Saki's" wit and encouraged and
exploited him for all he was worth. Not that other publishers
let political prejudice affect their judgment; but Lane seemed
always to find an additional piquant appeal in authors whose
views differed violently from his own on political or religious
grounds (he was a scathingly outspoken anti-Catholic). He
didn't allow even his aesthetic tastes to govern his decisions.
He was, for example, puzzled and slightly nauseated by the
gasconading excesses of Futurism, which at that time had
become a fashionable joke, but he consented to publish
Wyndham Lewis's huge, pink and garish journal *Blast*. To
me was assigned the job of devising the publicity and after I
had taken stock of the contents I thought the best policy
would be to disarm the defamation and ridicule, which Lane
would be bound to incur, by a subtle indication that he was
supporting the venture with his tongue in his cheek. Lane

would have none of this, so I asked him frankly whether he really admired and subscribed to the frantic aberrations of *Blast*. He gave me a patient, non-committal smile and said decisively, "No, no, no." He paused a moment and the burr dropped to a whisper. "But you never know—there may be something in it."

Lane suffered from that ailment so common among the elderly, of being unable to remember people's names. This particularly applied to the names of authors, except for those of the chosen and familiar few. He had a quite automatic and unaffected habit of referring to authors by the titles of their books, but since he was often unable to remember the book-title too there were frequent occasions when the individual to be discussed had to be established by a process of deduction and elimination, in the course of which he would show increasing impatience with himself for his own lack of concentration and even more with me for my stupidity in being unable to guess the name of the person he wanted to talk about. But on the whole he was a good deal better at the book-titles than the authors' names. While we were in America he took a trip to Montreal and from the University Club in that city I received a letter from him which began:

"DEAR BEN,
"I have lunched here with Leacock and I am to dine here with him and the husband of the Red Lantern tonight—tomorrow I dine at the Red Lanterns'."

Though a complete autocrat Lane was a benign and at times an intimate autocrat. His manner towards me was never that of the boss towards an employee. It was the engaging if exigent manner of some old master craftsman of tradition towards his pupil. If in the course of conversation he asked me for my opinion he gave the impression that this wasn't because he thought I could offer him the smallest help in forming his own; but rather that he was just trying me out. If I gave what he considered was the wrong answer he would crow with exultant dissent. Yet there was no suggestion of unkindness or arrogance in this rather patronising habit. On the contrary it was a sure sign of his interest and affection.

I well remember one such test question. I don't know how the subject arose, but he suddenly asked me which I considered the greater, George Meredith or Thomas Hardy. He fixed his watery eyes on me and waited in gleeful anticipation to bash my indiscreet judgment to bits. If I had been candid I would have answered, "I've read very little by either of them, and I strongly suspect that your own estimates are based almost entirely on the sixth sense." But having at least come across *Lucifer in Starlight* in an anthology, I guessed boldly and without hesitation. Lane's look of challenge dissolved into a smile of approval. "Of course," he murmured.

I was with Lane for exactly three years before I went off in 1914 to serve in the war. I said that Teignmouth Shore's letter of introduction to Lane altered the whole course of my existence. It did. It is true that those three years were the whole of my experience in the publishing trade. Nor was my later career as a writer materially influenced by any of the Bodley Head authors; I had learned more in a few weeks from Pinero than in my three years of publishing, and through it all I still clung to my ambition to become a playwright. But that letter of Shore's had landed me definitely and permanently in the world of literature. I knew now that somewhere—there was no telling at what odd spot, but somewhere—in that world was where my future lay. At the time it was quite understood that I should return to the Bodley Head after the war, but destiny had other ideas.

Destiny meanwhile hit on an extremely whimsical idea concerning my immediate employment. My father had acquired a house at Burford Bridge where my brother and I were living with him in the circumstances which the average type of fairly prosperous business man could, in those days, quite comfortably afford. That is to say it was a spacious house with a billiard-room and a three- or four-acre garden; and the domestic staff consisted of a butler, old King, and the butler's cook-wife and the cook-wife's housekeeper sister and two maids and a whole-time gardener and a chauffeur who drove our early specimen of a Straker Squire car and used to ogle the prettier of the two maids and, I remember, I didn't blame him. Old King was one of the vanished race of butlers, born to his job. Only once did his dignity forsake him. He dashed into my bedroom early one morning, crying wildly "Hairship . . . hairship." I scrambled grumpily from bed to the window and set eyes for the first time on an aeroplane. It was, of course, of the primitive box-kite type and was staggering over the garden at its ceiling of about one hundred and fifty feet.

I looked at it dispassionately. Interesting, yes—any phenomenon is interesting. But even such advanced and madcap prodigies of science and mechanics could never become any active concern of mine. I just wasn't made that way. Why, I'd never had the smallest inclination even to try to drive the Straker Squire car. I thanked old King, rather curtly I'm afraid, and went back to bed.

About a year later, in the autumn of 1914, I was a Probationary-Flight-sub-Lieutenant in the Royal Naval Air Service.

CHAPTER IV

Pilot Irving

M R. WINSTON CHURCHILL stood beneath the open cockpit of my aeroplane and looked up at me with the expression of a viva-voce examiner who isn't himself quite sure of the right answers. It was in the last days of May, 1915; so he would have been about forty years old. He was First Lord of the Admiralty. Information had reached him that the Germans were about to launch the first Zeppelin airship raid on London. He had come to inspect the one Hendon aircraft which had been finally detailed and equipped to engage the enemy and to admonish its pilot and crew. I was the crew.

It was an exceptionally large and ponderous two-seater biplane known familiarly as the Sopwith gun-bus. It was of the pusher type, having its heavy stationary engine behind the pilot. The observer or gunner sat in front of the pilot and right out in the nose of the machine. So by standing and leaning over I was able to talk quite confidentially to Mr. Churchill.

He questioned me about my armament and I exhibited the rifle with which I had been served out for the purpose of shooting down the Zeppelin. I didn't tell him that I had never handled a rifle in my life and hadn't the slightest idea how to reload it. He asked me whether it was conjectured that a rifle would prove an adequate weapon for shooting down Zeppelins. I leant a trifle farther over my cockpit and lowered my voice.

"It's got incendiary bullets, sir," I said.

"Ah," said Mr. Churchill in a tone which seemed to imply

74

that this settled the whole problem. He must have realised the pitiable inadequacy of the entire outfit but there was nothing in his demeanour calculated to dampen my zeal and optimism. On the contrary, as though satisfied with all he had seen and heard, he changed the subject to ask after my cousin, Jim Travers, who was a pioneer of flying and with whom he himself had, I think, taken the air in a characteristic spirit of adventure.

There was less chance of my knocking out a Zeppelin than there was of my knocking out Jack Johnson. I don't suppose for a moment that this was in any way Mr. Churchill's fault. He had, no doubt, taken office to find that, so far as the Royal Naval Air Service was concerned, the preparations to meet the impending air attack on London were typified by the figure I must have presented to him, as I stood brandishing my rifle in the nose of the Sopwith gun-bus.

But the nod of encouragement Mr. Churchill gave me also typified his strength of purpose in inspiring confidence at home and, with any luck, in intimidating the enemy. It had been openly stated that if a Zeppelin ventured to invade our skies it would fly into a nest of hornets. A small deputation of M.P.s had visited Hendon and had been shown a row of box-kite training machines, lined up in weatherbound and oilstained dilapidation, some of them incapable of soaring beyond the few feet required for taking-off and landing practice. But the ordinary citizen knew nothing of types and performances. An aeroplane was an aeroplane. The M.P.s had gone away with winks and whispers of sage reassurance. It was true enough. The hornets were there. They'd seen them for themselves.

Flight-Lieutenant Douglas Barnes was a big, slow, charming character of about my own age, which was eight or nine years above the age of most of the volunteers accepted for flying duties in the R.N.A.S. He was invariably referred to and addressed as "Auntie", a tribute to the benignity of his nature. He and I had been left at Hendon during a transition period in which our training squadron was being transferred to the neighbouring and affiliated station at Chingford. The authorities had recently selected and established the latter site as being ideal for training purposes, it being a strip of fogbound and soggy meadowland at Ponders End, situated between a reservoir and a sewage farm.

Auntie Barnes undoubtedly saved my life by exercising his authority as senior officer at Hendon. It had been originally laid on that in the anti-Zepp operations I should pilot a Caudron biplane, accompanied presumably by some ill-fated air-mechanic who was to crouch close behind me and direct a stream of incendiary bullets either through or just to one side of my shoulder. But I had never flown after dark and Auntie declared my Caudron unfit for flying. It wasn't; but no doubt he well knew it would have been very soon after my take-off; to say nothing of how unfit I and the wretched air-mechanic would have been. Grounded from my Caudron I compromised by persuading Auntie Barnes to cast me for the role of gunner in his Sopwith—and there I was, all made-up and accoutred, just in time for Mr. Churchill.

It was late on the night of the 31st May, 1915, and darkness had set in when our signal came from the Admiralty by telephone "Stand by and await further orders". We stood by and awaited. The Zeppelin chugged its laborious way to a destination somewhere over Victoria Station where it dropped a bomb or two and chugged away again, maintaining throughout a height of about 10,000 feet. Chingford duly received its further orders and some half-dozen pilots and their riflemen took off in a variety of training aircraft. One of them relied even on his box-kite and had to confine himself to a protracted series of furious circuits round and round the roofs of the Chingford huts.

At Hendon I waited with Auntie and eyed the silent telephone, conscious of a gradual evaporation of my urgent lust for battle. On the aerodrome miscellaneous mechanics made well-intentioned but ineffective efforts to illumine the ground for our take-off with acetylene searchlights which all spluttered out and contributed only an execrable stink. At length Auntie made bold to go to the telephone and prompt the hesitant Admiralty. "What?" came the reply. "Haven't you gone up yet? Go up forthwith." I later ascertained that by this time the Zeppelin was well on its homeward journey somewhere over the North Sea.

I don't know how long we were in the air. I don't know at what height we cruised, peering in conscientious ineptitude through the mist. I suppose the gun-bus may have been encouraged by slow degrees to attain a ceiling of a sulky 5,000 feet. Eventually Auntie decided on a forced landing and nose-dived into a field at Hatfield. I had the presence of mind to slip out of my safety-belt on the way down and was shot like a stone from a catapult ahead of the wreckage.

It may seem strange and reprehensible that I can look back at the tragedy of that night with a light heart. Perhaps it is because my memory still hears the echo of the laughter and gaiety which inspired us all through our struggles with the risks and inexperience of those days. And, after all, if, when memory comes to rest on some old friend of the past, one's first instinct is to laugh, what more genuine proof can there be of one's affection?

Moreover, I myself went through the most ludicrous performance on regaining consciousness; one which should, I think, be briefly reported if only to show how odd may be the immediate effects of concussion. Perhaps the oddest feature of it all is that I have remembered many of the details so clearly, though only half my brain was functioning at the time. This half of my intelligence bade me first investigate what had taken place in the midst of the shattered gun-bus. Then for some time I was obsessed by the spiritual sense of duty in the tragic circumstances. This was quite as it should be, but my observances took the form of walking round and round in widening circles and singing a variety of hymns. Presently I found a stile and after gazing at it suspiciously for a minute or so I clambered with difficulty through the hedge alongside it. I found a cottage and my rambling soliloquies were heard by the inmates of the bedroom above. The husband naturally contented himself with sitting up in bed and shouting some terse and testy comments on whichever of his drunken neighbours was at it again. Fortunately the wife favoured more practical and energetic measures. She rose, pulled up the window and looked out, pausing no doubt on the way to arm herself with the water-jug.

She went and got hold of Mr. Smith-Bingham who lived close by. He came and propped me up as we reeled along to his house. I was muttering all the time, "I must telephone; I must telephone." "You shall telephone," he said—I remember the quiet reassurance in his tone and exactly the position I sat in when I flopped into a chair in his study and every syllable that was said, and yet by this time I was hanging desperately on to the last shred of consciousness.

"Now—who d'you want to telephone to?"

"I can't remember."

He asked to be put through to the Admiralty. "Now, what's your name?"

"Barnes," I said.

"Barnes. And what's the name of the other poor chap— the one we went and saw out there?"

"Travers."

That was my last word for twenty-four hours or more. I didn't remain officially dead for long. Smith-Bingham must have seen the name-tabs on my clothes when he put me to bed and telephoned the Admiralty again. He and his wife put me up in their house until I was convalescent. I duly remember their kindness, but I remember nothing about the whole incident so clearly as all that went on while I was almost as extinct as I said I was.

Some who are elderly enough to possess memories of those days may maintain that the administration and equipment of the R.N.A.S. were not so bad as this implies. After all, I myself, a few days before Mr. Churchill's visit, had urged a Henri Farman biplane to a height of 7,500 feet, to beat the existing Hendon height record. And while I was yet on my three-weeks sick leave Warneford actually brought down a Zeppelin in France and gained his V.C. Even his achievement would have been forestalled if the bomb dropped by Bigsworth on a previous Zeppelin had hit something solid enough to explode it. So conditions surely couldn't have been as bad as I suggest.

But the fact is that, all through the war, the Army dominated the flying services; and when these were combined into the R.A.F. in 1917 the R.N.A.S. was simply merged into the Royal Flying Corps and given military ranks. And this was because many of the senior officers of the senior service were stubbornly and foul-mouthedly shocked by the almost sacrilegious suggestion that these preposterous flying-machines, manned by a levy of lunatic landsmen, could ever aspire to render reinforcement to the Royal Navy. Some of them knew better and, later in the war, Admiral Beatty initiated, or at any rate approved, the formation of a squadron of land-based, carrier-borne torpedo aircraft with the rather optimistic idea that they should undertake a surprise attack on the German fleet in Kiel Harbour. But many old sea-dogs, their judgment and tempers methodically undermined by gin, carried their grumbling resentment of the R.N.A.S. with them throughout the whole contest and, indeed, to their dying day.

Warneford trained with me at Hendon, a brash character, half, or perhaps wholly, American by birth. His cocksure and boastful nature annoyed us all and fairly infuriated the Naval Officer who had been transferred from the Fleet to instil service tradition and discipline into our uninitiated civilian understanding. Warneford's final offence was to land one precious training box-kite effectively on to another which was remaining stationary on the aerodrome. He was forthwith dismissed the station with a strong recommendation that he should be dismissed the Service. Instead, the Admiralty ordered him to France; a decision which, it was generally anticipated, meant only a brief postponement of his farewell to arms. A month or so later he was a national hero.

But I? Many of my associates have wondered what sudden incongruous circumstance—what sudden rush of fevered patriotism, whimsicality or wine to the head—induced the utterly incompatible me to become an air pilot. Some of the more candid have added, "Even so, how the devil did you manage to remain one?"

It was November, 1914. My brother and most of my friends were already in the Army. Why wasn't I? Simply out of conscientious allegiance to Lane. At the outbreak of war, three months earlier, he had once more beetled off to America. He had besought me to remain at the Bodley Head until he got back. He wouldn't be long. Oh, wouldn't he? The months passed. I became every day more conscious of my patriotic impatience and of the eyebrows of some of my father's acquaintances (themselves nicely beyond the age-limit) raised in exasperating unspoken comment.

But I admit I nursed a certain foreboding. Army training involved, amongst other things, undertaking a continuous series of very long and very strenuous walks, a form of occupation which I had always regarded with the utmost disdain and still do. Nor was I confident that I would take kindly to the use of firearms. Some odd little kink in my nervous system had always prompted me to shrink instinctively from fire-arms, rather in the way that one may shrink instinctively from snakes. I wasn't a coward. I could and would gladly over-come this aversion and brace myself to face the battlefield. It was just that I deplored the dismal prospect of being taught, rather discourteously, how to get there.

But it was the unavoidable course which lay before me and patriotism reprimanded my qualms. Then, one day, when I was, as usual, lunching at the Public Schools Club, I met one of my fellow-members who was resplendent in a full R.N. sub-lieutenant's uniform. Full. None of your wiggly R.N.V.R. stripes.

"Good Lord," I said. "Where did you get that outfit?"

"Gieves'," he replied. "R.N.A.S. It's easy. They want chaps badly. I'll tell you how to apply."

I applied. I was accepted. My medical examination held one awful moment when I was bidden to climb up a suspended rope. I waited until the supervisor was looking elsewhere and took a flying leap at the rope, landing over half-way up. The supervisor turned and saw me up there and said, "All right, that'll do." I went to Gieves. I walked down Piccadilly, myself in the uniform of a R.N. sub-lieutenant, varied only by the addition of a small gilt eagle on the left sleeve. I didn't know how even to exchange a Naval salute.

As for the perils of learning to fly—pooh! It wasn't peril I was secretly so anxious to avoid. It was that walking. I had dodged that anyhow. My lack of the first faint glimmer of knowledge of aeronautics dismayed me as little as my abrupt renunciation of Lane. But I must almost certainly have been the first individual who learned to fly an aeroplane before he ever learned to drive a car.

At the age of twenty-eight I found myself back in a class-room, learning logarithms, the theory of flight (I never got within a mile of that one) and navigation from a dug-out Naval Instructor and putting up my hand when I wanted to leave the room. Away flew all the intervening years, in Singapore, in the City, in the Bodley Head. Back came my boyhood with its obsessions and presentiments.

What was I doing here? My companions were hearty youths whose whole outlook and baffling technical conversation showed them to be well-equipped for potential airmanship. I could have entertained them with a graphic comparison between the respective style and artistry of Clem Hill and Frank Woolley, or, if they preferred, could have quoted for their benefit the whole of Arthur Bourchier's acting version of *The Merchant of Venice*, with a critical commentary on the side. But they were concerned only with such questions as the theoretical advantage of dispensing with inlet-valve springs in a Monosoupape engine and Chinese of that sort.

My flying tuition was undertaken by Merriam, a name which will be familiar to collectors of flying memoirs and curios. I drove him nearly frantic. But here again I was handicapped by my inner sense of inadaptability rather than by lack of skill. Eventually Merriam's somewhat uncouth perseverence was rewarded; although, by the time I yanked my spluttering box-kite off the ground single-handed, I had been under instruction for what was then the preposterously lengthy period of two hours and six minutes.

Favoured as I was by an absolutely first-class ignorance of why and how aircraft flew—and consequently unaware of any probable source of disaster—I became an accomplished pilot. When, following my sick-leave, I reported back at Chingford they were on the look-out for instructors. A pilot of six weeks standing, returning slightly haunted and unnerved by a narrow escape from death in an appalling crash, was held to be obviously the very man for the job. As it turned out I proved to be an outstanding success as an instructor and was retained at Chingford until the Spring of 1918.

Ivor Novello, who joined the R.N.A.S. in 1915 was one of my pupils. He had just written *Keep the Home Fires Burning* and was welcomed as a promising recruit for the entertainments branch of the station's activities, as indeed he proved. His first experience of flying entranced him to such an extent that it stimulated him into song. His voice trilled in ecstasy above the less dulcet roar of the engine. But after a few nerve-racking experiences I firmly ruled that, however lofty his artistic aspirations, as a pilot the ground was his limit. To have preserved the life of Ivor Novello at the outset of his career will probably be regarded by some as the one useful thing I ever did.

One morning at the outset of my training at Hendon the attenuated figure of a rather pallid eighteen-year-old trailed his long flying-boots into my company. I scrutinised him with that instinctive antagonism with which human nature is apt to prompt our first impression of any stranger of the same sex. "They want chaps badly," my club friend had told me. "Indeed they must," I thought.

But his conversation, conducted in a drawling tone in keeping with his stringy appearance, showed perspicacity and an undeniable sense of humour; and, after all, here we were in the midst of a war and it was necessary to associate and co-operate with various freakish assortments of one's fellow-man and I gradually decided very decently, if tentatively, to tolerate this springald youth. A few hours later it was revealed to me that he was the only son of my favourite actor, H. B. Irving. I adjusted my first impressions automatically. Here, surely, was one member of the Hendon party who might be able and willing to steer clear of thrust and dihedrals and centrifugal force and pitot tubes and all that gibberish and to give me some really worth-while information on the subjects nearest my heart. He became and remains the greatest friend I have ever had or ever will have.

Laurence Irving came back to Chingford from service in France in 1916 with a Croix de Guerre and impaired health. That in later years he developed into a man of such hale and striking appearance from the delicate creature he was then is a very good advertisement for something; enthusiasm perhaps. Even then his experiences at the front had not affected his inherent gaiety of spirit. Ivor Novello, now safely seconded to some essential but air-proof duties on the staff, collaborated with us in a revue and wrote some original numbers for it. We performed it at the air-station to the officers and their relations and friends and its success encouraged us to write a Chingford pantomime. But before this could be produced I was posted to East Fortune, not as may be supposed on account of my pantomime script but because Admiral Beatty's forthright plans for discommoding the German fleet were in process of gestation and I was to command one of the squadrons. These exercises in writing at odd moments when I wasn't engaged in teaching people to fly or when the aerodrome was under water or fogbound, as it often was for several days in succession, at least helped to keep the poor derelict old Ambition alive. They were, of course, essentially extravagant and local-topical, but this didn't make them any easier or less profitable as exercises. I still remember the concluding lines of the dismal soliloquy of the pantomime principal boy who had forced-landed in some god-forsaken back of beyond and was bewailing his impending fate:

> Marooned, without a drink, without a friend:
> And doomed, like Ponder, to a filthy end.

In the middle of the war, when air combat had become a regular and ferocious feature of hostilities, someone hit on the

THE CUCKOO
AIR TORPEDO

THE AUTHOR IN THE PILOT
SEAT OF A 60 H.P. BRISTOL
BOX-KITE TRAINER,
CHINGFORD, 1916

bright idea of inventing a parachute for the use of pilots in
trouble. I was appointed to carry out some tests of this
brainwave. An outsize toy teddy-bear, weighted up to
about fourteen stone was strapped beneath the fuselage of a
BE2C. A 20-foot coil of rope attached it to a parachute
designed to open as it left the aeroplane. On the first test
I released this elaborate bag of tricks at 1,000 feet. It worked
perfectly and the teddy-bear sailed gracefully and without
any severe bounce to the ground. I was then requested to
repeat the experiment from 500 feet. They rewound and
re-strapped the teddy-bear and parachute to the fuselage but
they (and, needless to say, I) had failed to take into consideration the fact that the surface of Chingford aerodrome was
in its normal state of soaking wetness. The rope had become
saturated and although, on the second run, the teddy-bear duly
fell out, the parachute refused to budge. I found myself
flying around with a fourteen-stone burden swinging twenty
feet below me. The only course was to make as slow a landing
as possible so that when the weight of the bear pulled off my
undercarriage (as duly happened) I should avoid going over on
my nose. It was a very minor disaster involving small risk;
but to-day, when I sit and watch news-reels of operations which
congest the skies with whole battalions of descending personnel,
to say nothing of their guns, lorries and tanks, I recall with
mixed emotions the aboriginal joint efforts of myself and
Messrs. Hamley.

Frederic Weld-Blundell, a distinguished R.N. torpedo-man,
had been transferred to the R.A.F. (as it had now become) to
take charge of the projective torpedo operations. I had taught
him to fly and it was he who offered me command of one of
the two squadrons in slow process of formation. The other
squadron was allotted to Conway Pulford, who was destined
long afterwards to be the ill-fated Air Vice Marshal of the
R.A.F. in Singapore at the time of the Japanese invasion.

Sopwith had designed a special aircraft for the torpedo job, the Cuckoo, probably to this day the largest single-seater machine ever put into service. We used Belhaven sands, near Dunbar, as an aerodrome and made practice runs, aiming at a stationary drifter and gradually working up into formation attacks on co-operative destroyers steaming full-speed-ahead.

I initiated this enterprise when, on July 4th, 1918, I deposited into the Firth of Forth the first torpedo ever to be dropped from a land-based aircraft. How odd it seems that so improbable a character as I should have figured in these elementary but portentous affairs.

The armistice mercifully curtailed our preparations but in the early spring of 1919, when I had got over the Spanish 'flu and my almost miraculous escape from succumbing to this ghastly scourge, I was sent on a mission to South Russia. This, I'm afraid, was not because a generous Air Ministry wanted to provide me with a rest cure. We were still—for some obscure reason which I forget now if I ever knew—lending military support to the White Russians against the Red ones. Someone in authority conceived the idea that we might torpedo the Red Russian fleet which was lying iced-up in Astrakhan harbour. The operation was not intended to anticipate a now popular form of entertainment and to be performed on ice; we were to be prepared to strike at the outset of the melting season.

Someone had to go and prepare the way for this nightmare sortie. If only the inspired and pugnacious Air Ministry chieftain had decided, as a preliminary, to consult the nearest geography master he would have ascertained that the Caspian Sea is a lake with a depth of about fifteen feet and was therefore impracticable for the reception of torpedos. As it was, I was dispatched to spend three dilatory and excessively uncomfortable months of travel.

In the course of this I journeyed from Batum to Baku by the

Trans-Caucasian railway in a train which covered some two hundred miles in a week. I was one of a British party recruited from all three services whose dozen members were making the journey impelled by a variety of biddings and motives. They ranged from an R.N. post-captain to a Scots private in a kilt.

The natives of Aserbijan were enjoying a private feud with their neighbours of Georgia and our train was held up at the frontier by a hostile gang of Georgians, bristling with fur and firearms, who declined to allow an engine driven by an Aserbijan to proceed along their territorial track. Our naval captain dealt with the emergency in characteristic style. He sent the Scots private along to the engine accompanied by a fixed bayonet and an interpreter. The interpreter was told to reassure the engine-driver that the Scots private would protect him from molestation; the Scots private was told that if we did not forthwith get up steam and blind ahead he was to give the engine-driver himself a good prod up the backside with the bayonet. We proceeded.

I eventually got home and issued to the Air Ministry my strictly confidential report on the depth of the Caspian Sea. I had been set several other questions as well. One, I recall, was "What was the surface condition of Tiflis Aerodrome when you saw it?" the answer being "I didn't. It was under eight feet of snow."

I got demobilised. I closed my fifth and final Pilot's Flying Log Book with a hearty snap. Compared with that of hundreds of other pilots my war record was a very modest one; for one thing I had never, thank heaven, been called upon to engage in aerial combat. I had survived only eight crashes, including one picturesque pancake into the Firth of Forth. But I had made 3,523 flights as pilot and had averaged three-quarters of an hour in the air for every day of the war. At the end of it all I found my sentiments towards aviation to be almost exactly the same as they had been on that early morning, some years before, when old King had come panting into my bedroom with his precipitant "Hairship. . . . Hairship."

Throughout the war I received many favours from Fortune or, as I prefer to believe, from Providence; but one of them was boundless and everlasting. Like my friendship with Laurence Irving this favour received a very lukewarm initial reception from my grudging and resistive nature. At Chingford on Sunday afternoons accredited visitors were allowed to come and be shown round the place, but I could never be bothered with them. One day a lady and her daughter turned up to bring us news, which they had somehow or other received, of an ex-Chingford officer who had gone abroad and was a prisoner-of-war. It was a thoughtful action on their part, but when I, on the strength of having known the officer in question, was told off to greet and escort them I protested in brief, futile soliloquy and went to do so cursing my luck.

At the first moment of our meeting I uncursed it. By the time I had recruited some lounging nonentity to deal with the mother and had walked twenty yards with the daughter I was busily blessing it. We were married on April 29th, 1916. If, as I honestly believe, I have spent a happier life than anybody else I know, that is the reason.

"I am giving up," said John Lane. "I am turning the Bodley Head into a private limited company. Now—I will make you an offer."

A brief pregnant pause. The lymphatic smile dwelt upon me with genuine warmth of affection. I wondered what the offer would be. He might be giving up but from what I knew of him the dear old boy wouldn't be likely to be giving very much more.

The offer came. I was to work for the firm. I couldn't, of

course, hope to participate in any profits but I would be paid a salary of five hundred pounds a year.

Well, that didn't sound so bad. But that wasn't quite all. "My dear boy," said my father when I told him about it, "I can't possibly afford to raise ten thousand pounds."

My father-in-law was a dapper, well-dressed, highly-coloured, sharp-tempered little man who possessed private means sufficient, in those days, to enable him to live in comfort without having to earn his living. This was fortunate because I don't think he could have. Every hour of his life was regulated by a punctilious time-table, devised to enable him to spend each completely profitless day to his satisfaction. My mother-in-law did not contribute much brain-power to the ordering of the methodical menage, but she was the soul of good nature and enjoyed being laughed at, which always made her very easy for me to get along with.

It had been my father-in-law's pre-war custom to spend the late summer months, accompanied by his wife and daughter, at Burnham-on-sea, in Somerset, where, to a strictly pre-scribed routine, he would associate with its disused residents and thrash its celebrated links.

I was now, of course, out of a job and circumstances seemed to recommend my finding one pretty quickly. Still, I had a handsome war gratuity and some savings. "First of all," I said, "I mean to have a go at writing." "All right," said my wife. "Let's go to Burnham while you have it."

We had been in Burnham together on a week's leave during the war. We now rented a small furnished house there; but it can't have been so very small, for it accommodated us two, my one-year-old daughter and her nanny, a cook-general and, for many delectable weeks, Laurence Irving.

Under his exhilarating influence the go at writing took a preliminary excursion into an exciting but unexplored line of country. Motion pictures, belonging to what are now referred to as "the old silent days", were by this time so universal a form of entertainment that they had reached even Burnham. Laurence Irving was so obsessed with them that he easily persuaded me to collaborate with him in writing a film script. All I can remember about it is that it was sternly and solemnly dramatic in theme, that it bore the title of *Priests' Land*, that it had something to do with an unfortunate priory house which had managed to land itself with a curse in the days of Henry VIIIth's abolition of the monasteries, and that its harrowing proceedings were presided over by a forbidding priest named Sarpax. I don't think the script ever got beyond our sitting-room until one day we decided to submit it to the judgment of Laurence Irving's good-natured mother, Dorothea Baird.

She did me the first of two very good turns. "For goodness' sake," she wrote back to her son, "tell your friend Ben to try his hand at something funny. I'm sure it's much more in his line and there's always a much better market for it."

But so long as Laurence Irving was staying with us the pictures were the thing. We used regularly to attend the abandoned shop which had been converted into The Majestic Cinema and sit gloating in an indescribable fugg while the redheaded daughter of the manager accompanied the films on a piano which would have been faulty anyhow. One particularly spectacular picture of the *Quo Vadis* species animated Laurence Irving's gift as a cartoonist. He depicted two lions leaving the Roman arena. One of them, wearing a very wry expression on his face, was turning to his partner and inquiring apprehensively: "Did you notice anything queer about that last Christian?"

I had met Mrs. H. B. Irving several times during and just after the war. Her extraordinary experience of having emerged practically from the schoolroom to create the part of

Trilby and her long stage career which followed had left her the most untheatrical person imaginable. She was gentle and gracious, as, indeed, are many successful actresses, but I don't believe she had any great love for the profession. Later on I used to try to get her to come to my first nights, and she sometimes said she would for my sake; but she always asked me to let her back out of it at the last moment. She said the environment of a first night made her feel physically sick.

She and my wife had been the only two feminine members of the audience at a memorable special performance of *The Bells* which H. B. had given to the troops in war-time and which marked the stage début of his daughter Elizabeth, Laurence's sister, who later married Felix Brunner. Elizabeth Brunner has always presented a problem. Is she more beautiful in looks than she is kind at heart or the other way about? I think the only solution is that it's a dead heat.

The preliminary stage of my beneficial friendship with the Irving family was rounded off by my being taken with my wife to visit H. B. in his house at Harrow. There he was, sitting and talking to me, primate of all the high priests who had for so many years performed the rites while I had sat, an obscure little worshipper embedded in the pit. I felt like Anatole France—"*je ne sais pas que je ne rêve*". I was to experience this same queer sensation of incredulity on every occasion when I found myself for the first time in the company of others of the high priests—Hawtrey, Maude, du Maurier. They materialised into a still half-fantastic reality from the treasured Mystery of my boyhood.

H. B. Irving died in early middle age and I met him only a few times. I remember on this first occasion his asking me what impressions I had formed on my trip to South Russia.

I said, "It's all very cold and uncomfortable. The food and living conditions are shocking. The country is crowded out with all manner of people of all nations and with nondescript

refugees belonging to none. Their habits are indescribably
dirty and their dispositions are most unreliable. You can
never be sure whether anyone is your friend or foe."

"H'm," said H. B. "It sounds very like England."

Laurence Irving married soon after this and our friendship
with him became immediately and permanently duplicated.
I have now known him for well over forty years and to me his
friendship grows a more valuable and dependable possession
the older it gets.

"Something funny", Mrs. H. B. had said. A farce then,
obviously I had never envisaged myself as farce writer, but
after all Pinero himself had explored and civilised that line of
country before he discovered *The Second Mrs. Tanqueray*.
Moreover, I was under the delusion still shared by many people
that farce was the easiest sort of play to write. I was soon to
find out, and to continue finding out, that no form of stage
entertainment is more difficult successfully to write, to produce
or to act.

Anyhow, I knew the formula for farce—and here I was right
enough. Act 2—the sympathetic and guileless hero is landed
into the thick of some grievous dilemma or adversity. Act 1
—he gets into it. Act 3—he gets out of it. Right. Then
what type of hero? Why not aim high? It was prodigious
odds against my getting Charles Hawtrey even to consider my
first and as yet unwritten farce, but he gave me a definite and
objective type to work on. And the particular form of
adversity or dilemma? Suppose I myself were suddenly
called upon to face up to some novel, topical, social obligation?
Wasn't there one which would strike me as being peculiarly
nightmarish?

Ballroom dancing of the sort known as "specialty", originated by Vernon and Irene Castle and featured by their many
proselytes after Castle's death in the war, was all the rage.

What about a Mrs. Vernon Castle, suddenly let down by her normal opposite number and roping in a kind and susceptible gentleman who undertakes to act as her partner before he realises what he is getting himself in for? Not bad for Hawtrey. The setting could be a county ball, given by an inflated, titled war-profiteer (another topicality). Once committed, the hero would, of course, remain loyal to the lady, engage in altercations with the host and in bewildered argument with the leader of the coon band (topicality again). And no sooner has he scored in a comedy variation of the specialty dance that he is exposed by the belated arrival of the genuine husband. And is not his fiancée an unforeseen member of the house party?

I set to work. Pinero gave me my construction; the good old standard text-book still held good. But the West End theatre had become thoroughly du Maurier'd by this time and there must be none of the Pinero grandiloquence. I started as I always went on all through my farce writing, making the characters recognisable types of human beings. The funniness must be in the situations and circumstances in which these human beings find themselves, and these are only funny because the characters are so recognisably human.

This sounds very dogmatic and pretentious and I don't for a moment claim that I discovered it. But I do claim that I found it out for myself. And to be quite honest I think there have been quite a few people rather given to airing this, their theory, about the secret of Farce who are a little apt to forget who put them wise to it in the first place.

I finished my first edition of the farce. I didn't think it was bad but I funked the issue. A sort of lack of bounce and the sensitive apprehension of having my own feelings hurt, which were always lurking in my nature as the result of the timorous littleness of my boyhood, made me shrink from the prospect of having the Ambition blighted in its first youth. But it seemed a pity to waste the material. What about writing it up as a novel? John Lane would probably be prepared to show a certain amount of indulgence in my case. So I wrote it as a novel, called *The Dippers*—the Castle characters in the story were named Hank and Pauline Dipper. And, sure enough, before long I had the curious experience of myself entering from Vigo Street and edging into the still teeming outer office of the Bodley Head to sidle my way through and be interviewed, as a prospective author, by John Lane in the doorway of his congested sanctum.

The private limited company did not seem to have materialised as yet and I wasn't altogether surprised. At any rate, Lane had given up giving up for the time being and was still running the business in exactly the same way. He produced a contract undertaking to publish *The Dippers* and five subsequent novels. It would be tedious to enter into details about the terms. I will content myself with remarking that that contract ought to be placed, as an historic document, on public exhibit in some appropriate berth, preferably the Black Museum at Scotland Yard.

But I signed it without hesitation. At least it meant my official acknowledgment and establishment as a professional author. And in the buoyancy of that feeling I assured myself that the alarming number of copies which would have to be sold before I began to receive my first modest royalty would be pretty certain to be wolfed up by a clamorous public in next to no time.

I confided to Lane that I was toying with the idea of writing a stage farce on the subject of *The Dippers*. He looked at me as though he feared that the favour he had just conferred on me had gone to my head. "Oh, I wouldn't try to do that," he replied. I said no more but his words and manner seemed a direct challenge. Already, since finishing the novel, I had rewritten the farce, and now another of Laurence Irving's visits spurred, or rather propelled me, to destiny. He put a stop to all my indecision and sent the script off to his mother.

Before this happened we had temporarily left Burnham. My prolonged struggle with *The Dippers* had used up my war bonus. That we could still go on subsisting was largely due to my wife's long deceased grandmother.

My wife's grandmother must have been a wise old soul. She had taken shrewd measure of her only child, my wife's father. She had concluded that a meticulous attention to doing nothing with a methodical regularity did not argue very reliable strength of character and with the most gratifying common sense she had left a moderate sum of money in trust to my wife on her marriage.

Had I been the hero of a story by a Victorian lady novelist we would never, of course, have been married at all. On being accepted as a suitor, only to learn of my wife's financial prospects, I would have buried my face in my hands, have bade her a choking farewell and have disappeared over the horizon like a scalded and broken-hearted Walt Disney cat. As it was, I was duly grateful to the shade of the grandmother, and I will say for my father-in-law that, far from resenting the old lady's adjudication, he welcomed and heartily encouraged the idea that I, too, should settle down to a steady and scrupulous programme of systematic unemployment.

But by now I had decided that the time had come for me to take a regular job. The Dippers and others could continue their inconclusive antics, but this would have to be in my spare time. The trouble was that, at this juncture, it was nearly as difficult to find a decent regular job as it was to place a first farce. I scoured the publishing trade in vain and eventually had to agree to try my hand at the only available job, which consisted of touting a series of unwieldy and voluminous records of 'Varsity sport on commission. We took a small furnished house at Hayes in Kent while I endured the horrors of this undignified occupation and my wife brought forth our elder son, Benjamin the Eighth.

One morning, some months after this event and early in the year 1921, I was in my bath before setting forth to fail to sell some records of 'Varsity sport. I heard my wife in conversation on the telephone below, and presently she paused to call excitedly up to me. "It's about the play," she cried. "It's about the play."

Like Archimedes in his moment of supreme enlightenment, I leapt from the bath. Unlike Archimedes, I stopped to wrap myself in a towel before dashing forth from the bathroom. By the time I reached her my wife had finished telephoning and was on her way to bring me the news.

Who had been on the telephone but the staunch and invaluable Laurence Irving. But what had happened, what had happened? Just this.

Mrs. H. B. had sent the script of the farce to the leading play-agent in London, Golding Bright. Golding Bright, discerning in it potentialities for Hawtrey, had sent the script to Hawtrey. Hawtrey had read the farce and had considered it and had approved it. And at length, in due course, he had entered the building in Leicester Square and passed the ground-floor Leicester Galleries, and had mounted the stairs to the first-floor offices which later I was to know so well. And there he had finally clinched the purchase of *The Dippers* by presenting Golding Bright with two post-dated cheques.

The incredible had come to pass. My first farce—written for Charles Hawtrey—accepted by Charles Hawtrey. I swung the bath-towel round my shoulders with a sweep of triumph and embraced my wife. At length—at long length—I released her. And then I turned and shook hands with Pinero.

CHAPTER V

"Quite Extraordinary People"

REGINALD GOLDING BRIGHT was a short pudgy man with both the appearance and the qualities of a singularly complacent bull-dog. He was never, never perturbed. In all his dealings with professional eccentrics and vehement impresarios he maintained an unruffled and practical dispassion. His method of dealing with antagonism or disappointment was unfailingly polite but very definite; he merely showed them civilly out of his office and consideration until such time as they chose to return in a chastened state of mind. He never gave way. Once he had made a decision it was always quite affably understood that this decision was the accepted and unalterable starting-point of any discussion.

He was very secretive; he would confirm or deny some fragment of information or rumour but he would never initiate it. It was this habit of his, in the course of his dealings with *The Dippers*, which was to bring me such resentment that I temporarily forsook his counsel; but I soon found myself back in his office and he received me with a bland amiability which did not seem merely to ignore my fit of pique but to be totally unaware that I had had one.

Thereafter, until his death in 1942, he was to be my constant guide, if guide is not too subservient a word for a sort of consultant superintendent. For even later on when I was finding my own way he always kept one watchful eye on my progress and another even more watchful eye on my returns.

He was agent for nearly all the leading dramatists of his time; but it was not because he played so important a part in my own career that remembrance loves to linger in his company. Even in the jungle of the theatrical world, with so many exceptional individual specimens roaming at large, he remained an unique and immutable personality. Every first night discovered him in his stall and, by the time the play was half-way through, in an unvarying attitude, with his hands, encased in white washleather gloves, propping up his gold-knobbed cane, his chin resting on the knob and his eyes closed in apparent, and often genuine, slumber.

He enjoyed being a *bon viveur*, but in a strictly intimate fashion—one never seems to have heard of Golding Bright being at a party. He also delighted in exercising what he thought was his skill as a punter; though I suspect that his judgment in spotting likely winners was limited to plays. He had some remarkable theatrical treasures; once in his flat he showed me Barrie's original prompt-script of *Peter Pan*, with marginal comments and instructions as to how it should be produced and acted; and an eight- or ten-page letter written in red pencil on pages apparently torn from a child's exercise book, in which George Bernard Shaw implored the recognition and patronage which would promote him to success in the commercial theatre.

But my most impressive memory of that visit was gained by a glance into Golding Bright's bedroom. There is something characteristically engaging about a man whose bedside reading consists of only two volumes—the Holy Bible and *Ruff's Guide to the Turf*.

On my second visit to Bright's office I met Charles Hawtrey. He seemed to have stepped off the stage into the room and to be playing one of his usual characters; courtly, suave and complimentary. He congratulated me upon the farce. It was admirably conceived and well-written. Indeed, he adjudged it to be quite perfect for his purpose. All that was required now was for it to be thoroughly and almost totally revised.

My memory is vague about the number of revisions I made and submitted to Charles Hawtrey in the course of the next few months. But I remember he arranged that I should be invited to meet him one Sunday at a luncheon-party given by Lord and Lady Tichborne at their house in the Thames Valley. I was to bring the first of the revised versions with me and Hawtrey and I could discuss it together after the meal. It was an extraordinary party with about a dozen guests so diverse that they might have been invited by lottery. They ranged from Hawtrey and Pouishnoff, the pianist, to Sammy Woods. I had known the latter quite well at Burnham and he still enjoyed the reputation he had earned in past years for a remarkable proficiency in games; though it was perhaps fortunate for him that modesty was not a game. He monopolised the conversation during luncheon with reminiscences of his prowess in two of the pastimes which had contributed to his fame, namely cricket and drinking. At the end of it all Pouishnoff was roused to challenge and in a tone of defiance to which his slightly foreign accent seemed to lend additional emphasis he cried, "Mr. Woods. In this cricket, no; I cannot compete with you. But please to take notice that I am willing to join issue with you at any time in the matter of this lotion."

I suspect that Charles Hawtrey had been giving himself a quiet try-out as a potential rival to Sammy Woods in the course of the luncheon. At any rate, when he and I withdrew and he read through *The Dippers* again, he sat and laughed until the tears ran down his face. But more revisions were evidently called for. In a letter to me dated May 4th (1921) he wrote from the Playhouse, where he was appearing in *Up in Mabel's Room:*

"I am delighted to get your letter. I hope to read your new version this week"

which surely must relate to yet another revision from that which was the subject of another letter, written at the Orleans Club on Friday, whenever Friday was:

"If you get this in time will you look round at 37 Hertford St. to-morrow, Saturday? I have just got your new version and shall read it tonight."

Eventually, however, a final pre-production new version was achieved and agreed. By this time I had abandoned touting 'Varsity Sports records and we had gone back to Burnham. There I remained, finishing the novel *A Cuckoo in the Nest* and awaiting patiently but rapturously the wonderful forthcoming consummation of the Ambition.

And then suddenly one morning I had tidings of the Ambition's immediate prospects. My eye fell upon a head-line in the paper:

Mr. Charles Hawtrey for the Criterion

Ah. And then:

Mr. Charles Hawtrey will shortly appear at the Criterion Theatre under the management of Mr. T. C. Dagnall in a new comedy by Mr. Walter Hackett, entitled *Ambrose Applejohn's Adventure*."

Of course, it goes without saying that Golding Bright should have told me. But it was against Golding Bright's principles to tell anybody anything. I might have felt a little less aggrieved about it if Golding Bright hadn't been Walter Hackett's agent too, besides being the close friend and adviser of Mr. T. C. Dagnall. I am not saying for a moment that they were not right to pick on *Ambrose Applejohn's Adventure* in preference to my farce or any other farce on the market at that time. It gave Hawtrey one of the best parts he ever had. But that didn't alter the fact that every line and inflexion and reaction that I had written was perfect Hawtrey too. But there it was; and after *Ambrose Applejohn* had been running triumphantly for a month or two I was asked to call and see Hawtrey in his dressing-room. I went very despondently, knowing what was coming. He was going to relinquish his option on *The Dippers*.

I might have known my Hawtrey better. Relinquish his option? When he'd paid for it—with his heart's blood— with earnings filched from beneath the very noses of the bookmakers—and disbursed triumphantly in two post-dated cheques? No, indeed. But what Hawtrey could do was to *sell* his option on *The Dippers*. And had done so. It had all been most cordially arranged. Golding Bright, sitting pretty with the Hackett farce doing roaring business but saddled with *The Dippers* to sell for Hawtrey, had shrewdly sold *The Dippers* to Mr. T. C. Dagnall as well. Mr. T. C. Dagnall was looking for a new farce for Cyril Maude. So there it was. What could be better? To judge by Hawtrey's demeanour cordial was an utterly inadequate word for the arrangement.

I knew I was still tremendously lucky—my first farce still definitely accepted, still definitely going into production. But it meant giving up what I had set my heart on—and not only my heart, my whole imagination and purpose. Every line, mannerism, glance had been devised for Charles Hawtrey, to say nothing of my devotions to the task and new versions and the glory of having had the last of them accomplished and approved and blessed. Even the two post-dated cheques had been duly honoured.

I stood in the dressing-room rather disillusioned and dubious. Hawtrey for the first time became a little bit testy with me.

Clad, not inappropriately, in full pirate's rig, he spread his hands at me emphatically.

"Think, my dear fellow, think. Here am I—for another year or more—not a hope of doing your play, I'm afraid; not a hope. But Cyril Maude—an excellent fellow—and very popular—who better? And Mr. Dagnall has agreed to buy the play from me. He wants to make it a condition that I shall produce it." He sighed, as though he found this prospect a tedious obligation and the little matter of a pro-ducer's fee had not even crossed his mind. "Oh, very well, I suppose if he wants me to—I *will* produce it. There! What more do you want?"

So it came about that one Monday morning in February, 1922, I was again summoned to the Criterion Theatre; this time to attend the first rehearsal. I arrived late on purpose, being too self-conscious to face preliminary introductions and discussions. I found my way through the stage-door, down narrow stairs and along ominously silent inhospitable sub-terranean corridors, feeling rather like a lone passenger in the Ghost Train at a fair. I discovered the stage and halted, peering nervously from the wings.

The rehearsal had not yet started. The company was standing about in scattered little groups of twos and threes, engaged in subdued gossip. Seated in an upright chair mid-stage was Charles Hawtrey, shrouded in a heavy overcoat and a Homburg hat. Horn-rimmed glasses, resting almost on the tip of his nose, were bent over my script on his knees. A massive red pencil was in his hand and was methodically employed in scoring line after line of dialogue from the pages.

A sudden wave of resentment overcame my shyness. I advanced and inspected. On what passage of the play was the monstrous pencil at work? Yes—I might have guessed—one of my best scenes—and there it was going piecemeal—out—out.

This was too much. I had been belittled and ignored and treated as a catspaw for the Hawtrey-Bright machinations and had submitted pliantly. But at least the play had been there, completed and finally approved for them to do their surreptitious deals with. And here was Charles Hawtrey's endorsement of the completion and approval—in red pencil. So much for all his enthusiasm and delight and congratulations, my dear fellow. So much for the tears of laughter after the Tichborne lotion and fervid receptions of new versions from up in Mabel's room and from the Orleans Club Friday. I took a step nearer.

He didn't see me; he was too busy scoring out the dialogue—swish, swish. The next line? M'yes, swish. So naturally the dependent following line went too—swish. Another moment and that devastating pencil was hovering above my favourite line in the whole play—that brilliant riposte which had been chewed over and chuckled over in bathroom soliloquies for so many months past. The pencil duly hovered—struck. Out. A cry of anguish burst from my lips.

"Oh, Mr. Hawtrey——"

He glanced up at me over his glasses. His countenance softened in a smile of welcome—"Oh, there you are?"

"Mr. Hawtrey—that last line. Must that go? I'm sorry, but really I always thought it was—rather a good line."

He gazed at me. He spoke in a tone of gentle incredulity.

"A good line?" he said, emphasising each syllable. "A—good—line? My dear boy, it is an *excellent* line. Don't on any account lose it. Put it in another play."

But whatever was retained or cut it soon became obvious that the original Hawtrey farce was destined never to materialise. Cyril Maude's stage presence was that of the pathetic, appealing and unimpeachably respectable type which could never invest the part with the Hawtrey qualities of bemusement, blinking doubt about the causes and results of what he was doing and, above all, a subconscious awareness of possible amatory compensation for the same. Hawtrey's was the beloved tradition of the gay deceiver and sympathetic rake. Maude's was the established and incorruptible tradition of the *Flag Lieutenant* and the *Second in Command*. I don't think Maude was really a farce actor at all. I would add that, as leading man, especially in an anxious author's first play, he was a perfect god-send. From first to last he was unfailingly considerate and encouraging.

The Dippers introduced a little song, whose melody was supposed to be overheard from the ballroom to be picked up and crooned by the leading lady in the preoccupations of her dressing-room. I suggested asking Ivor Novello to supply the tune and was duly sent along to discuss it with him.

Preserved from the carolling indiscretions of airmanship and any subsequent jeapodies of warfare, Ivor Novello had emerged to distinction not only as a composer but as an actor. He was indeed at the outset of a career which was to be unique in the history of the modern theatre. At this time he was already playing juvenile lead, if only at the Kingsway Theatre and in one of those rather flaccid Anglo-Chinese pastiches of the "Oh, my chelly-blossom" variety. I called to see him in his dressing-room after a matinée and he was as charming and co-operative as ever and asked me to sit down and write out the lyric of the song. While I was engaged in doing this the door opened and another very personable stripling of the theatrical world entered to salute his colleague.

I recognised him as the mature edition of a boy actor who had already blossomed forth as the author of a couple of promising light comedies. His name escaped me for the moment—then, as Ivor Novello introduced me, of course—I knew I hadn't really forgotten it; Noel Coward. They left me to my writing and went into a little huddle of candid and completely genuine mutual admiration.

"You're wonderful. Oh, I wish I were as wonderful as you are."

"Oh, don't be so silly. You're much more wonderful than I am. You're marvellous."

No matter which character spoke which line. They were both equally sincere and, ah, how right. It amuses me to recall the three of us that afternoon in that pokey little dressing-room, all as yet on the threshold of our careers. I myself was going to enjoy a certain distinctive measure of success in the theatre; but just think what the future held for the other two. Destiny must have peeped through the dingy window and lingered for a moment to dwell upon us with a knowledgeable smile.

Meanwhile, rehearsals—and there was Charles Hawtrey seated stolidly every morning on the Criterion stage, with me on the edge of an adjacent chair. He seemed rather bored and listless; I think he knew that the whole thing was doomed now to be a second-best. He groaned and grunted a good deal; though occasionally he perked up to treat me to some ripe aside. Once, when he caught some mumbled protest from my direction, he called a temporary halt to the rehearsal in order to forefinger me in admonition.

"My dear boy. I have been at this game for forty years. And there is one thing I have never finished learning and which I never will finish learning. And that thing is learning. Thank you. Now—come along then—who speaks?"

We had great difficulty in finding the right actress for the principal Irene Castle, or rather Pauline Dipper, part. The lady originally cast and two or three tentative successors had come, read and been defeated. One morning an attractive girl of a particularly dashing type arrived to try her luck. I had no idea who she was but I made a good guess about her favourite line of business; she was obviously a pantomime principal boy.

"What do you think of her?" asked Hawtrey aside to me.

I said, "I think she would make a very good Dick Whittington. But I'm afraid she is not for us."

Hawtrey seemed very struck by this judgment. He looked into my face as though he had suddenly discovered there a gleam of unsuspected intelligence. "Yes," he murmured, "yes."

A moment later the lady found a line in the script which she could really get her teeth into. She swung into an attitude and got them into it. Hawtrey clapped a hand on my knee and exclaimed excitedly, "Thrice."

"I beg your pardon?"

"Thrice."

"I don't quite——"

"Thrice. Thrice, my dear fellow. Thrice Lord Mayor."

A morning or two later a girl came along who not only made the part her own within five minutes but who brought fresh interest and hope to the whole rather bedraggled proceedings. She was Binnie Hale.

Binnie Hale may have inherited some of her talent but she herself has been responsible for most of it. Whatever her material has been she has always used it to give the best performance imaginable. Others—Mary Martin in *South Pacific* for example—may have soared to heights which seem beyond the measure of comparison or even of calculation. But Binnie Hale is like the proprietor of some exclusive West End shop offering a wide variety of goods of which every specimen is the best on the market. In private life she has always loved to discard, not without conscious effort, the artificiality of her stage surroundings and to lapse into a natural enjoyment of being the most sparkling and the favourite relative-by-adoption of somebody's happy family, as she has always been of mine.

She was just as clever and creative as a young girl as she was later on; and thank goodness she was. *The Dippers* was a moderate success and had a London run of 167 shows. But it was due to Binnie Hale that this, my first play, had any success at all.

Another lady who has since achieved great esteem and popularity was in the company—Hermione Gingold. But at this time her gifts were only being employed as a walking-on-cum-understudy character, and her only marked contribution to the production was an occasional caustic appreciation of it back-stage.

The Dippers had duly appeared as a novel. I read it through again the other day and wondered who, besides my father and my mother-in-law, could have been the few hundred people who bought copies of the original edition. My father-in-law read it and expressed himself agreeably surprised. The surprise was mutual, as I was sure that his scrupulous design for living did not yield him any spare time for the reading of fiction and he must, for my sake, have consented to some special dislocation of his set programme of unemployment. I am glad he made this generous effort, for it was almost the last thing he did. Early in 1921 this charming character took to his bed and soon made an ordered and punctual departure to his well-rehearsed rest.

When the novel had been on the market for a month or so Jerome Kern came across a copy in New York and told the manager of Lane's American branch that he would like to use it as the theme of a musical comedy. The manager, knowing nothing about my aspirations as a playwright, naturally told Kern to go right ahead and cabled the glad tidings to the London office. But by this time the Hawtrey deal had gone through and the New York branch must have been devastated to receive a letter from Golding Bright telling them in the most unctuous terms that they were wasting their time.

Whereupon Jerome Kern threw the novel aside (or, more probably, at the head of the New York manager) and the matter ended.

I suppose I couldn't have it both ways, though I have never quite been able to see why not; but it was a pity. Jerome Kern had already established himself in England, where some of his numbers, beginning with *They'd never believe me,* had been introduced to bolster up some of our musical scores and I had always been a particularly declamatory admirer of his outstanding gifts. Moreover, at the very outset of my efforts as a writer my name might have become at least noted down in the U.S.A., whereas it remains as unknown there now as it was then. My first four novels were published there but with remarkable non-success; and even later on when William McFee, who liked them, managed to promote a new uniform edition and got Thorne Smith to write a special introduction to one of them, they still fell completely flat. Nor has there ever been a single professional perform-ance of any of my plays in the States. An amateur society once produced *Rookery Nook* in Boston, Mass; but the results seem to indicate that the operative word is "once".

The first public performance of my first play took place in what, for a farce, was not perhaps a particularly hilarious environment, namely the Royal Court Theatre, Liverpool, on the Monday of Holy Week. Liverpool tolerated rather than acclaimed the production. I sat with my wife in the stalls and endured the full ordeal, which I have always shunned ever since, of seeing the whole performance through, sensitive to the comments of unwitting neighbours, with my own lips muttering the lines a beat ahead of the actors, like Hamlet in the play scene, and breaking off to engage in frequent, hurried and intense moments of prayer. Later on, at the Aldwych and elsewhere, I always managed to get a box for first nights, so that I could sneak from the side of my unflinching wife in order to avoid any particular scene or episode which seemed likely to result in a foozle and to spend a few moments in consultation with some lurking commissionaire or, if the risk seemed really pressing, with the Almighty.

But the only vivid recollection I have of that Liverpool first night is the memory of my father. Since my dismal showing as a business man he had always been filled with an intense desire that—for my sake, not his—I should achieve a public success that would show the City that I wasn't such a damn fool after all. His anxiety on that first night was greater even than my own, for his hopes and fears had that special poignancy which springs from a parental love. Modest and retiring man that he was, he became almost assertive in his emphatic enjoyment of the farce and in his glances of challenge at any who did not seem to be sharing it. Later when the play was running in London, his pride and affection would bear him to the theatre in this enchanting mood of rapturous defiance. I remember sitting with him one night in the front row of the dress circle when, shortly before the play was due to start, a gentleman beside us remarked to his wife, "H'm. Don't seem to be many people coming to see this." An audible snort escaped my father. He allowed a minute or so to elapse; then half rose and, leaning over the front of the circle, surveyed the stalls below. "A *packed* house," he exclaimed almost savagely and sat down again.

The Dippers staggered along to three or four provincial cities. I was too inexperienced to foresee the inevitable and, so far as I was concerned, unheralded arrival upon the scene— which was Brighton, I think—of the jolly boisterous play-doctor, Sydney Blow, along with his accustomed partner, Douglas Hoare. Between them they had written several successes and were, no doubt, well qualified to resuscitate an ailing farce. Sydney Blow was, it seemed, to perform the energetic and practical part of the job; Douglas Hoare appeared to fulfil rather the duties of bottle-holder and anæsthetist of the medical team. For Blow had been engaged not merely to overhaul the play but to reproduce it. He was—as I am sure he remains today—a most amiable man; but I was indignant at having been left entirely in the dark about Mr. T. C. Dagnall's quite justifiable decision and went speeding in hot haste to London to inform Golding Bright and seek his advice.

Golding Bright, of course, knew all about it beforehand. Hawtrey, who followed me into his office, knew all about it beforehand. I seemed to be the only person who didn't know the first thing about it beforehand. · I asked Bright whether I ought to consent and he replied, rather more acidly than was his wont, that that all depended on whether I wanted the play brought to the West End. Damped and somewhat despairing, I turned to Hawtrey for support. For he, too, was affected. Apart from what Blow was going to do to my script, he proposed to overhaul Hawtrey's production. What had Hawtrey to say about that?

Hawtrey said nothing about himself. Perhaps he knew that, whatever happened, Mr. T. C. Dagnall would judiciously keep "the play produced by Sir Charles Hawtrey" (he had recently been knighted) in the London programme. But so far as I was concerned his manner, like Bright's, was a trifle terse. "My dear fellow, your name, as a dramatist, will be remembered long after all this little trouble has been forgotten." I looked at him in amazement. Did he really mean it? He seemed to. His tone grew more gentle and almost rhapsodical. "Looking back over the wide vista of the years——"

He broke off with a friendly smile and we parted. I never met him again. Between the first exultant moment of its acceptance and the adequate success of its first night at the Criterion *The Dippers* had brought me a good few disappointments and frustrations, but in one respect it was the most rewarding play I ever wrote. To have known and worked with Charles Hawtrey, at his best moments and at his worst, must remain one of the richest experiences of anybody's lifetime.

I soon became infected with Blow's chortling enthusiasms. He and Hoare made a good job of reconstructing bits of the play while I wrote whatever new dialogue was called for. I had never had any real intention of opposing Mr. Dagnall's abrupt ultimatum and it resulted in very few altercations for me to give way about. Binnie Hale made her big hit with the first-night audience at the Criterion and with the critics next morning; and the mangled but still animated Dippers had a very respectable reception. So I could afford to forget what might have been and to regard the whole long laborious and tantalising record of the production of my first play with grateful satisfaction. At least it assured me that I possessed two assets of great value to an aspiring playwright—a sense of the theatre and a weak nature.

I have always longed to know what Mr. and Mrs. Thompson thought of *The Dippers*. I don't suppose Mr. Thompson laughed much at it; for he seems to have been a morose and captious man; but I hope it provided a certain exhilaration for him in the last hour of his life before Bywaters stabbed him on his way home. As for Mrs. Thompson, it is obvious that unless she were definitely a party to the actual murder she should never have been executed. So, if the verdict passed upon her had any justification, she must have sat at the Criterion that night putting up a specious and discreet show of carefree merriment in order to conceal her Medea-like broodings over the forthcoming and prearranged assassination. What nonsense. It may be self-interest on my part, but I could never understand why the defence completely ignored the incredibility of her gratuitously seeking to face this frightful ordeal, which she must have imposed on herself had she really been a guilty accomplice.

Poor Edith Thompson—it has often intrigued me to reflect upon the association of her tragedy with my farce and I have journeyed specially to Ilford to have a look at the scene of the murder and at the house in which she sat and wrote her preposterous suburban fabrications. Ernest Trimmingham, a coloured disciple of Thespis who performed the extravagant duties of the leader of the Dippers' coon band, propounded a theory that the Thompson murder resulted in a hoodoo affecting the farce. After it, he declared, business was never so good either on stage or in front. On the other hand I sometimes wonder whether Edith Thompson ever found cause to reflect on the last play she was ever destined to see and to decide that *The Dippers* had been a bit of a hoodoo to *her*. I hope not.

J. L. Sacks was a remarkable being who had originally issued from some Polish corridor and had found or wheedled his way, via South Africa, to the West End of London, where his transactions as a theatrical impresario remain a legendary joke. They were no joke to me.

He was short and hunched and his lower lip protruded almost to the level of his not inconsiderable nose. He could at least write his name but was reputed to be unable to read English which, however, he spoke with a fluent eccentricity. A blend of acuteness and effrontery soon gained him an impressive position in the musical-comedy world. He must have won the confidence of some of those mysterious men of substance who put up large sums of money to finance musical shows. His projects were exorbitant and in some cases ostensibly very successful. There was a sly, humorous philosophy in him which was appealing even when it was ludicrous and any number of people fell for him. Many of them fell with a wallop and I was one of them.

On one occasion he found himself in such reduced circumstances that he had to resort to a fruit machine in order to raise his railway fare from London to Manchester, where he bought up (with goodness knows whose money) an enormous musical play which subsequently had a long run in the West End. But it was common knowledge that the current state of J. L. Sacks's finances at any given time was somewhat suspect. It certainly must have been so at the time when I encountered him.

He or some beguiled backer had bought the English rights of a comic opera by Franz Lehar. This was to be produced in London by Tom Reynolds, who was Binnie Hale's uncle and an old hand at this sort of game.

In the autumn of 1923, some months after *The Dippers* had surrendered to the hoodoo, Tom Reynolds asked me whether I'd like to have a shot at supplying the English libretto of this opera, *The Three Graces*, for which Sacks had already secured an option on the Empire Theatre. Impulsively I replied of course I would. I rather fancied myself as a librettist and the vision of taking a bow at the dazzling Empire as collaborator with Franz Lehar was, to say the least, exciting.

But there was an unusual feature about the proffered task. There was nothing to serve as a basis for adaptation. The original German libretto had apparently been so unspeakably awful that the opera had either been stillborn or had died in earliest infancy—nobody seemed quite certain which. Never mind—I felt confident I could devise some story to fit the vocal characters and some appropriate words for them to get vocal about in Lehar's numbers.

My enthusiasm was irked by misgivings about the trust-worthiness of Mr. J. L. Sacks and I told Tom Reynolds I had better consult Golding Bright. Tom Reynolds, who himself possessed something of Golding Bright's habit of thinking more than he said, but in a humorous and philosophical sort of way, said he was afraid that would mean the end of it.

He had a presentiment that Golding Bright would not favour my undertaking a commission for Sacks. But he quite agreed that I'd better take due precautions. By this time I was so eager to begin that I was incensed by the very thought of opposition. I recalled to myself my resentment of Bright's secretive manipulation of *The Dippers* and now it exaggerated itself almost to the proportions of a feud. All right then—I was through with Golding Bright anyhow. I'd consult my solicitor and get him to draw up a good stiff contract with Sacks.

My solicitor was one of those solicitors who was my solicitor because his father had been my father's solicitor. He is dead now and I will not say anything derogatory about him except that I wish he had been dead then. He received my apprehensions with a derisive smile. He knew how to deal with people like Mr. Sacks. Leave it to him. And sure enough the good stiff contract was duly drawn up and delivered, bearing J. L. Sacks's outlandish autograph.

I worked away and eventually completed the most difficult and painstaking job I have ever known. I laboured for months inventing a story, writing the play, and scribbling nonsense words to indicate the intricate metre of the required lyrics while an obliging lady thrummed the tunes on an office piano. Presently I inquired of my solicitor whether he had completed his difficult painstaking job too. He had not. There was no sign of my cheque for advance royalties from Mr. Sacks.

I attended rehearsals and watched the promising preliminary efforts of such considerable contemporary performers as Winifred Barnes, Thorpe Bates and Morris Harvey. The leading comedian had been recruited by Sacks from America and appeared somewhat distrait but said he would be all right on the night. Meanwhile whole ranks of immense but symmetrical show ladies posed to order; chorus singers trilled my distinguished lyrics; male and female dancers bounded and twinkled. The American comedian still said he'd be all right on the night and everybody seemed to be going ahead splendidly—with one exception. My solicitor wasn't.

On the day before the show was due to open—cold—at the Empire I called on my solicitor and told him he'd better apply for an injunction. The costumier had just done so and had been paid on the nail. But my solicitor thought it would be as well to give Mr. Sacks a last chance. This he gave him in the form of some facetious sarcasm over the telephone. It was all very exasperating, but I decided that it might be well to refrain from taking any action which might mar the prospects of the morrow's triumph. Better, perhaps, triumph first and injunct later. Even Sacks would be bound to hav some cash by then.

He had certainly put the show on regardless of somebody else's expense. The sets and effects and costumes were superlative. The orchestra was too large and too noisy. My poor lyrics were utterly inaudible; but perhaps this didn't matter much. I re-read and rewrote the whole libretto not long ago at the request of the George Dance Company and, having seen a production with the present script substituted for the precocious original, I realise that the triumph might well have come to pass. For Lehar had written some beautiful numbers, though, with the exception of the still remembered *Gigolette*, they didn't seem to make much impression on the rather saturnine first-night audience. Morris Harvey had some funny moments as a Dutchman and got the one big laugh of the night with my original version of an oft-repeated joke about his encounter with a Highlander in a Scotch mist: "So thick was the mist that at first I did not know whether he was a short man with a beard or a tall man with a sporran." But gradually and unmistakably I felt the icy presence of failure pervading the huge auditorium and, at the finish, the booing from the gallery drowned the polite half-hearted applause from the stalls. Lehar was mistaken enough to make an appearance and the booing waxed in an angry crescendo. I wasn't such a fool as to venture from the wings. My first and only essay in musical comedy was a decisive enough flop without my being personally informed so from the audience. On the second night a modicum of disgruntled advance-bookers and curiosity-seekers duly corroborated the press notices.

The American comedian was not as all right on the night as he had hoped to be. He was soon replaced by W. H. Berry, complete with Arthur Wimperis and Nat Ayer as his song-writers, and although between them they greatly improved the show they couldn't redeem it. Morris Harvey was extremely piqued by the introduction of Berry. Harvey had practically monopolised what laughs there had been and he objected to a star comedian being brought in to raise some bigger and better ones. "After all," Harvey protested to Sacks, "I saved the show on the first night." Sacks snapped back at him. "You did, eh? And who saved it on de second?"

The failure evidently confirmed Sacks in the opinion that I need not, and had much better not, be paid anything. No doubt this production, like many of its kind, was run by a company specially formed for the occasion and could have sidled into its predestined liquidation at any convenient moment; and to have started legal proceedings would have been throwing good money after none. But the show ran for altogether 130 performances and I never received one single Polish rouble. In view of my solicitor's confident contempt of my qualms at the outset I thought his final pronouncement on the disaster was particularly choice. "Let this be a lesson to you never again to have any dealings with a man like that," said my solicitor. But there—he is dead.

So is Sacks. But only fairly recently. In his old age he was sustained and provided for by a sympathetic associate of the past and he still shuffled round the fringe of the theatre world and past the buildings where, to give him his due, his name had shone in lights above the titles of many musical shows renowned in their time. My own association with him had finished up, all those years ago, in a heated and futile exchange of abuse in a café. But I am sure that had I met him again in his latter days I would have yielded once more to the subtle appeal of his quaint personality. And this would not have been in any spirit of heaping coals of fire. For the very improbity of Sacks had in it a whimsical and mischievous attractiveness which awakened in one an instinct of illogical charity and even of indignant affection.

Some years after the Empire disaster, when I was fairly established at the Aldwych, a friend of mine happened to mention my name to Sacks.

"Him?" cried Sacks. "I made him. I gave him his first yob. But for me he vill never have been heard about."

And a little later still I was dining one night with Harry Graham, whose many successes as author and librettist never robbed him of the appearance and manner of some traditional Guards' officer engaged in a rather bewildering but tolerable civilian enterprise.

"Has it ever struck you," Graham suddenly asked me, "what really quite extraordinary people one is called upon to deal with in the theatrical profession?"

"Yes," I said. "It has."

CHAPTER VI

Aldwych Entrée

I CAN'T work out how I managed to remain solvent at that time, even with my wife's grandmother contributing from the tomb. Directly we had heard about Golding Bright selling *The Dippers* we had hastened back to Burnham and settled there for good. We bought and furnished a house— or, rather, my wife did, as two-thirds of the cost came from Granny's capital and the other third from the sale of my wartime car. For this was long before I started earning money and even when I did the royalties from my first two plays were no fortune; since by Mr. T. C. Dagnall I got paid in all about thirteen hundred pounds and by Mr. Sacks nihil.

Lane had published *A Cuckoo in the Nest*, which got some really exceptional notices and sold moderately well for a second novel; well enough, perhaps, even to reach the figure at which the author in Lane's contract began to participate in the returns. But if so the author's share did not present any problem in mathematics to our old friend, the bearded teetotal accountant, Mr. Harris.

But somehow we lived in comfort and had a cook and a housemaid, Elizabeth Bradbeer (the sister of all those golf professionals), who eventually stayed with us for thirty-five years; and a nanny and a nursemaid and an occasional old gardener on a tricycle, to say nothing of a third baby, our second son; and I simply don't know how we managed but we did manage and very happily.

Once back at Burnham I finished the novel of *Rookery*

Nook, which caused a great deal of local discussion in a residential community of which local discussion was practically the staple industry. The novel was obviously about Burnham; there could be no denying that; so everybody started claiming to recognise their neighbours in its characters, while the recognisers were in their turn recognised by the recognisees.

I was, I admit, guilty in one instance. There was a certain old resident whom I couldn't resist putting into *Rookery Nook* in the guise of the fire-eating, retired Admiral Juddy. To my dismay this formidable model halted me one morning in the main road and squared up to me in a very challenging manner.

"Now then, young feller," he said. "This book of yours. Won't do, you know. That Admiral. Eh? What have you got to say for yourself?"

I had a dreadful presentiment that he was going to sue me for defamation of character or something. I murmured some obvious lie about being sorry I didn't know what he meant.

"Oh, stuff," he cried. "Won't wash. Not for a minute. That Admiral, he's nothing but a damn lampoon. The whole place is saying so. Everybody knows he's meant to be poor old Hart."

Now that the reviewers labelled me a humorist I realised to my surprise that this seemed to be the line of business I was most likely to suceed in—at any rate to begin with. In the novel of *The Dippers* I had studiously observed the conventions of style and narrative, and the result when examined today is pretty smug. I think some of my early dramatic efforts were even worse. Directly Golding Bright had placed the farce version of *The Dippers* I decided to show him that I possessed the qualifications of the fashionable comedy author and, in the interim before its production I wrote a play (I forget the title) on the subject of some current social problem (I forget which) whose serious purport was enlivened by the tea-table banter of stage dowagers and discursive stage dudes. I gave it to Bright and asked him eagerly what he thought of it. He replied in the most non-committal way that it gave further proof of my promise as a playwright, and he refrained from damping my enthusiasm by handing it back. I can only suppose that he shoved it away in some cupboard-limbo which he kept specially for the abortive scripts of playwrights who shouldn't be damped. There it was subsequently joined by at least two more of these early sparkling horrors. Then, in writing my second and third novels, I learned to use my own initiative in my methods and devices and the results showed a great improvement. Up to then, like so many beginners, I had made the mistake of trying to compete with established authors on their own ground.

Even the good little stage version of *The Dippers* had been careful to comply with the farcical formalities; but the adaptations I made of *A Cuckoo in the Nest* and *Rookery Nook* cut right adrift from them. Somehow, without renouncing Pinero and the principles of technique, I seemed suddenly to have struck the knack of being my natural self and of giving the impression that I enjoyed being it. I felt confident that the new farces showed an immense advance on those pretentious comedies which Golding Bright had so shrewdly withheld and had submitted for the consideration only of his mice.

On that ill-fated night at the Empire I had stood with my wife at the head of the staircase leading to the famous prom and watched the leisurely arrival of an audience as resplendent in its full-dress deportment in the vestibule as it was to be uncongenial in the stalls. Sure enough, there in its midst had appeared the portentous figure of Golding Bright with his gold-headed cane and his white washleather gloves; so I knew that he must have witnessed my downfall during his short grim snatches of wakefulness.

So, even now, when after two or three full-length experiments I had got the stage version of the *Cuckoo* to my liking, I couldn't bring myself to show it to Bright. Not only did I feel shamefaced; I was afraid that following the Empire flop he might have written me off as a failure and that the script of the *Cuckoo* might be consigned automatically to the cupboard.

Then I had a letter from Lawrence Grossmith, whom I had seen on the stage but had never met. He had read the Cuckoo novel. He lavished effusive praise on it and wanted me to write him an adaptation. He got his headstrong copy of the script by return post. Then I sat and wondered whether I hadn't been a little hasty. Lawrence Grossmith was recognised as a competent light comedian, but that was all. He had played a leading part in one or two plays which had been successes but not for that reason. In other words his name was acceptable at the box-office but was not magnetic; and the *Cuckoo* was, at that stage, essentially a one-man farce. Now, if only he had been his uncle Weedon——Oh, dear. Had I been impulsive again?

Shortly afterwards I had another letter from Grossmith readily accepting the farce.

Well, there was one thing about it. This gave me the chance of renewing my relationship with Golding Bright without my having to make airy observations about bygones being bygones and would he consent to have a look at my new play? I could now just walk casually in and say, "Oh, hallo, Golding. Look. Here's a thing I've sold. Would you care to handle it for me?"

I seem to remember, however, that my reconciliatory speech did not quite take this form and that the interview consisted chiefly in my confessing what I had been up to. I asked Golding what he thought of Lawrence Grossmith as a potential star for my farce and he told me. But he agreed to act for me and was quite cordial and conciliatory. I think he considered the whole proposition to be second-rate.

It might have been unjust to call Lawrence Grossmith a vain man but, if so, it would have been only a slight miscarriage of justice. He possessed a pompous self-contentment which was attractive to me, as he seemed to regard any stroke of good fortune as only to be expected as his normal due. But he was no fool and good company in his impressive way. One day he informed me quite dispassionately that he wanted to take me to meet a great friend of his, to whom he had given the farce to read. The friend was wildly enthusiastic about it, he said, and wanted to be allowed to produce it. Oh? Who? Grossmith told me who in the same casual tone—Gerald du Maurier. Perhaps he was purposely underplaying slightly in order to make an effect on me; but his manner suggested that it was only being a friend of Lawrence Grossmith's that qualified du Maurier for liking the play.

It all turned out to be true. I duly met du Maurier. The *Cuckoo* had made a particular and extraordinary appeal to him. He seemed to look on it as an escape from the standard type of play and on the prospect of producing it as a holiday rather than as a job. He got very bored by the theatre, he told me. Acting, he said, held only one remaining ambition for him, which was to make an entrance, stroll down to the footlights, survey the audience and deliver himself of some frightfully indecent impromptu.

He was not universally liked. As his faithful public were grieved to gather from his daughter's book, *Gerald*, he had a candid way of showing his impatience with people and things that antagonised him. Though it was severely criticised I thought *Gerald* gave a sincere and attractive portrait of this man, who, whether he sought it or not, was the most influential actor of the half-century. Daphne du Maurier's description of a typical first night at Wyndham's is one of the most vivid and moving passages in any biography I know.

I loved him. From the first moment his manner to me was not merely friendly; in his discussions of the play with me there was always an intimate, almost conspiratorial suggestion that what we were doing was a bit of fun. While we visualised some of the scenes and characters he would smile his slightly crooked smile and twitch his nose in that particular way of his, in keeping with his thoughts. But at one moment he became very serious. There seemed to be no immediate prospect of our getting a theatre; and he noticed my disappointment on hearing this. He faced up to me and said, "All right, I'll promise you something. I'll promise you this play shall be done in the West End." That was good enough for me. I went back to Burnham to await, like Browning's Artemis, "in fitting silence, the event".

I didn't have to await it for long but it came in an unexpected form. A wire from Grossmith bade me please come without fail to the Badminton Club for luncheon next day to meet Tom Walls. The message implied an unwonted urgency on Grossmith's part. For once the favoured votary of Kismet seemed slightly agitated.

What was all *this* about? I arrived in good time at the club next day and Grossmith informed me. His accustomed manner of trenchant composure and verbiage always favoured a marked indulgence in the cliché. It was thus that he explained the situation:

It had come to his knowledge that Tom Walls, at the Aldwych, was in pressing need of a successor to *It Pays to Advertise*, which had outrun its popularity. He, Grossmith, had accordingly submitted the script of the *Cuckoo*, intimating that should it fill the gap he might be prepared to surrender his option for a reasonable consideration. All concerned at the Aldwych had signified their approval of the script to a man and Walls was straining at the leash to set the ball in motion. Gerald du Maurier had immediately been informed and had given his blessing to the proposed transaction which he applauded to the echo.

Grossmith ended his ornate, prefabricated recitation and I sat torn between exultation and disquiet. When I think what the acceptance of that offer was destined to mean to me for the whole of the rest of my life it seems unreasonable that any author, especially so tractable an author as I, should have hesitated for a moment. But my first thought was that I wouldn't agree to sacrifice du Maurier without some ample compensation. What compensation was offered?

Tom Walls? I had seen him sometimes in past years as an unfunny and too red-nosed comedian playing small parts in musical shows. The father-in-law, who was the leading support character in my sophisticated farce, called for a straight comedy actor, and I had sounded Gerald du Maurier about approaching Charles V. France. The idea of Tom Walls red-nosing and reeling his way through the part was decidedly unnerving. When I think of the glorious study Tom Walls made of Major George Bone it makes me fear I must have been rather a prig about the values of my characters; but perhaps it was only that I was trying hard to stick to my principles about making them recognisable human types.

The other and more conspicuous Aldwych comedian, an individual named Ralph Lynn, I had seen only once and that had been in a music-hall sketch. He specialised in types who were the direct descendants of the Edwardian "nut" and he had a monocled fatuity about him which had gained him a moderate reputation as a funny man in his own particular line, until he had suddenly, one night in 1922, sailed up to join the stars.

But there again—wouldn't this mean that the conscientious, embroiled, misunderstood young husband of my play would be caricatured and nincompooped into unreality? So there I sat, an ambitious and questing farce-writer, in a state of rueful irresolution about joining forces with the greatest farce-actor of our time.

The Aldwych. To get in with the Aldwych. That was the thing that mattered. That was a big consideration if you like.

On that night in 1922 a farce called *Tons of Money*, at the Shaftesbury Theatre, had achieved one of those rare, genuine, overwhelming first-night successes which drive minor dramatic critics to their dictionaries to see how to spell "unparalleled". *The Dippers* was then still in its penultimate Blowing and Hoaring stage in the provinces and I remember reading the notices of *Tons of Money* with frankly jealous dismay.

Before long it was transferred from the Shaftesbury and settled down in rooted occupation of the Aldwych. Eventually, as the years went by, *It Pays to Advertise* took its place and although this play was now showing marked signs of exhaustion it had good reason to, for it had been on for about eighteen months. The Lynn-Walls combination at the Aldwych was already almost a regular theatrical institution.

To have one's farce chosen to be the next production— think what that meant. Surely the very thought of it should banish any misgivings about red noses and monocles.

But within five minutes my mixed and indefinite feelings about the proposition had ceased to matter. Tom Walls arrived. The terms of Lawrence Grossmith's reasonable consideration must have been settled beforehand; for Tom Walls made it clear at once that he had decided to produce the farce. I learned for the first of many times that, so far as I was concerned at any rate, once Tom Walls had decided on anything, that settled it.

He was much younger than I had supposed—it turned out that he was only two or three years older than myself. The

shape of his head and one or two tricks of his speech denoted
that he derived from Yeoman stock; this being, in those days,
an expression used to indicate somebody who was obviously
not out of the top drawer but was shrewd enough to qualify
for the second.

He had great virility. He tended to lead, if not to mono-
polise, the conversation. His affability was perhaps a little
studied to suit the occasion; yet even at that first meeting he
showed glimpses of the redeeming qualities I was to value so
greatly in his unique character—his prepossessing instinct for
companionship and his invincible sense of humour.

It became clear, without his saying so, that he was in sole
and absolute control of the affairs of the company leasing the
Aldwych Theatre. But then, in my riper knowledge of him
I could never imagine Tom Walls being on the Board of any
company of which he was not Chairman, Managing Director,
head of every department, general supervisor, production
overseer and unchallengeable authority on every detail of
policy and procedure.

The boss having issued his preliminary and felicitous decrees,
I hurried to Golding Bright to impart my news. He received
it with a nonchalant satisfaction which rather suggested that
he had initiated the whole thing. He never claimed to have
done so but, being also the agent of Walter Hackett, part-
author of *It Pays to Advertise*, he must have been acquainted
with the state of affairs at the Aldwych, and he was remarkably
prompt in conjuring up my substitute agreement.

I regret I saw but little more of Lawrence Grossmith. He
retired from the scenes of my further progress, though when
Rookery Nook was successfully presented a year later he wrote
trying to make out that he ought to participate in the returns
for that play as well and received in reply a masterpiece of
restrained repudiation drafted for me by Golding Bright. I
hope I have not overemphasised the predestinate self-confidence

of Lawrence Grossmith, which was by no means a disagreeable quality. I always enjoyed his society and his grave appreciation of a joke. And in any case I have not forgotten that it was he alone who spotted the dramatic possibilities of *A Cuckoo in the Nest* and that his doing so led to the start of my Aldwych career. As regards the *Cuckoo* he thoroughly earned my eternal gratitude and his two per cent of the gross takings.

During the next nine years I wrote nine of the eleven farces produced at the Aldwych. I supplied six in a row; then, in the autumn of 1930, Tom Walls had a dispute with Golding Bright which led to a temporary breach, though dispute is hardly a possible description of any fracas in which Golding Bright was one of the parties concerned. I returned to provide two more and then, after another lapse of a few months, the final farce to round off the series. My complete Aldwych tally during this whole period reads:

NAME OF PLAY	PRODUCED	NUMBER OF PERFORMANCES
A Cuckoo in the Nest	22nd July 1925	376
Rookery Nook	30th June 1926	409
Thark	4th July 1927	401
Plunder	26th June 1928	344
A Cup of Kindness	7th May 1929	291
A Night like This	18th Feb. 1930	268
Turkey Time	26th May 1931	263
Dirty Work	7th Mar. 1932	195
A Bit of a Test	30th Jan. 1933	142

Tom Walls did not appear in the last two. If truth be told he did not appear at a good many performances of the others. Rehearsals of the *Cuckoo*, which began five days after I had first met Tom Walls, gave me my first experience of some of his singular methods as actor-producer. For the first two of the three-weeks rehearsal he sat and directed the rest of the company, including his understudy. At the beginning of the third week he resigned himself, with a groan of effort, to participation in the acting. But during the past fortnight he had, of course, been much too busy to study his lines; and when the play started out on its one week's probation at some provincial theatre his performance was liable to hiatus. This didn't embarrass him at all. He would cross to the prompt corner and rally the dithering stage-manager with a rasping and resounding aside—"Come on, Bobbie—let's have it, can't you?" He had no compunction or shame about this. He took a contemptuous view of audiences at the best of times. But it is only fair to say that on first nights in London he was not only word-perfect but gave what was probably his best performance of the entire run of a play. "In every play there's only one show that really matters," he used to say; a candid admission of his cynical outlook on the whole concern. But he never hesitated to be candid about himself when he chose to be; just as he was always ready to see the funny side of his own mistakes and discomfitures.

Another of his peculiar practices was to ignore the third act completely until the last week of rehearsals. In the case of the *Cuckoo* this resulted in the most distressing ordeal for me. By the end of the second week the first and second acts had been cut, re-invented, transcribed, gagged and generally tinkered into fairly promising shape. On the Saturday—or was it the Sunday?—morning the company read through the original third act. What they read or the way they read it or both made it sound like a prolonged incantation to Gloom. I sat squirming in self-conscious anguish. The material had been in keeping with the original first two acts, but by now the first two acts had been translated into Aldwych and the poor little original third seemed about as applicable as a death-knell. Tom Walls handed me a script of it. "Go back to your room," he said, "and rewrite the whole bloody thing. Don't strain yourself. Thursday morning will do, so long as you get it right."

My wife was down at Burnham with the three children who all had whooping-cough. So had I. I was lodging in a bed-sitting-room somewhere in London and it was quite bad enough to have to spend the next fifty-four hours hard at work and without a thought of sleep; let alone having to jump up from my chair every few minutes to pace the room, beating my chest and fighting for breath. But Tom Walls got his rewritten—and in fact completely re-devised—third act by the middle of the week, and a very successful one it proved to be.

Ralph Lynn was an exception to all the others in being given a free hand in the way he acted his part. Tom Walls might occasionally criticise this but he refrained from inter-fering. Ralph delighted me at the very outset when we were talking together about the farce and he told me he had agreed to play in it after reading only the first act, having rejected scores of other scripts submitted to him for his opinion. His reason was that the character in the *Cuckoo* didn't try to be funny and was actuated by honest and serious motives. This won my heart at once. Here was somebody who really appreciated my theory about farce. I remember thinking at the time how mistaken I had been in suspecting that monocle.

And it is true that Ralph Lynn has always been funniest in characters impelled by the most earnest and striving motives; and it goes without saying that these characters must be the victims of embroilment or menace. I have never seen or heard of any actor with so instinctive and unerring a gift for timing; and in writing for him I have always exploited another distinctive and inimitable feature of his, the throw-away line; or perhaps what, in his case, would more aptly be called the give-away line. He makes a deliberate, unfunny, definite and convincing declaration; then, unable to contain his self-satisfaction, he ruins its whole effect by some ill-considered afterthought.

He has also always relied to a great degree on instinct and impromptu, taking the form of a sudden whim during any one performance, momentary and almost unintentional. Often in the course of our long years together I have looked into his dressing-room after a show and said, "That was a lovely bit of business tonight in the second act. Don't forget to keep it in." And he has asked blankly, "Why, what did I do?" The bit of business or the extraneous remark may not always have been so lovely, but he has only had to be told that it was out of character for him to spurn it with remorse and shame. When, before I became acclimatised to the Aldwych, I sat at rehearsals of the *Cuckoo* racked with suspense and whooping-cough, I listened to Ralph's interpolations with aversion. Some, admittedly, were good; but I felt uneasy about taking the nominal responsibility for a line like this: when, having written a false name in the inn visitors' book, his entry is inspected by the puritanical landlady:

"You don't write very clear."
"No, I've just had some very thick soup."

I gently protested but Ralph said he'd like to try it, and it always got a big laugh. And after all it's exactly the sort of thing Ralph himself would have said in the circumstances.

A Cuckoo in the Nest was topical in a way. It was a comment, in very jaunty form, on the contemporary state of the divorce laws. It had always been taken for granted that any unmarried couple who spent a night together in an hotel must, incontestably, be guilty of adultery; as in most cases no doubt they were. But at this time divorce judges were beginning to get rather restive and inclined to hanker after some pretty solid evidence. I thought it might be a good idea to show a couple fortuitously separated from their respective spouses and compelled by circumstances to spend a completely blameless night together not only in the same inn but in the same bedroom. And a good idea it was, though little did I foresee—in my pitiable moments of diffidence before my first meeting with Tom Walls—that the essential absurdity of the situation could not possibly be better brought out than by having Ralph Lynn and Yvonne Arnaud as the joint occupants of my bedroom.

The credit for getting them there must go entirely to Tom Walls. He had an extraordinary gift for sensing the potentialities. I think he must have persuaded, or perhaps even bluffed, Yvonne Arnaud into accepting her part in the *Cuckoo* on the strength of her successful association with Ralph in *Tons of Money*; for it wasn't worthy of her. But the fact that she was little better than a picturesque foil for Ralph never seemed to occur to anybody, and if any tribute were needed to Yvonne Arnaud's abilities this in itself would seem to suffice. But tribute should also be paid to Tom Walls' perception of how immensely valuable her very presence and personality would be to the scene.

All she had to do was to sit up in bed, looking very attractive in the midst of her primitive and forbidding surroundings, and complacently to read a book, while Ralph wandered about, irresolute and woebegone, with a blanket and a pillow. Nobody but Yvonne Arnaud could have conveyed so perfectly the sheer impossibility of there being anything morally wrong in the situation and at the same time her mischievous amusement at their joint dilemma. And yet almost every line she was given to speak was a feed line:

"My husband hasn't got a nasty mind. Has your wife got a nasty mind?"

"No, but she's got a nasty mother."

"To any decent-minded person there's nothing wrong in your sleeping on the floor of my bedroom, is there?"

"No. But where's the decent-minded person?"

The Lord Chamberlain's Office expressed great concern about this bedroom scene when the script was presented for consideration. So much so that, for the only time in my experience, a special (and very inconvenient) rehearsal was called for inspection by a representative of the Censorship Department. The genial major detailed to pass final judgment did so without hesitation and almost apologetically; which was in itself a further unspoken, and perhaps unconscious, compliment to the art of Yvonne Arnaud.

The first night in London took place during a violent thunderstorm, which must have upset the calculations of any Roman augurs who happened to be about; for the farce was a definite success. Tom Walls did not discard his red nose; but his glorious study of a Major of Yeomanry in decay quite justified this. He was the sort of old fellow who would be bound to have had a red nose in real life. Mary Brough had been in *Tons of Money*, but it was her landlady in the *Cuckoo* that constituted her an indispensable member of the Aldwych team from this time onwards. She was in all nine of my Aldwych farces and had one remarkable trait. She always retained and observed the traditional but by this time archaic attitude of deference to the author from the actor when on duty. All through the nine years, once we were in the theatre she would address me as "Sir". I never told her not to; I knew that would be asking her to forsake her principles. It must have been Mary Brough, or someone very like her, who inspired the original use of the term "trouper".

She lived—the object I am sure of enormous local esteem—at Clapham. Every night during the run of the *Cuckoo* she used to be hoisted into the sidecar of a motor bicycle and conveyed to her home by a young member of the company, who was no less a person than Roger Livesey. He played Alfred, the inn barman and general factotum—another example of Tom Walls' genius for casting. I always remember Roger Livesey in one particular moment, typifying the obstinate density of my home-grown Somerset chawbacon at cross-purposes with the hero's clamorous mother-in-law:

"Where is the landlady?"
"Gone to get some milk."
"Where from?"
"From the cow."
"Yes, but where *is* the cow?"
"Being milked."
"Yes, but *where* is the cow being milked?"
"Wull, you knows whurr to milk a cow, don't 'ee?"

There were two others in that cast who, with Ralph Lynn and Mary Brough, appeared in all nine of the farces. One was Ralph's elder brother, Sydney Lynn, who acted under the name of Gordon James. The other was, at that time, a conscientious and punctilious little support-player named Robertson Hare.

People of middle age and upwards still sometimes talk about the Aldwych of those nine years as a landmark in theatrical history. My own memory dwells perhaps less on the plays themselves than on my association with Tom and Ralph and, beyond everything else, the participation in their laughter. Tom might be despotic and, at times, arrogant and quick to assert his position as the boss of the place, but he would no more let this interfere with his laughter than he would let it interfere with his methodical, and apparently quite innocuous, patronage of the bottle. As for Ralph, he has always had a nimbleness of wit as individual as his methods on-stage. He not only sees the ridiculous side of things; he searches for it. His first instinctive thought is to spot something funny in anything he sees or hears or reads. Usually his sallies are as unpremeditated as his stage gags; but sometimes he will remain silent and pensive for a moment or two, looking as if he were trying to work out a sum in his head and then suddenly produce some odd quip. He originated, in the course of everyday conversation with me, one very familiar joke—the one about the Elephant Old Bailey, with the disreputable-looking elephant accused giving evidence on his own behalf and, asked what he had been up to on the night of the crime, protesting, "I can't remember." I was always fond, too, of Ralph's bookmaker caught in a shipwreck on board a liner, running up and down the deck and shouting, "Women and children third."

I once spent a few days with Ralph in Paris. Oh, *mon Dieu.* Ralph understood only one attitude towards France—I don't think he knew that any other existed. This was the splendidly insular, Gilbertian "darned mounseer" attitude, which considered that the sole function of Paris was to serve as a playground for the light-hearted English visitor and that its citizens were the natural and legitimate butt for his persiflage. Ralph was liable at any time to accost a middle-aged Parisian stranger of either sex with a toothsome smile and some personal and unrefined jocularity in broken English and with a wealth of gesture.

My worst moment with him was when he noticed a gendarme on duty in the middle of one of the busiest avenues, armed with truncheon and whistle and trying to regulate the Paris traffic with the non-stop vigour of a frantic marionette.

Ralph immediately stepped into the road and began dodging his way towards him. I felt bound to follow, and both of us, after escaping death by inches from a dozen cars, eventually arrived intact beside the gendarme. He was too busy whistling and flourishing his truncheon to give us more than a fleeting and furious glance; but at length, during a momentary lull, he turned his head and shot out a sharp interrogation. At this Ralph performed the elaborate gesture of the conventional stage Frenchman, with the high-shouldered shrug and outspread palms. He leaned towards the gendarme and spoke in confidential and expectant inquiry. "Feelthy pictures?" he asked.

But Ralph has always been tremendously painstaking about his work. He was never satisfied so long as there was a single line in any of his scenes which wasn't right. All through the run of a farce he would worry and experiment until he got the thing to his liking. In those moments there were none of the waggeries and wisecracks of his leisure hours; we were concentrating on the solemn problem of creating laughter. Nobody ever appreciated so well as Ralph how intensely serious is the job of being funny.

When the general strike of 1926 closed the theatres for a week or so Tom and Ralph motored down to stay with us at Burnham and I read aloud to them the first act of *Rookery Nook*, which I was readapting for them on Aldwych lines. They were by this time labelled and regarded as co-star comedians of equal standing, and the first result of this was that they had become, and were always to remain, extremely sensitive and wary—not about their own individual material so much, but about each other's. I had not merely to write farces containing two leading male characters of equal importance, but to organise my scripts so that in their scenes together, if one were given a line calculated to raise a laugh the next laugh had to go to the other. Or if, unavoidably, A got two laughs in succession B must forthwith be allowed to bring the score level. It was an intriguing exercise and, although my primary object was always to avoid criticism and reproach, it probably proved very beneficial to the farces. They soon learned to rely on me, but at the outset they kept a pretty sharp look-out about it The only time I was interrupted in my reading of *Rookery Nook* was when, at one point, I had given Ralph what sounded like three to nil, and my drawing-room rang with Tom's quick challenge: "Hi, hi—what's all *this*?"

There is some peculiar quality about *Rookery Nook* which has made a lasting appeal to the British public. I will not divulge what this quality is, but only because I don't know. It has been acted by repertory and amateur companies, all over the country and in the Dominions, more or less habitually for the past thirty years. I have no idea how many times in all it has endured the inspection of urban and rural district audiences, but the total number of its performances has been many times greater than that of all my other plays put together. And yet it could not have survived and might never even have been produced at all if my gate at Burnham had not opened one morning at the psychological moment when the "Hand ever above my shoulder" gently pushed into my front garden a girl we knew named Betty Tucker, selling flags for the life-boat.

The first two acts, as written, had been accepted as quite promising. They planted and developed the situation of the innocent maiden, driven from home by her Anglo-Prussian step-father and forced to seek sanctuary, wearing only her pyjamas, with our old friend, the migrant but loyal and well-intentioned husband. But the third act just ambled along, limping as it went and showing ever-increasing signs of fatigue. It was Ralph Lynn who hit on the idea of enlivening

136

the proceedings by introducing a new and unheralded young woman, to be inveigled into the house as a substitute for the original refugee, without the knowledge of the husband. As usual, I agreed readily to experiment with any suggestion offered, without pausing to calculate the problems it involved. The procedure of the new young woman had to be odd, to say the least. She had to pay a morning call at the house of a man who was a complete stranger to her. Once inside, she had to agree to lend her frock to another girl whom she'd never met, and to remain there to explain. Well, I felt I could account for her behaviour when she'd got into the house; but her motive for coming along there in the first place had, in keeping with my principles, to be unimpeachably reasonable and probable. Perhaps I was rather dense, but I couldn't for the life of me determine what that motive could be. Then—click—the gate; and in walked Betty Tucker.

I jumped up, hurried out and must, I think, have aroused suspicions in the breast of Betty Tucker by the lavish abandon with which I purchased her flags for the life-boat. Festooned and elated I returned to my study. The rest was easy. Poppy Dickey arrived and knocked at the front of Rookery Nook, and the whole situation blossomed forth into what proved to be a really triumphant dénouement. It was one of the best bits of farce-writing I ever brought off; but it would never have materialised (quite apart from Betty Tucker) if it hadn't been for that vague and speculative inspiration of Ralph's.

I have often been asked how Winifred Shotter came to be discovered for the leading girl's part in *Rookery Nook*. It was due to Leslie Henson, who had been a co-director with Tom Walls in the management, ever since the start of *Tons of Money*. Winifred Shotter was in the chorus of one of his musical shows and he thought she looked the sort of girl for the part. He thought rightly; she looked ideal for it. But it wasn't just a matter of looks—the way this part was played affected the whole action and justification of the story and the humour of the situations. The girl had to be seductive enough to justify the gossip of the "residential seaside cats" but at the same time quite without guile and, as the Ralph Lynn character asserted "like Potiphar's wife—above suspicion". She might look a bit of a little play-girl, but the game she played was as innocent as "Old Maid".

Winifred Shotter brought exactly the right blend of charm and *naïveté* to the part. She immediately won the approval of critics and audiences and very soon was commanding a record proportion of wall-space in studies at Public Schools. It became taken for granted, rather than decided, that she should stay on and appear in future Aldwych productions. It was a useful additional asset to have a young and very attractive leading girl; especially as Ralph invariably stuck to what are known as "juvenile" characters, and whatever the juvenile in any of the farces got up to was inevitably the outcome of romantic feminine inducement. But, although this turned out to be a very useful and delightful arrangement, I don't think it did justice to Winifred Shotter. It resulted in her becoming "typed" as some ingenuous fiancée or engaging young person of unassailable virtue in urgent need of equally decorous male championship. Only in *A Cup of Kindness* was she given a chance to show how good an actress she is. Perhaps, however, her having had to impersonate a succession of young women of undesigning maidenhood is one of the reasons why she doesn't look a day older to-day than she did then.

The success of *Rookery Nook* seemed to confirm the appointments, as it were, of several other members of the company. The farces that followed it were, to a large extent, cast before they were written. They had to contain worthy or suitable parts for Ralph Lynn, Tom Walls, Mary Brough, Robertson Hare, Winifred Shotter, Gordon James and Ethel Coleridge.

Another standard feature of the future Aldwych farces had its origin in this play—namely the traditional victimisation of Robertson Hare.

So far as *Rookery Nook* was concerned, his character of the intimidated little male relative who becomes entangled in the trouble was written as a subsidiary "feed" part. I had certainly no idea of exploiting the personality of Robertson Hare. It never crossed my mind that he would be given the part; and, in view of the results, it is interesting to record that he wasn't Tom Walls' first choice for it.

But he played it; and the fact that he played it initiated and practically dictated a new feature in Aldwych policy. The farces thereafter generally had to contain a situation in which he stood between an inexorable Walls and a more plausible but no less ruinous Lynn, to be fleeced of his fair repute, of his cash, of his trousers. In *Turkey Time* the biggest laugh of the whole play was when, Tom and Ralph having rehearsed their fell designs upon him, he made his entrance and duly arrived, beaming and unsuspecting, for the slaughter.

I am quite convinced that this standard victimisation joke would never have found its way into the subsequent farces if the third person had been any other actor than Robertson Hare. There is nothing the farce-going public loves to laugh at more than the sight of the familiar, next-door-neighbour type of earnest little citizen in tribulation or being "put upon". I was recently asked to write about Robertson Hare, and I can only repeat what I said of him then. He has been endowed by Nature with the personality and physique of the ideal "put-uponee". And he lives next door to everybody.

"The lack of inches—offset by a cocksure sort of confidence that he is as big as they come; the lack of hair—offset by a cocksure sort of confidence that he is bald because he prefers to be; the pedantic, almost clerical intonation in which he voices his ready assent to some calamitous proposal or his bootless distrust of the same; the expression of his face, puckered in instinctive doubt about the integrity of some interlocutor (and pucker in doubt well it may after all he has been through)—yes, Nature has certainly contributed. . . ."

In farce the object of the audience's derision quickly becomes the object of its affection. With *Rookery Nook* Robertson Hare rose from being one of the useful Aldwych hangers-on into becoming one of its popular attractions.

The bare subject of my third Aldwych farce was suggested to me by Tom Walls. When I say suggested I don't mean that Tom put his arm round my shoulder and said, "Listen, Ben—don't you think there might be something in the idea of Ralph and me getting mixed up in a ghost story? If you agree, would you like to have a shot at it?" or anything quite like that. What he did say was, "The next one has got to be about a haunted house; so get on with it." But he said it in a very friendly way and, coming from Tom Walls, the peremptory order meant exactly the same thing as a polite, tentative approach. Besides, it saved time. Also, it was satisfactory to feel I had reached a position when I was no longer considered to be a likely candidate for the authorship of the next farce. I was just told bluntly what I'd got to write it about. The Ambition was enjoying excellent health.

But it must not appear that I was still at the stage of hanging about at the Aldwych waiting for orders. By this time I was intimate with Tom Walls and I had got the measure of him and knew all his foibles and he knew I knew them and trusted me. And, notwithstanding the abrupt word of command regarding the subject of the next farce, he was always, from now onwards, readily prepared to accept any major projects of mine; and his imagination and sense of humour would often improve on them. So long as I didn't try to improve on *his* projects all was well. I have said he trusted me; and one of the things he trusted me not to do was, ever at rehearsals or in company, to say anything which might appear to challenge his judgment.

He wasn't just a crude egotist—it wasn't as simple as that. And he didn't mind so much having his decisions criticised or opposed. What sent him up in a blaze was to have them criticised or opposed in front of other people. For this might lead the other people to think (and perhaps to whisper) that somebody else knew better than he did.

At one rehearsal (of which of the plays I can't remember) I felt convinced that he was all wrong in his direction of some important piece of action. I was determined to get it done my way. If I had said, "Tom, don't you think it would be better if——" that is as far as I would have got. He would have said quickly, "All right, all *right*—d'you think I don't know what I'm doing? Who the hell's producing this play?" So what I did say was this:

"Tom—half a tick. You've forgotten something."

"Eh? I've forgotten? What d'you mean?"

"Last time we did this bit you said you were going to alter it and have so-and-so do such-and-such."

"Eh? I don't remember that."

"Yes, you *do*. I said at the time what à good idea."

"Oh? Oh, yes, I think I remember now. Hold on then. Here—Coley—go back to where you were. I've decided to do this another way."

I was undignified and obsequious? Worse perhaps. One might suspect—I have suspected it myself—that I let myself be dominated and even sometimes humiliated as the best diplomatic means to a profitable end. Or was it just my weak nature—unable to offer resistance to Tom's self-protective

141

arrogance? That perhaps was nearer the mark; but there were other considerations.

Tom's gift for getting the best out of my farces was an absolute revelation. It didn't show itself in flashes; he had a steady almost lazy application and foresight in discovering possibilities which had never occurred to me. Frankly, I think my Aldwych farces were excellent material which owed a great deal to Ralph's preliminary help; but the material could not have been more keenly appreciated or put into better trim to be presented as a finished article. And never, never did Tom fail to give me full credit for my efforts.

Quite apart from his talent as a producer Tom Walls was the actuating force which drove Aldwych farce to flourish as it did. Nor could it have done so had not Tom Walls been exactly the Tom Walls he was. That same self-protective arrogance was an essential and guiding factor in the character of this rather coarse, wrong-shaped-headed, ruthless, inclined to be dissipated, utterly extravagant, optimistic, entertaining, laughing, irresistible man.

Once, at the Garrick Club, I heard a distinguished actor describe Tom Walls as a beggar on horseback. Well, a beggar on horseback he may have been. But nobody ever gave him a leg up—nobody could. He alone hoisted himself to the saddle. And even the horse won the Derby.

CHAPTER VII

Aldwych Heyday

IN private conversation my wife and I always spoke of Burnham as "Burtle". This sounds rather whimsy and tiresome but it wasn't. It originated as a mild joke but it came to have a deep and lasting sentimental significance.

Burtle was, and is, a Somerset village some miles from Burnham. One of Burtle's middle-aged rustic male inhabitants decided, one day, that the time had come to spend his life's savings in satisfying his life's ambition. He blew the lot on a week's visit to London. Asked, on his return, what he thought of the metropolis, he answered, "Ah, she be a foine town; a foine town to be sure. But give I Burtle."

My wife was by nature graced with the lovely quality which I would call simplicity of outlook. I don't mean that she was in the least parsimonious—she wasn't even very economical. As our prosperity increased she loved to share with me full enjoyment of all the accepted pleasures of life that we could afford. What I mean by her simplicity of outlook is her knowledge that all the genuine full enjoyment of life must be rooted in contentment. Contentment was home. And home was Burnham.

In 1921, at Hayes, when we heard about Hawtrey buying *The Dippers*, almost our first word to each other had been spoken simultaneously—"Burtle". During the 1930's my film work made it necessary for me to live for nearly a year within easy range of the studios, and we moved the household temporarily to Rothamstead in Hertfordshire. But it was never more than a home from home. "Give I Burtle." We counted the hours.

The reason why Burnham exercised this spell over us was because, for all the earlier part of our life there, it retained a delightful, slow-witted, unconsciously humorous, West-country complacency. In the latter years it made continuously costly efforts to disavow its true character and to attain the status of a popular seaside resort, but it always failed. Now, since the last war, it has become no better than a secondary port of call for democracy on tour. All its old appeal has disappeared with all its old residents; and part of the former, battle-scarred Ladies' Golf-Links is now a caravan site.

Even in its old days Burnham was always a bit of a failure; and while it was content to be a failure it possessed this ingenuous charm of its own. We often went to London and enjoyed London. But we wouldn't have enjoyed London half so much if we hadn't had Burnham—and nowhere else —to go back to. It was a blissful experience to live in a place which was always a little behind the rest of the world, at a time when the rest of the world was already beginning to speed ahead of tranquillity.

There were three postmen in Burnham. One was our children's nanny's brother-in-law with a cleft palate; one used to umpire the local side to victory in our village cricket matches; and one was lame. It was characteristic of Burnham to employ a lame postman.

Every week one or other of the postmen brought me a fat envelope from Golding Bright—my returns from the Aldwych and a delectable cheque. To all appearances no comparatively graduate playwright could hope to attain to greater prosperity; for I had the assurance that the fat envelope would be delivered with unfailing regularity for the best part of a year on end. At the worst it would continue in only slightly modified degrees of fatness, for as each farce was launched at the Aldwych three touring companies were organised and were presently on the road simultaneously. All I had to do, it was thought, was, for some brief intensive period during the year, to sit down and rattle off the next farce for the next year's run.

It was true that I was very fortunately placed. The mistake some of my acquaintances and others made was regarding this rattling business. Its period was certainly intensive but it was not brief. Very few of those farces ran for much longer than they took to write.

For the five farces which followed *Rookery Nook* I had to invent a subject calculated to give full and equal scope to the two main male characters. Well, this wasn't very difficult perhaps, though I always found it quite difficult enough. When this subject had been submitted, discussed and provisionally approved, I had to devise a story round this subject, not only doing justice to the two leading men but containing characters to suit the special personalities of Mary Brough, Robertson Hare, Winifred Shotter and two or three other of the licensed habituées of the Aldwych stage. It wasn't the actual writing of the play which was the really difficult part of the job; it was the knitting together of that infernal story. Morning after morning, for days, weeks, months, I would return to the blank, demoralising prospect—with only a little situation here, a likely piece of business there, to be preserved and docketed and worked in somehow when the story at length struggled into existence. I never tried to write a line of the play until I had completed a detailed synopsis covering every moment of the action as I foresaw it, though the completed article invariably wandered off from this detailed synopsis during the five or six editions which I wrote of the farce itself, and wandered off still further when the last of the five or six editions came to be rehearsed. I wonder how many torn-up pages went to contribute to the compilation, from first to last, of one of my Aldwych farces. And I wonder what the local Burnham dustman thought I did with myself.

So far as I can determine there are three varieties of authors' wives. The first is the wife who is the assiduous consultant and critic and sometimes collaborator. In the case of a married couple of middle age, with no small children and few domestic responsibilities, there are, no doubt, many instances of such a wife proving a treasure. There are also, no doubt, many instances in which the husband is tempted to leave the wife to get on with their joint effort while he sneaks out and buys a few large-size tins of weed-killer. The second wife is she whose husband, like a damn fool, incites her to take a zealous interest in his literary aims and achievements prior to her own domestic and social responsibilities. However greatly she may admire his work it is not long before her chief interest in it becomes purely financial. How much can she expect to get for alimony? My wife was the ideal third.

My home life was supremely happy because my wife regarded all my workaday labours and preoccupations with a deeply affectionate, cherishing, facilitating unconcern. They were nothing to make any special provisions for or any allowances for. They were just part of the daily and, on occasions of my inspired overtime, nightly routine. For my part, I was never bothered or distracted by working in the midst of the regular and not by any means inaudible activities of a cheerful household featuring three growing children. If I had been, my wife would have seen to it that I wasn't; but she knew that I loved my domestic life to be just what she had made it. There was never any question of my putting up with it—I counted on it.

Thank goodness I am not by nature temperamental. I dare say I might have been more gifted a playwright if I had been temperamental, but I would never have been such a happy one. I can still picture myself sitting at my study table, devising and composing no less contentedly and inventively because someone had managed to take time off from the vigilance of nanny and had looked in on me and was driving a train round the room or something of the sort. It didn't last long or happen often; just an interlude, just a reminder that the place and conditions in which I worked were already part of the happiness I was working for.

And I couldn't in justice complain even if I had wanted to; for although it was never by any means a noisy household I contributed to any unwonted clamour that might be going on. I acquired and have always practised the habit of writing plays aloud. My wife always treated this as a perfectly reasonable proceeding and the servants got used to it. But occasional visiting neighbours were surprised to hear loud exclamations and snatches of altercation issuing from my study, and even more surprised when my wife showed her calm surprise at their being surprised. Thinking it over, I suppose our homestead must have struck some of the local Juddies as a pretty extraordinary set-up. To all appearances it was what it seemed, a normal, practical, sensible, sociable habitation, liable suddenly to be afflicted by the assumed voices of Tom and Ralph engaging in a vehement exchange of experimental badinage. It must have afforded our fellow residents a good deal of delectable concern. "If you ask me, that little woman has a lot to put up with."

Beyond wanting always to know that I was happy and interested in what I was writing, my wife never tried to find out what it was all about until I told her for myself. Even then, the readiness and pleasure with which she read a semi-accomplished script back to me was genuine only because she was sharing in my pleasure. She was the most untheatrical person imaginable. She enjoyed going to plays well enough but no more. She never had any great desire or curiosity to participate in the professional and technical side of the theatre, but the human side interested her enormously. For this reason she was of immense help and value to me at the Aldwych and in any of my subsequent plays. Theatre people soon found out it was no use trying to talk their eternal shop to her. It wasn't due to any lack of sympathy; simply she didn't pretend to know anything about it. On the other hand she loved nothing better than to spend an evening backstage and have a good old gossipy and not necessarily very decorous discussion about mutual domestic affairs with anybody who was glad to escape from the artificiality of their surroundings. And oh, how they all delighted to escape into her company.

There was never a suspicion of insincerity about her. She didn't bother about who the people were or what they did; she just enjoyed the people. She was equally at ease and natural and good company when Tom Walls entertained us on a Sunday evening at his newly-acquired house at Ewell and escorted us round his stables—with a good deal of formal inspection of the horses, which bored me no little—as she was when one of the dressers at the theatre was telling her about her daughter's expectation of her third in four years. When my wife called for me at the Aldwych towards the end of a day's rehearsal, she would leave with very little idea of what had been perpetrated on the stage but full of the latest information about the understudies' dogs.

She was beloved by everybody in the world of the theatre who ever knew her, from her close friends like Binnie Hale to the stage hands and the cloakroom women.

Rookery Nook was the last of my plays which my father saw, for he died suddenly in January, 1927. One night, in the very last month of his life, he shared with me one of the funny little boxes, designed for two, which are tucked away along-

148

THE STANDARD ALDWYCH VICTIMISATION SCENE
Tom Walls, Robertson Hare and Ralph Lynn in *Plunder*

side the circle at the Aldwych. It was the only part of the
house that hadn't been sold. There was no need for him now
to reconnoitre anxiously and to direct critical glances at people
and announce emphatically "A packed house". I am always
thankful that he lived long enough to see the fulfilment of
his hopes for me and of his loyal insistence that I had the
ability to do well at something, if only we could discover
what thing.

He had the further satisfaction of knowing that I was
already busy writing the next Aldwych farce; for this was
some time after Tom Walls had issued his decree, "The next
one has got to be about a haunted house", and had, for the
only time, saved me the initial pains of finding a subject. A
promising enough subject too. I remember receiving the
decree with my usual compliant enthusiasm and returning to
Burnham to begin the intricate process of working out how
to treat it.

A haunted house—all right—where? Somewhere in cold,
windswept isolation. Norfolk? Yes, Norfolk seemed to
supply the right blend of the civilised and the remote. A
bleak old Norfolk manor then—bleak—stark. It must have
a name implying bleak, stark, weird bogyness. Got it—
Thark Manor. *Thark*. As in the case of *Rookery Nook*, the
first line I wrote of *Thark* was its title.

I suggested it to Tom and he was greatly taken with it, so
that, at least, was decided. But when, eventually, after many
testing months of gestation and fruition, the title of the
forthcoming farce was published it met with a lot of adverse
comment. *Thark?* The gentlemen representing the Theatre-
ticket Libraries put their heads together in a huddle of dismay.
They jointly warned Tom Walls that they strongly protested
against this baffling and unattractive title and that their negotiations might be seriously affected unless it were changed.
Tom told them, in effect, to go to hell, and the title stood.

What they didn't appreciate was that, even if he had agreed
with their views, the fact that they had tried to find fault with
a Walls edict was enough to settle their well-intentioned hash
from the start. In so many ways he was really the most
splendid man to work with.

So long as there was plenty of money about Tom never
spared expense in staging and costumes and effects. The set
representing the dining-hall at Thark was the most elaborate
ever built for the Aldwych. It conveyed exactly the right
atmosphere of spacious eerieness and provided an effective
background for the ever-increasing state of funk which had
to be displayed by Ralph. Commissioned, as usual, by
Winifred Shotter, he had agreed to spend a night in the
haunted bedroom at Thark and lay the ghost. In this undertaking he was badgered rather than sustained by the sceptical
incitements of his middle-aged, well-to-do and, this time,
only slightly red-nosed uncle.

"Ghosts? Rubbish. Have you ever met anybody who's
seen a ghost?"

"No; but I've never met anybody who hasn't met somebody who has."

Some playgoers of mature vintage may remember that the
situation called for a gaunt and nightmare-ridden old male
retainer, who had so absorbed Thark's spirit of place that he
himself resembled some gloating and hollow-voiced spectre.
For once I had to forsake my principle of introducing only
characters whom one might encounter in the everyday walk
of life; but James Agate, who greatly approved my Thark
butler, aptly described him as "Brontë-esque", which seemed
to give him and me a certain justification. Gordon James
(Sydney Lynn) made the hit of his life in the part and cherished
its memory for ever after.

The episode in which he first appeared provided a good example of Tom's prodigious and unsparing methods of giving full effect to a scene. Immediately following the revelation of his name by this sepulchral butler to the nephew and uncle there had to be a loud and prolonged roll of thunder. This was the context:

"You—let me see, what's your name again?"

"Mrs. Frush wouldn't call me by my real name, sir; so she calls me Jones."

"Oh, a sort of pet name. But what is your real name, Jones?"

"My real name, sir?"

"Yes."

"Death."

(*Thunder. When at length it has subsided it is Uncle's turn.*)

"I don't care a damn. I knew a feller named Death. Major Death—he was in the Blues", etc.

While production was in hand Tom decided that he was going to promote a roll of thunder which would be the end of all rolls of stage thunder for all time. Learning with elation from me that my first cousin, Dan Burges, V.C., was Governor of the Tower, he commissioned me to apply for the loan of two dozen cannon balls. He then erected in a permanent position half-way up to the flies a long and solid flight of wooden stairs. The cannon balls were discharged from aloft, one by one, down the wooden stairs. I forget exactly how they finished up, but I suppose they ran into some elaborate slot or network or perhaps were collected by a hard-pressed fielding side of stage hands in the wings. Meanwhile other stage hands simultaneously performed on thunder sheets for good measure. Tom got what he wanted.

The last scene of *Thark* was laid in the haunted bedroom. The uncle has consented to share the ordeal, armed with a duck gun, though the nephew plaintively protests that he doesn't believe the trouble is caused by ducks. The incident of Tom and Ralph as joint occupants of a small double bed produced a longer and louder sequence of laughs than any other scene between the two in the history of Aldwych farce. In the try-out week at Southsea Tom was, as usual, extremely uncertain of his lines, and this time—for the first two or three shows at least—Bobbie Dunn, the stage-manager, had to remain hidden under the bed, holding the script in one hand and a flash-lamp in the other and doing his tormented best to keep Tom informed of his part. His conscientious but incoherent promptings were mostly drowned by the laughs; and it was difficult to determine which lines were actually meant to be in the play and which were the rather profane incitements shouted by Tom to Bobbie Dunn.

With each new farce Tom alternated between playing someone of his own age and real-life appearance and an elderly character part. He preferred the former, but he was incomparably funnier and easier to cater for as gentlemen of riper years; and in *Thark* he was at his best. He had one line which has been quoted at me more than anything I ever wrote. It was in a short scene in which the sporty baronet is thanking his maidservant for some act of domestic diplomacy:

"You're a very good girl. (*He pauses briefly and appraises her.*) I suppose? Are you a good girl?"
"Yes, sir."
"Then don't waste my time."

This and Mary Brough's line from *Rookery Nook*—"I will come at eight-thirty in the morning; earlier than that I cannot be"—seem to be the two relics of dialogue which, for some reason or other, planted themselves in the public memories of the old Aldwych days.

Kenneth Kove drifted back into the company for the run of *Thark*. I had seen him in *It Pays to Advertise* and shrewdly guessed that his pallid, weedy personality and piping monotone would provide a good feed for the scathing reactions of the Tom Walls character; e.g.:

"Well how do I get out?"
"You can walk downstairs or you can take the lift. Or you can fall over the banisters and break your bloody neck."

Kove's potentialities were limited, but he trailed his thin umbrella in and out of three of my Aldwych farces. I always thought him an acquisition and many of the audience took a particular delight in him. But his spindle-shanked appearance and immutability of style tended to make him an interesting exhibit rather than a recognised member of the team.

Plunder, which followed *Thark*, was received with greater and more unanimous enthusiasm by Press and public than any play I have ever written. It played to capacity for the first five months of its run and even at the time of its premature withdrawal after 344 performances its returns were still showing an ample profit. Its story was straight drama and it had the distinction of being the first farce in which the action revolved round a violent death. In a moment of inspiration I visualised Tom Walls and Ralph Lynn suspected of a serious crime and being grilled by the police authorities at Scotland Yard. Obviously the crime of which they were justly accused had to be the most serious crime in the catalogue. Only if the crime involved the maximum penalty would the situation contain the maximum of menace. And only the maximum of menace could provide the maximum of laughter. The charge against Tom and Ralph had to be one of wilful murder. The penalty—the rope.

So they had, in fact, to be murderers. And the audience, from whom none of their secrets were hidden, had to know they were murderers and to watch them entering the death-trap of Scotland Yard and to witness their agonising ordeal with an intense desire that they should bluff and wriggle their respective ways out of it. It was a stiff task I had set myself. I accomplished it mainly by exploiting the contrast in the personalities of Ralph and Tom. In the course of the action leading up to the Scotland Yard scene the audience had seen them planning and executing a burglary. They came up a ladder into Mary Brough's bedroom and looted her jewel-case while she remained wrapped in porcine slumber. Ralph was, of course, actuated by the highest principles and Winifred Shotter. The jewellery was morally and, as it eventually transpired, legally hers. But the murder?

I contrived the murder by having a detestable old male relative of Mary Brough's spot the ladder and climb up it to investigate. In a brief bedroom struggle he was gagged with a towel, lost his footing at the top of the ladder and fell off it into the next world. This made his welcome decease, though unforeseen and accidental, wilful murder in the eyes of the law, since Ralph and Tom were engaged in perpetrating a felony at the time. I had got what I set out for and the situation gave full effect to the hazardous subterfuges of Ralph and the unflinching acumen of Tom in facing the ordeal of the third degree. As I have said, Ralph would never have been able to get the last ounce of comedy out of it, as he did, if he hadn't stood to be hanged.

Tom's character in this play was written in flat and undis-guised defiance of the moral principles and, needless to say, he revelled in it. He had to be the instigator of the whole criminal procedure—a genuine society crook, who was going to steal the stuff in any case and had unwillingly to consent to rope the woefully inefficient Ralph into partnership. He had to be so attractive an individual that he could retain not only the sympathy of the audience but, against all stage precepts, his unwarranted share of the loot. Moreover, still with the inexpert assistance of Ralph, he had finally to turn the tables on Scotland Yard by the prescribed expedient of blackmailing Hare. It was a nice study in ethics. If any actor could carry it off that actor was Tom Walls. And he did.

Once again Tom showed his thoroughness as a producer. He agreed with me that in order to get full value from the scene in Scotland Yard the personnel, setting and procedure must all combine to give a life-like reproduction of the real thing. Before I wrote it, he and I got an introduction to Chief Constable Wensley and spent a couple of hours in consultation with him. Wensley had risen to his high position from the ranks and was by then in late middle age, a man of slow, impressive speech and ponderous, almost mournful manner. He might well have been a successful undertaker; as, in a sense, he was.

Wensley took the utmost pains to instruct us. He said he had often seen Scotland Yard on the stage and it had never been anything like it. He told us he never acted as the leading questioner of any unfortunate suspect who was escorted into his room. He contented himself with offering him the most comfortable—in fact, the only comfortable—chair, and studying the victim's reaction to this unexpected courtesy. "I see you casting an eye upon that screen in the corner," he said. "They all of 'em do that. But they've no reason to. It's put there to hide a washhand-stand. There's nothing like that goes on here. And there are no Sherlock Holmeses here either. It's all just straightforward hard work."

I told him I wanted two characters suspected of joint participation in a crime to be interrogated together. He shook his head. "You can't do that. We always have 'em in one by one. I don't deal with 'em both together." "I'm sorry, but you've got to this time," I said. "Please think of a way."

"Ah, well now, yes, you could have it like this," Wensley said. "You would have the Chief Detective Inspector who's doing the interrogation say to whomsoever he's got there at the time, 'I don't think you're telling me the truth. I'm going to have your friend in and ask him the same question and see what he replies.' I remember," he went on, "having to do that in the case of Bywaters and Mrs. Thompson."

I made no comment but I found this an interesting sidelight on the grim, secret ordeal which must have been endured by that unhappy couple in the very room where I was sitting.

One gratifying result of our visit was that, after one matinée performance a few months later, old Wensley was able to assert—very gravely—that at last the theatre had succeeded in providing a flawless representation of the aspect and ritual of his gruesome headquarters—not that he put it quite like that. Tom crowned his precautions as producer by choosing Herbert Waring to play the inquisitorial Chief Inspector. This delighted me, because Waring had been one of my favourite actors for something like thirty years. It never occurred to me that one of his distinction would be considered for—or would consider—a one-scene feed part. But Waring was long past his prime and was glad to accept it. He contributed tremendously to the success of the scene. Nobody could better have provided the authentic, steely menace which made Tom's procrastinations and Ralph's squirming evasions so effective and so funny. I always tried to tell Herbert Waring I was greatly obliged to him but his gracious nature would never allow this. He said it should be the other way about and did me the favour of getting me elected a member of the Garrick Club, just to show that he meant what he said.

Another great actor made an even more spectacular comeback to the West End theatre at about this time. *Plunder* was tried out at Southsea for a week in the middle of June, and Tom transported his spacious Rolls Royce car one day to the Isle of Wight, luxuriously to patrol its pleasant leas. Personally, I don't care for motoring for so-called pleasure, but I do like shell fish; so I went with him, and so did my wife and Golding Bright. As we purred along, piloted by Tom's chauffeur, who bore the extraordinarily appropriate name of Pacey, we approached a sign-post which stood on a little island of grass at a fork in the road. On the grass was stretched a strikingly picturesque figure. It was that of a lightly-clad, bronzed, gipsy-like and remarkably handsome man, lying there oblivious of cars or care or anything but an opportune place in the sun. I remarked, "Look at that chap—he looks like Harry Ainley." As Pacey slowed down to something like 40 m.p.h. in order to select the right prong of the fork, I said, "Hold on—it *is* Harry Ainley." We halted. Golding dismounted and trudged for a considerable distance back to the grass plot. Next day he told the Haymarket management that Henry Ainley's long rest-cure was complete and that their problem of finding the right actor to play opposite Marie Tempest in *The First Mrs. Fraser* had been solved. Henry Ainley duly returned to the theatre and, for some years, to what the world regarded as his rightful place in the sun. Later on he faltered again; his nerve forsook him at a critical moment; the sun went down. The last I saw of him was in a film production of *As You Like It*, when in the minor part of the Banished Duke he outclassed everybody else concerned.

He was an enthusiast for the Aldwych farces and I possess and cherish the long exuberant letters he used to write to me. He was, perhaps, as used to be said of him, his own worst enemy. But I sometimes wonder whether *I* wasn't; and whether it might not have been better if I hadn't spotted that handsome gipsy sunning himself on his blissful patch of grass.

Plunder called for four sets and involved quick change of scene and was beyond the scope of repertory companies and amateur societies or its popularity might have been as lasting as that of *Rookery Nook*. Why, then, should it have come to an untimely and premature end?

Well, I have depicted Tom Walls as a genius, and so far as his qualities as actor and producer are concerned I think this is justified. But he was no genius of finance. In fact, I am almost tempted to think that he knew less about finance than I did. Because although I invested and lost two thousand pounds in the company he formed to take a lease of the Fortune Theatre on lunatic terms, and thousands more in another company he formed to purchase some infernal quarry somewhere or other, and could therefore myself claim distinction as a mug of the very highest order, Tom's was, after all, the master-mind of muggery which originated these lamentable ventures. And I never really had any sound belief in them; it was simply that I let my disgustingly weak nature be dragooned into participation. But Tom thought he was infallible; and when he began his Fortune Theatre tenancy with the successful run of *On Approval*, by Frederick Lonsdale, he thought so with even greater ease than before.

When I say "successful" run, *On Approval* may have exemplified Lonsdale's peculiar skill and declared Tom to be a theatrical wizard; but it didn't result in any more material declaration in the form of a dividend. And when the play chosen to succeed *On Approval* turned out to be an utter flop and had to be withdrawn after losing money steadily for six weeks, the Fortune Theatre, if still a going concern, showed pretty clearly where it was going to. But I couldn't very well complain about this, because I was the author of the flop.

Some years earlier Lane had published the fourth and easily the best of my novels, *Mischief.* Knowing that a new comedy would soon be wanted for the Fortune, I greedily and far more hastily than usual adapted some of the main incidents of *Mischief* into a mistake in three acts. It had a brilliant first scene which did it more harm than good; because Yvonne Arnaud came on and delighted everybody with a matrimonial squabble; but from then onwards what I had intended to be sophisticated and amusing, when produced (even by Tom Walls) and interpreted (even by Yvonne Arnaud) became unsympathetic and irritating. It was a meagre and inconclusive little affair in any case. Perhaps I, too, had begun to think that I was infallible.

So that prize misnomer, the Fortune Theatre, swallowed my two thousand pounds. I could afford to write off the loss. *Plunder* was bringing me in ample returns and was so settled a success that it couldn't fail to do so for another year or more; besides which there were royalties from the tours of the other farces. Just as well—because I had planned to go to Australia in the winter of 1928-9 and the passages were already booked. I also had to face the prospect of sending my daughter, Josephine, to an expensive school for girls and my son, Ben, to old Tom Pellatt's school, Durnford, near Swanage; and there may still be about some poverty-stricken old gentlemen like myself who will remember what that used to cost, even in those days. My second son, known as Burtie (he was named Daniel Burton, after that delightful master of applied indolence, his mother's father), would be following along there in another year or two—yes, it was just as well that I had dug my heels in so firmly at the Aldwych.

But if the Fortune Theatre dealt a painful glancing blow to

my financial resources, what about Tom's? He still carried on there and produced several more unsuccessful plays; but already the project must have cost him a weighty packet. He was to lose plenty more in the years to come. That damned quarry hadn't yet hove in sight; and, however gruesome was the appearance of his banking account at any given time, Tom always pursued a mode of life which was an unvarying pattern of glorious extravagance.

He must, however, just about this time, have been called upon to face one of the more vexatious of his many crises. After the Christmas holidays season of 1928-9 the returns from *Plunder* began to show a falling off, as theatre returns are wont to do. They were still good, but they didn't represent capacity business by any means. That was no use to Tom. For his purpose it was necessary that the Aldwych should go on playing to capacity for another four or five months to come. There was only one prescription for this—a new farce.

By that time I was in Australia, enjoying myself and thinking about the subject and story for the next farce only at odd, disjointed moments. I could think it out on my way home and write it when I got there. It didn't matter how long it took. *Plunder* would still be running. As it turned out, I was cabled for at the end of January, snatched some last-minute non-starter's berth in an Orient liner and spent most of the homeward voyage looking for inspiration. I had carefully labelled it "wanted on voyage", but it had disappeared.

Tom said, "This has got to be the cheapest production we've ever had. Just one set throughout and a pretty simple one. The smallest cast you can manage." I said, "After *Plunder* they'll be expecting something elaborate." He said, "I don't care what they expect, they're not going to get it." I said, "All right; we'll go for contrast. Something domestic." It suited my book. The only time when I had discovered anything like an idea on board was when I suddenly recalled a subject I had experimented with in the old old days. On one of those evenings, nearly twenty years before, when I had come back from giving sultanas to City policemen and had settled down to the real business of the day, I had written the first three pages or so of a play which was to treat of a respected and apparently perfectly innocuous young man being arrested at his wedding reception. The idea had been consigned, like so many others, to perish in its infancy and the waste-paper basket. But now, with Ralph on hand, it resurrected itself and throve.

A Cup of Kindness fulfilled all Tom's stipulations and gave him the results he wanted. I made it a Romeo and Juliet story of the suburbs. The Montagues were Tom Walls, as Mr. Tutt; Mary Brough, as his wife, Mrs. Tutt (an ex-barmaid) and his two sons, played by Ralph Lynn and Kenneth Kove. The Capulets were Robertson Hare, Marie Wright and Winifred Shotter, as Mr., Mrs. and Miss Ramsbotham respectively. There were also a revolting old invalid Mr. Ramsbotham, senior, with bits of pineapple on the front of his dressing-gown, for Gordon James; an elderly skivvy for Ethel Coleridge; and a good-looking nurse who was supposed to attend to old Mr. Ramsbotham and was attended to in her turn, needless to say, by Tom Walls. The arrest of Ralph for an unintentional breach of the law governing outside brokerage was timed to take place just as the parties were posing for a wedding group, and to throw an already restive inter-family party into absolute chaos.

The by now traditional Aldwych favourites were all well catered for and it was, as intended, a very funny little farce on frugal lines. During its run there occurred a minor incident which provides a good example of how Tom Walls could combine his sense of authority with his sense of humour. It came to his ears (everything came to his ears) that Kenneth

Kove was going about saying that the people who really contributed most to the success of the show were some of the support-players, including, naturally, himself. Kove was perhaps betrayed into this assumption by the laughter throughout the scene of his first entrance. Ralph was just on the point of persuading his stubborn and irascible father, Tom, to give his approval and financial aid to his (Charlie Tutt's) marriage with Betty Ramsbotham. At this moment the lamentable younger Tutt son arrived, in the shape of Kenneth Kove, having just been sent down from the 'Varsity.

Tom: What for? What did you do? And who is she?
Kove: A girl called Robinson. I met her and her people last year at Winter Sports.
Ralph: The Swiss Family Robinson.
Tom: Shut up, you. Well?
Kove: They found her in my bathroom, but I wasn't there at the time.
Tom: Why not?

At the end of the scene Kove concluded that he had better leave the Ramsbothams' house and return home. To this Tom had, of course, only one answer—"Go to hell." "Right-ho," said Kove. "Then I'll see you later."

His exit on this line always got a good laugh and a round of applause. On the night when Tom had heard of Kove's indiscreet remark he refrained from comment; but when the cue came for him to say "Go to hell", he contented himself by saying "Go away." "Right-ho," replied Kove, somewhat flabbergasted. "Then I'll see you later." He withdrew without a sound from the audience. A few minutes later, the picture of wan and injured perplexity, he was confronted by Tom in the wings. "*Now* who contributes the big laughs to the show, you——?"

This was 1929. The picture-houses, still displaying their visual wares in an atmosphere of orchestral decorum, were destined in the near future to be rent asunder by a cacophony which sounded like machine-gun practice in a parrot-house. The first "talkies" arrived.

Herbert Wilcox may have been a loss to the diplomatic service but I am one of many who had cause to be glad that he took to the motion-picture business. His astuteness was matched only by his amity. He immediately seized on Aldwych farce as being the most promising material for the new medium. I know little about the course of his negotiations with Tom Walls, but I do know that Tom would only come to terms on condition that he should take command of the shooting. He entirely lacked experience but never confidence in his own ability, and the results of his first and subsequent efforts, though often assailed by critics and rivals, provided picture-houses all over the country with customers for years to come. But it was characteristic of Tom Walls that on the first occasion he entered a film studio it was to direct a picture.

For my part I, for once, insisted on something. My suggestion that it would be effective if there was musical accompaniment to some of the action was regarded with disfavour. The introduction of musical noises into a straight farce would be inappropriate and unrealistic. But I eventually prevailed and Tom and I interviewed, on Wilcox's recommendation, a man I had never heard of—a gentle, modest, stammering American named Carroll Gibbons.

Twenty-three years later, in 1952, after the first night of *Wild Horses*, I took my family and Laurence Irving and his wife to supper at the Savoy. When he saw me there Carroll Gibbons delivered from his piano a long impromptu calypso about me. I can't think of any tribute that has ever pleased me more. We had made friends over that *Rookery Nook* film all those years before; and once you became a friend of Carroll Gibbons you stayed his friend.

Rookery Nook was one of the very first British talkies. I saw a public try-out of it with the Aldwych company while we were in Glasgow for a preliminary week with my next farce. It filled me with horror and headache. It was a great success all over the country and later was used as the opening attraction of the largest picture-house in the Empire, the State Theatre, Sydney. To me it always remained a painful, distorted version of the genuine article, even when I had to walk on to the stage of the New Gallery in Regent Street with Ralph Lynn and Winifred Shotter and receive a prize for my contribution towards the best British talkie of the year. The prize was an inscribed scroll and I haven't the slightest idea what has become of it.

There was no further call for immediate frugality at the Aldwych now. *A Night Like This* was an elaborate affair with a large cast and six sets. One of these represented a London exterior in a thick fog which was well suggested by means of a gauze curtain and skilful lighting. An old-fashioned growler with a real cab-horse was discovered and, the cabby having temporarily deserted it, the horse moved off at a given moment and was supposed to home, like a pigeon, to its mews, carrying Ralph and Tom inside the cab. This was easily managed, with the genuine cab-driver in the wings to instruct the horse; but the poor old horse, though otherwise an excellent actor, persistently declined to behave itself on stage and before long we had to appoint an artificial substitute. Regrettable—but the genuine horse's offence not only embarrassed the audience but prolonged the interval during a quick change. Besides, it always tempted Ralph to stray beyond the recognised bounds of impromptu.

Soon after the opening performance of *A Night Like This*

"DEATH"

Mary Brough, Ralph Lynn, Winifred Shotter, Robertson Hare, Tom Walls, Ethel
Coleridge and Gordon James in a scene from *Thark*

THE AUTHOR WITH TOM WALLS AND RALPH LYNN ON LOCATION

Queen Mary attended a special matinée which was given for some distinguished charity or other. I was commanded to be received in her box during the second interval. This interval immediately followed a scene in which Ralph and Tom, desirous of keeping Robertson Hare imprisoned in a room, decided that the best way of doing this was to remove his trousers and take them along with them. This was the farce's moment of most blatant frivolity, but a good deal that had preceded it had not been exactly puritanical. I awaited the comments which Her Majesty might graciously be pleased to make with some disquietude.

She said, "It is very amusing and very interesting." I bowed my acknowledgment, though I couldn't help wondering whether "interesting" was a compliment to myself or to Robertson Hare. Then, with a slightly quizzical smile, she added, "Is it an adaptation from the French?" Who else could have found so humorous a way of expressing indulgent reproof? No wonder they called it a charity matinée.

A few months later Golding Bright heard from Gilbert Miller, who said he was thinking of producing *Plunder* on Broadway with two English actors, Stanley Logan and Lionel Atwill, both well known in the States. Golding Bright told him to go ahead, but as usual I was told nothing about it. Golding only presented his authors with the *fait accompli*.

Then Tom Walls said, "Come on; it's time we got busy with the next picture" and told Golding Bright he was going to film *Plunder*. Golding said he was sorry but *Plunder* must be held in reserve. Unwillingly he had to tell the insistent Tom the reason why. If Gilbert Miller did *Plunder* on Broadway the talkie rights would be tied up with the American agreement.

Tom Walls was furious. His authority had been challenged. I suppose he thought I had been keeping him in the dark or something. Whereas the first thing I heard was that Tom had signed an agreement with two other authors for their farce to be the next Aldwych production. The second thing I heard was what all the trouble had been about. The third thing I heard was that the Gilbert Miller project had been abandoned.

I sat with my wife on the first night of the new farce. Tom made a complimentary curtain-speech about me. The farce was adjudged to be rather below Aldwych standard and I received, by inference, some of the best notices I'd ever had. Tom and I soon laughed it off.

But as time went by the ill-feeling between Tom and Ralph at the theatre became more acute and more persistent. They weren't jealous of each other; each had quite sufficient confidence in himself to prevent him from resenting the other's success. But they bore an irksome grudge against each other. I think the real trouble was that they had got weary of their long year-in, year-out stage partnership and by the perpetual pinpricking differences in their characters and standards. Ralph's approach to his work was intensely and unceasingly conscientious. Tom's was blasé and feckless. He would constantly prolong the interval between acts while he entertained desirable guests in his dressing-room, leaving Ralph and the others—to say nothing of the audience—chafing to get on with the job. Ralph loved to make his laughing comments to me on Tom's ambitions as a social climber and of where he had climbed from. When I was writing the next farce, *Turkey Time*, I wanted Tom to appear in another of his elderly character parts. But he wouldn't; he said he wanted to play a man about town. I was consulting Ralph on my plans and reported this to him and his remark was not only characteristic of Ralph but typical of his attitude towards Tom. He simply asked, "What part of town?"

Turkey Time was the last of my stage farces in which Tom

performed. He had an illness during the run but, in any case, he had always been in the habit of taking a lot of time off. I have met an Aldwych customer who stated that he had visited every one of my farces without ever seeing Tom Walls act. In the case of *Turkey Time* his absence one night wrung a lament from my London daily woman which, as a non-sequitur, would be difficult to rival even in the world of daily women. I had given her and her husband seats at the Aldwych and, next morning she said to me, "Oh, it was lovely—lovely it was. But Mr. Walls he wasn't there, and my husband, who'd seen it before, he said that last night's gentleman wasn't as good as what Mr. Walls was. It's a small world, isn't it?" Many disappointed clients were less obscure and far less lenient in what they had to say about Tom's incurable practice of working undertime.

Herbert Wilcox had quite sufficient faith in Ralph's popularity as an individual comedian, especially in partnership with Winifred Shotter. I wrote two very successful little films for them. The first, called *The Chance of a Night-time*, was an adaptation of the good old *Dippers* and it was kept for three weeks at the Plaza. The second was *Mischief*, which redeemed the stage fate of that subject by sticking more closely to the comedy material of the novel. For its first performance at the Carlton Wilcox, with his unsurpassed instinct for showmanship, managed to organise one of those ostentatious full-dress charity crushes, now so accepted a feature of the motion-picture business. The Duke of Windsor, who was then Prince of Wales, honoured the occasion. It was, in some respects, a most satisfactory one. The crushers were generous and the Press quite enthusiastic. But when we came to rehearse the next Aldwych farce not only had Tom himself withdrawn from the cast but Winifred Shotter had been supplanted.

If I am unfair in relating this bluntly as a case of cause and effect—if, as Tom afterwards maintained, the change at the Aldwych had nothing to do with the success of the two Lynn-Shotter films, I can only remark in justification that his timing was unfortunate; for he telephoned to me at Burnham and told me heatedly that he was engaging a new leading girl for the next farce two days after the acclaimed first showing of *Mischief* at the Carlton. Why then, it may be asked, should anyone consent to go on working with a man who was prone to these autocratic, sweeping fits of pique? I can only repeat that they were just the weak and misguided expressions of his determination to assert and maintain his position. That position he filled not only with brilliance in achievement and results; but also with immense charm and allurement. Over and over again I went to Tom Walls' dressing-room to tell him that I would not tolerate something or other that he had done. I was never with him more than five minutes before we were having a drink together and shaking with laughter.

Both Ralph and I thought at first that the choice of Winifred Shotter's successor was an unpromising one. We were proved wrong, for the girl Tom had appointed, on the recommendation of Charles B. Cochran, was a very jolly person to have in the company and was quite good in her part by the time we opened. But after about the second rehearsal Ralph persuaded me to tell Tom that we didn't think she would do. Tom refused to have his judgment questioned and brushed me aside: "Oh, nonsense; she's as clever as a monkey."

I returned to Ralph. "It's no good, Ralph; Tom won't change her. He says she's as clever as a monkey."

That morning, while Miss Carpenter was still engaged in her rather unpromising attempts to rehearse one of her scenes, Ralph sidled across to my chair, stooped close to me and whispered, "Some monkeys are not so bloody clever."

But all turned out happily and the farce, *Dirty Work*, did well enough, considering that Tom was now officially and permanently an absentee. Robertson Hare was promoted to the position of joint leading comedian and the other regular members of the team were still going strong. These now included Archibald Batty who had understudied Tom in some of the plays and had appeared as his deputy goodness knows how many times. Henry Hewitt, who was recruited for this play, was to do me excellent service later on as well, and so was Margaretta Scott, whose talents, if already unmistakable, were given no chance to do her justice. But her youthful enthusiasm was a great asset at this rather drooping stage of the Aldwych story. We called her the Labrador puppy.

Again in my next farce, *A Bit of a Test*, there were two small-part players who today are leading West End actors, Clive Morton and Hyde White. This was my last play of that Aldwych series and it differed from all the others in its abandonment of the essential, true-to-type depiction of character. I couldn't even pretend to be sticking to my principles with a farce in which Robertson Hare was England's cricket captain on an Australian tour, with Ralph Lynn as the star batsman. Nor could their being kidnapped by bushrangers and rescued by Mary Brough in riding-breeches maintain the environment of stern reality which had been the secret of the Aldwych tradition. The whole thing was really an elaborate topical sketch, since it coincided with the English tour which gave rise to the great body-line controversy. The farce had a limited public but a number of people thought it very funny except in Australia. When some optimist subsequently produced it there it was regarded almost as a public scandal and was quickly slain. I am glad I was not in Australia at the time or I might have been slain as well. I had dared to joke about cricket.

This, then, so far as I was concerned was the catalogue of
Aldwych farce, now known perhaps to the majority as an
ambiguous theatrical term, but abiding and, I think, treasured
in the memories of some ladies still in full bloom and mellow-
ing male recorders of the good old days of fun. I had still
before me a long association with Ralph and Tom and the
others in the studios, and the farces enjoyed a second lease of
life. Tom, as film director, scouted the critics and contented
himself with photographing the stage versions; and a new
and wider public became familiar with the hollow tones of
"Death", and the traditional figure of Robertson Hare,
encompassed on either side by Tom and Ralph to be put
upon.

Mary Brough lived long enough to take part in this series
of reproductions but died soon afterwards. She was dear to
all of us and it was not from any lack of respect or affection
that her funeral, in a large suburban cemetery, proved so severe
a test of conflicting Aldwych emotions.

A public multitude had assembled but the adept Pacey
piloted the Rolls through a gap in the crowd and landed it
near the entrance to the chapel. Tom, Ralph and I alighted,
all already in a state of unnatural sensitivity. We were met
by the woebegone figure of Robertson Hare, who had been
doing some nervous perambulation in anticipation of our
arrival. With thousands of eyes feasting upon us Tom, for
once, became the victim of embarrassed aberration. He
made as though to shake hands with Bunny Hare, checked
himself, turned to Ralph and said, quite seriously, "You know,
Mr. Hare, I believe?" We began to quiver with suppressed
laughter. Hysteria had set in.

In the chapel we occupied the front pews of one of the aisles,
vis-à-vis the other aisle which was crammed by those of the
general public who had patronised the early doors. They
paid small heed to the service; they never took their eyes off

Tom and Ralph. They were accustomed to, and throve upon, such attention in restaurants and at race-meetings; but not at funerals. Ralph seemed particularly sensitive to such scrutiny at so genuinely distressing a moment. He made, from between his clenched teeth, a whispered attempt to side-track emotion:

"The second choir-boy on the right is like Madge Saunders."

But this didn't help very greatly.

After the service Ralph suddenly realised that he had left his wreath in the car. There was a prolonged hitch while we waited in the porch of the chapel and he explored indeterminately in several directions in the hope of finding it. Meanwhile the hearse drew up to convey the coffin some distance to the spot where the bearers awaited it and ran over the foot of an over-zealous press photographer. A small army of his more fortunate colleagues hastened to take up their positions at the graveside.

Ralph returned and we walked slowly, all four abreast, behind the hearse. And as we went, Tom, at last, delivered a line appropriate to the sad occasion. For if it were not a direct reference to dear old Mary Brough herself, it did at least express a sentiment charged with the spirit of Aldwych. Tom turned suddenly to Robertson Hare, pistoned a dictatorial forefinger into his ribs and spoke in a tone of severe command.

"When we get alongside that grave," he said, "don't you go and get yourself photographed standing between me and Ralph. They'll think it's a gag."

CHAPTER VIII

The Second Ambition

I SAT in the Mound Stand and watched the Middlesex side carry their captain on their shoulders into Lord's pavilion. It was the occasion of his retirement from the Middlesex captaincy and his side had just beaten Surrey for the championship. This was years before I ever met Sir Pelham Warner, but, long before this great day at Lord's even, he had been responsible for my having made a vow. For in 1905 I read a book called *How We Recovered The Ashes*, by Mr. P. F. Warner, and then and there I vowed that sooner or later I would go and watch a series of Test Matches in Australia. In 1928, when I was forty-two, I sailed in an Orient liner with England's team.

My wife came with me as far as Colombo, where we left the ship and spent a fortnight in Ceylon. She went back home to the children for Christmas and I pursued the cricketers and caught them up in Sydney. One of my fellow-passengers in the liner from Colombo onwards was another cricketer whose career had recently ended, fortunately for our touring team, for he was C. G. Macartney. He became the first great exponent of the game whom I got to know at all intimately—with the exception of the aforesaid and long retired Sam Woods, who was still reviving past glories in the fields of sport and lotion in his Somerset twilight.

When we got to Melbourne on our way to Sydney, Macartney took me to the offices of the Victorian Cricket Association and introduced me to the Secretary. In the first

Test Match I had ever seen, on the 10th to the 12th of August,
1896, I had watched that Secretary get 6 for 59 and 6 for 30 at
the Oval. England's second innings: W. G. Grace b Trumble,
9. F. S. Jackson b Trumble, 2. Abel (R) c Giffen b Trumble,
21. Hayward (T) c Trott b Trumble, 13 and so on. Hugh
Trumble. I had seen him make 64 not out, too, the old
nuisance, in Jessop's match in 1902. He was a dear, gentle old
fellow now. Presently into his Secretary's room came
another, not quite so gentle, cricketing celebrity—Warwick
Armstrong. Before I had seen a ball bowled in Australia I
was seated in the company of three of the greatest players in
history—Hugh Trumble, Warwick Armstrong, Charlie Macartney. I had that same feeling of incredibility which had
possessed me when I first met Charles Hawtrey and Gerald du
Maurier—*je ne sais pas que je ne rêve.*

I was amazed by the reception I got in Melbourne and
Sydney. I knew my name had been publicised and recognised
by this time in England, but in Australia I was treated as a
person of vastly greater importance. And used as such. One
of the Melbourne newspapers got me to write my impressions
of the Melbourne Cup. I was given the best seat to be had—
on the roof of the most imposing stand in a wide semicircle
of imposing stands, alongside the gentleman who was doing
the running commentary. I wrote a good article and only
finished while the newspaper's messenger stood over me in my
cabin, with the ship's siren impatiently announcing that we
were due to sail for Sydney. It may be that the article, which
was given a good deal of prominence, rather boosted my
prestige; but in any case the hospitality of Australia in those
days (and I expect the same holds good still) towards anyone
paying a gratuitous visit from England was surprising. I had
intended to come out on a quiet little jaunt to watch cricket;
and I was interviewed and cartooned and invited to broad-
casting stations and made an honorary member of one or two

clubs in each city and an honorary patron of considerably more than one or two bars.

But what gave me the greatest delight and surprise was the reception I got from the English cricket team at Sydney. Almost within a matter of hours I was made a member of the party. This was all the more gratifying because I hadn't set out with the smallest intention of tuft-hunting the touring side. If in the course of my camp-following I happened to get to know some of them, so much the more interesting; but I was completely innocent of that pathetic form of snobbery which appears, straining in self-assertion, on the fringes of unofficial photographic groups of sporting celebrities in ships and golf clubs and inspecting Blue Mountains.

Percy Chapman was captain of the English side, Jack White and Douglas Jardine being the only other amateurs. The others were Hobbs, Sutcliffe, Hendren, Hammond, Tate, Larwood, Duckworth, Geary, Mead, Ernest Tyldesley, Leyland, Ames, Freeman and Sam Staples; but Staples was taken ill very soon after the beginning of the tour and returned home.

At Sydney they played against New South Wales, and in a second game against a strong batch of Australian candidates for the Test Matches. I don't know how the Sydney cricket ground appears today, but on the Saturday which was the opening day of the State match in 1928 it impressed a visiting Englishman not only with its size but with some other unusual features. It made discriminating provision for the contrasted social strata of its patrons. Across the ground from my complimentary seat in the Members' Stand was the great expanse of the famous Hill, a vision of massed thousands, battling in the heat of uproarious and accumulated unrefinement. On my side of the ground, to my right, was the Ladies' Enclosure, an enchanting brainwave on the part of the local cricket administrators, since it allowed the male spectator to feast his eyes on a cross-section of the most beautiful feminine race in the world without having to listen to their conversation. Even their frequent outbursts of falsetto excitement sounded a soothing note against the hullabaloo from the Hill opposite; while in the less turbulent moments, when it could make itself heard, a decorously modulated brass band played selections from *The Gondoliers*.

Among the Australians being tried out in these two matches in Sydney was a youth whose name was already on everybody's lips, the Bowral boy wonder, Don Bradman. He looked a timid boy wonder, his shoulders carried high in a shrinking consciousness of public expectancy. But he rose to the occasion and played an innings which won him a place in the first Test. During this innings of Bradman's one enthusiast sitting near me in the Members' Stand was so carried away by a particularly brilliant stroke that he jumped to his feet and shouted a word of horrifying blasphemy.

He cried—"Trumper."

There was a sudden, deadly, shocked hush. However radiant this new prodigy might be there were limits to decent and permissible adulation. The delinquent was pulled violently back into his seat and driven half-way under it, collapsing beneath the unvarnished comments and black frowns of his neighbours. Time marches on.

Brisbane in 1928 was still in a stage of development. Some of its streets with their wooden shack-like dwellings were very like the settings of a Western film. I have not searched Brisbane's records to discover whether a mounted posse of bushrangers was ever liable to blow into its township and shoot up the sheriff, but in those days it looked as if it still might. The wooden hotel veranda where we sat in the tropical evening, while George Geary, not without opposition, played or nearly played his ukulele was very different from the academic and decorous modernity of Adelaide, the dignified and determinate modernity of Melbourne, the resplendent and exhilarating modernity of Sydney. In places where its transformation had already begun Brisbane was as imposing as anywhere else, but this only emphasised the Wild West aspect of its more primitive past. On one side of our hotel was a wide and stately white public building with tame kangaroos leaping between the palm-trees in its spacious gardens. On the other side, a short distance away, was a conglomerate wood-and-brick quarter devoted to the good old-fashioned beer and brothel business.

The arrival of the mail from England was still quite an event and since it was due on the morning of November 30th when the first Test was to begin, I expected that Percy Chapman would receive a sheaf of letters in addition to the inevitable deluge of wishful cables. I suppose I had become accustomed to the extravagant practices of the theatre, for Chapman received no cables at all and only one letter. This was from the British Inland Revenue authorities and referred to a claim for Income Tax. A nice message of encouragement for England's captain to get from the home government on such an occasion. Even in those days their first consideration seemed to be that every man that day was expected to pay his duty.

The cricket ground then used for the Queensland Test was as different from the other States' Test grounds as Brisbane was from the other cities and in very much the same way. The visiting players' dressing-room was in a sort of cellar beneath the level of the ground itself. I was given a seat in a small stand at one end of the members' enclosure, together with other privileged spectators, and with me was the one other accepted associate and friend of the English side, Colin Maesmore Morris, who was my close and ideal companion during most of my visit—a gloriously plump and convivial character.

The Brisbane ground may have been inadequate in its

accommodation and appointment, but it fairly sizzled with that pent-up anticipation and suspense which are peculiar to the opening of a Test Match in Australia as in nowhere else in the world. The humid air seemed to quiver almost visibly with tension. Long before the game started Maesmore Morris and I sat driven to silence by nervousness, as we waited for the all-important toss to be won or lost. At length I said, "If Percy Chapman wins it and we bat I shall feel physically sick." He replied briefly, "I'm feeling sick now." And we lapsed into silence again.

Chapman won the toss. Hobbs took guard. Suddenly there was no sound. Not a newsboy, not a bottle-boy dared raise his voice to break the ominous hush. Being Australian, he probably couldn't have at that moment even if he'd wanted to. All I could hear was my own heart beating. Jack Gregory began his splendid giant-stride run. Before he had gone two paces a great roaring thunderclap of encouragement burst from the crowd. The ball sped well outside Jack Hobbs' off-stump and he watched it with an air of respectful contemplation. He was the coolest—perhaps the only cool—man on the whole ground.

It had started. A Test Match in Australia and I was there. I was eighteen again, reading *How We Recovered The Ashes*, by Mr. P. F. Warner. Dear, good old Mr. P. F. Warner. Oh, what is there in this world to compare with the ecstatic thrill of cricket?

Hobbs made 49 and was run out. I condoled with him and he said placidly, "It was my own fault; I knew I was late; I ought to have taken a taxi." But Hendren made 169 and England made 521. At the end of the second day Australia had lost four very cheap wickets in their first innings. The first batsman to go was Woodfull, who was out to the most amazing catch I have ever seen or ever will see. Larwood was operating at full speed and Woodfull snicked him many feet to the left of Percy Chapman in the gully. Chapman flew like a swallow, caught the ball in his left hand and was carried by his own impetus past the slips and wicket and half-way to the square-leg umpire, where he fell, still clinging to the ball. Hobbs said it was the finest catch he had ever known in all his experience; so I am not over-estimating this astonishing performance.

As that second day's play ended I turned to the typically attractive Australian girl sitting beside me. "Well, well," I said indulgently. "Cricket's a funny game, isn't it?" "To *you* it is," she tartly replied.

Bradman made 18 and one and was left out of the Australian side for the second Test Match at Sydney. I don't think it is generally realised by cricket historians that Bradman, having once played in a Test, was promptly dropped. It was a shocking lapse of judgment on the part of the Australian selectors, particularly as Sydney was then Bradman's home ground. He was readmitted to the side for the third Test at Melbourne and his scores in the last three Test Matches of this, his first season, were: 79 and 112: 40 and run out 58: 123 and not out 37. Warren Bardsley, who was one of the selectors, was combining this form of occupation with a more profitable one, being a slightly ostentatious salesman of Yeast-Vite. I can only assume that after the first Test he took Don Bradman home with him and stuffed him with Yeast-Vite until he was ready for Melbourne. If so, this may have been of great benefit both to Bradman and Yeast-Vite; but it was of still greater benefit to the Englishmen at Sydney.

But Bradman was only one of the two names that were always being dinned into our ears, and the two names were not Bradman and Jackson, but Jackson and Bradman, in that order. Even so, Jackson did not play for Australia until after I had left for home, in the fourth Test at Adelaide, when he made 164. English crowds only had a brief glimpse of him

in 1930 and by then he was already a semi-invalid. If he had
been granted health and strength he would have been one of
the greatest batsmen Australia ever turned out.

It was on the first morning of the second Test at Sydney
that I witnessed the celebrated "Kippax incident". Kippax
was bowled by Geary but he thought the ball had missed his
wicket and had rebounded off George Duckworth's pads. So
he stayed where he was. The English eleven waited in
patient surprise for him to retire and Pat Hendren took
advantage of the unexpected lull to sit down on the grass. At
length it was decided that Kippax had been bowled and then
out he promptly went; but he didn't think he was out, so he
could not be blamed for anything he did, except perhaps for
getting bowled. The Australian public naturally shared
Kippax's illusion. Their only trouble was that they had
nobody to argue with or to bet with about it, since everybody
except the English visitors and, presumably, a pair of hesitant
umpires, knew for a certainty that the ball had hit the wicket
off Duckworth's pads. Indignant clubmen gave heated
demonstrations of how it happened and unexpectedly recalled
some erudite scientific formula to prove, by the position and
angle of the bail, as it lay on the ground in the press photo-
graphs, that it must have been knocked off from behind.
The Hill more philosophically contented itself with violently
barracking Duckworth. Not only for the rest of this match
but throughout the whole of the third Test at Melbourne
Duckworth never handled the ball on one single occasion
without being subjected to ironical cheers and shouts of "Why
don't you kick the wicket down?" George Duckworth
thrived on this. In England's first innings at Sydney he stayed
in for about a couple of hours and made 39 not out. "Aye,"
he said to me afterwards with a beam of contentment, "it's
very satisfactory when they have to coom to you on their
hands and knees."

This was Walter Hammond's great tour. In this Sydney match he was only called upon to bat once and made 251. His subsequent Test scores were: 200 and run out 32: not out 119 and 177: 38 and 16. After his Sydney innings of 251 he showed me his bat. It was unmarked, except that plumb in the middle of the sweet of the blade there was a small, perfectly circular indentation. It was an exhibit of unerring, almost mechanical accuracy. Of all the batsmen who favoured attacking methods Hammond, when he got going, must have been about the most heart-breaking man to bowl to in the history of the game. On this tour, innings after innings, he stood there and simply smashed the bowling with straight searing blows. All the bowlers could do to him was to make a neat little concavity in the middle of his white and crashing bat.

No doubt many striking changes have taken place in Sydney since I was there nearly thirty years ago, before even our bridge was anything like completed. And I dare say that, not only in Sydney but in the whole of Australia, there has, since those days, been a gradual easement of the somewhat challenging attitude towards the English visitor. This took the form of combining intense hospitality with an assiduous anxiety that the merits of Australia should be appreciated and admitted. The visitor was not required or expected to volunteer admiration, even if he were ever given the chance to. He had to undergo a preliminary course of instruction in his assessment of the Commonwealth, its scenery, its patriotism, its scoreboards, its harbour, its climate, Jackson and Bradman, the way its people sing, the way its people bet, its cattle stations and sheep stations, its landscapes, its seascapes, its seating accommodation at cricket grounds and race-meetings, the athleticism and physique of its young men, the unchallengeable beauty of its young women and anything else that happened to crop up.

CHAPMAN'S CATCH AT BRISBANE, 1928

NEW SOUTH WALES *v.* M.C.C., SYDNEY, 1928
Hendren, Hammond and "the Hill"

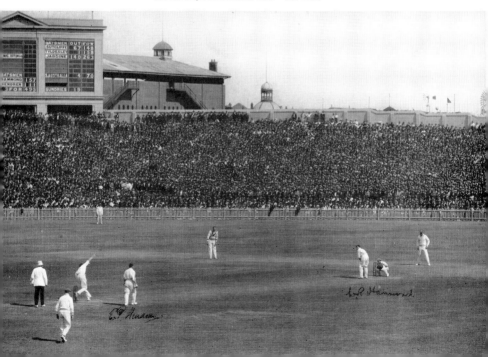

All these assets I most sincerely and enthusiastically came to admire (especially the scoreboards and the young women) when compared with our home products; but I got a little impatient sometimes at having my admiration so persistently prompted. On a particularly brilliant Sunday morning at Sydney one of my generous but over-impressive hosts motored me to a point of vantage from which I could view the whole stretch of Bondi beach in all its glory. Nowhere in the world had I ever seen a lovelier setting for the recreation-ground of thousands of magnificently proportioned young males with bronzed torsos, escorting an equal number of young females, who revealed, so far as the regulations allowed, that their forms were as attractive as their faces. Apart perhaps from the regulations the whole experience was Paradisiac.

But any attempt on my part to say so was cut short and rather damped by my host. He rallied me with an air of enthusiastic challenge.

"There. You haven't got anything like that in England."

"Nothing. I admit it. There can be few things like it anywhere."

"Your sky isn't as clear as this in England."

"Well—not very often, I suppose."

"The water isn't as blue in England."

"No, that's true."

"This whole beach—and it's only one of our beaches, mind you—this whole wonderful panorama—you've nothing like it."

"Nothing. I've said so. It's beyond anything."

"Look at those boys and girls—all that crowd o them. All their splendid, healthy bodies. Look at them."

"I'm looking. At some of them, anyhow."

I was finding this increasingly irksome. But he couldn't resist a crowning vainglorious claim.

"And healthy not only in their bodies. They only come here for hygiene and relaxation. There isn't a man or a girl on this beach with a thought of sex in their head."

"You can't say that now," I replied. "I'm here for one."

English people always accounted for this zealous trait by saying (but not to their faces) that Australians had an inferiority complex. Personally I think the whole explanation was far simpler than anything to do with complexes and far more appealing. Every one of us has known that stage of childhood which loves to have its achievements noticed and given full credit. It is the stage of "look, no hands", on our first bicycle. We can all remember the flush of pride we felt at having our skill admired, the difficulty of suppressing the smile of triumph and of assuming a grown-up, natural manner in accepting tribute. But the feat had to be performed and self-proclaimed; it could never be taken for granted. If some stupid aunt or somebody started to say how clever you were before you had shown how clever you were, it spoiled the whole effect. This, in 1928, was the attitude of the average male Australian towards the visiting representative of the mother-country. He had reached the proud, adolescent, clamorous stage of "look, no hands".

And just as a child is never so sharply hurt by any form of rebuke as by the first hint of ridicule, my Australian friends were keenly sensitive to any suggestion that they were being treated with levity. I suppose four years association with Ralph Lynn had accustomed my mind to search instinctively for the light side of things; but I'm afraid that at first I gave a good deal of offence in some of my well-intentioned and perhaps feeble attempts to be jocular. On the night I arrived in Sydney I was invited to broadcast my impressions. I was misguided enough to try to season my laudations with a slightly flippant reference to the city's proverbial glory. I said something about my never having realised how greatly my opinion was esteemed until, within half an hour of my arrival, I was asked by about two hundred people what I thought of their harbour. This was received very seriously, coldly, and in some cases with open resentment. I plunged even more deeply into trouble with a lady who proved herself to be my distant cousin. She asked me to inscribe a copy of one of my novels, and I obliged, in a moment of reprobate gaiety, by writing on the half-title page "To the convict branch of the family". There was the devil to pay.

Again, I played in a charity cricket match on some club ground at Sydney, and had the memorable experience of fielding while Clem Hill and M. A. Noble batted in partnership. But I was suspected from the first of an intention to clown. When I went in to bat I was greeted with derisive cries of "Rookery Nook" from the crowd. Clem Hill, who was bowling at the time, made things more difficult for me by tossing his first ball high into the air, and if only my partner had been more alert I might have turned the tables on Hill by snatching a quick run while the ball was still in flight. As it was, I was caught in two minds, and although the ball missed my stumps and I survived to make one not out, my quite serious efforts were regarded as a reprehensible attempt to be funny. Next morning one of the Sydney papers published a scathing reprimand of Clem Hill and myself for introducing an element of tomfoolery in the cricket field.

Clem Hill, like Hugh Trumble, had been a member of the Australian side which I had seen in my first Test Match, at the Oval in 1896. In a series of Tests in Australia in 1902 he made 99, 98 and 97 in three successive innings. Six more runs in all and he would have made seven centuries against England instead of four. He was one of the most cheerful Australian men I met in the whole of my visit, and he had a daughter who inherited his charm. So many of those

Australian girls must, it seemed, have taken mainly after their mothers.

I cannot help emphasising the contrast between the average feminine Australian and the average male, because, in her general outlook, in her natural eagerness to keep pace with the latest trends in the arts and fashions, in the thought she gave to her outward appearance and in her liveliness of spirit, the average Australian girl was well ahead of her opposite number in Great Britain; whereas in these respects the average Australian man was some way behind his. But this does not mean that the men who gave me such a welcome and showed me such hospitality were not individually very excellent company. From the first moment of my introduction by Charley Macartney to the kind, considerate old Hugh Trumble, I found the same friendship everywhere in the Australian cricketing community. And in one particular case this friendship was to become one of those especial, short-list friendships of my lifetime. A man who views the world at large, and cricket along with it, with a complete sense of proportion and a predominant sense of humour. Arthur Mailey.

Arthur Mailey has a unique place, not higher than some others but different to all others, in my affections and, I think, in many other people's. I still meet him on his occasional but regular visits to England and renew the immediate joy of being with him again. But his personality and indeed his influence are never far away from my thoughts or away for long. I don't think we have ever written to each other. He is perhaps not so much a friend as a sort of familiar spirit, no less genuine and permanent for being only sometimes visible.

Mailey is a pure and complete philosopher. None of my acquaintance sets my quick, mettlesome, falsely conscientious temperament a more valuable example. The exigencies of unnecessary speed and the frantic dictatorship of time-tables sap my energies and nervous system in the turmoil of a modern society whose motto is "Hurry-along-there-please". Mailey treats the rush of life with a quiet, impracticable practicability. Whenever it is necessary for him to go anywhere by train he waits until it is convenient for him to leave wherever he happens to be and then goes to the appropriate railway station. After all, that's where the trains are supposed to go from. And he seldom has to wait long. Waste time? He doesn't waste half as much time as I do. I get to a station long before the train is due to take me to a place that I don't really need to get to nearly so early. Or I hurry to catch a train which I hadn't noticed was marked "Saturdays only".

I mention Arthur Mailey's methods in dealing with his transport only as an example of his imperturbable way of dealing with life in general. Often, in a moment of anxiety over some quite trivial task or objective, I try to take myself in hand. After all, what am I really getting in such a state about? What is really at stake? "Mailey yourself," I say. "Mailey yourself."

There was some rule in force in Australia which debarred Mailey from playing in this series of Tests owing to his professional job as a journalist or something. But he had already done enough for glory as an Australian slow bowler. Here, too, his great technical skill was tremendously enhanced by his philosophy. He would work away, trying to get a batsman to make a particular faulty stroke which might result in a catch, and if he succeeded but the catch was dropped Mailey was quite satisfied—he'd succeeded. He didn't enjoy bowling to easy victims; he liked to match his wits against those of the really great, and he once bowled Jack Hobbs with a slow full-toss.

Never have I met a more natural and less offensive debunker. Soon after he emerged from a somewhat humble job in urban industrial life to bowl against England, the Australian eleven were being entertained at a reception held in their honour at a State Government House. Unintentionally, no doubt, the wife of His Excellency displayed a somewhat patronising manner. "I suppose, Mr. Mailey," she said, "that you've never set foot in Government House before?"

"Oh, yes, I have," said Mailey, in his slow, quiet voice.

"Indeed? And when was that?"

"A year or two ago," said Mailey. "I came to fix the gas."

When my mind tries to make a geographical survey of my three months in Australia all those years ago, Sydney stands out, resplendent still, from a background dim in the shadows of faded memory. But the reason for my visit was cricket, and so far as actual cricket was concerned Melbourne is the ground I remember best, because there, on the 29th December, 1928, began the greatest Test Match I have ever seen or hope to see.

England had followed up the overwhelming victory at Brisbane with a win by eight wickets at Sydney; so Australia had to win this match to keep the rubber alive. As at Sydney, Chapman lost the toss and Australia went in and lost three cheap wickets. I had never seen so many people on a ground because nobody had; the crowd beat all previous records for a cricket match anywhere in the world. Rather than stay away mothers, in scores, brought their babies. Several parked them over the pickets on the actual field of play; and at the opening the game was held up more than once while an umpire proceeded to the boundary, picked up a baby and firmly restored it to its owner. Australia's bad start depressed the crowd, which, like some gigantic animal, seemed all the more morose because of its vast size. But this applied equally to its reactive enthusiasm. Larwood had done most of the damage and Kippax went for Larwood and fairly collared him. A roar of encouragement followed every scoring stroke he made and when Kippax pulled Larwood for three fours off successive balls I have never heard such uproar. The men shouted, the women screamed and the babies yelled. Australians love to succeed in all games, particularly cricket. And why not? Some captious Britishers are fond of stating this as though it were to Australia's discredit, which always seems to me to be a very grudging and stupid attitude. I shall never forget the exhilaration of that moment when the record crowd gave abandoned and triumphant expression of its delight.

Well, Kippax made a century; so did Ryder the Australian captain and Bradman made 79 and the total was 397. England made 417, but considering that Hammond made two hundred of this number, Jardine 62 and Sutcliffe 58, the innings was a patchy affair and it was thought that a lead of twenty runs was little compensation for having to take the fourth turn at the wicket. It was thought so even more strongly at the end of the next day's play; for Woodfull and Bradman made centuries and Australia piled up a big lead in an atmosphere of steaming humidity and under skies which threatened to burst asunder in a violent thunderstorm. Burst they did. During the night the rain hammered down. But next morning the sun was blazing as strongly as ever, greedily burning up the sodden wicket; for this was in the days before they had taken to covering pitches. On a beach of sawdust Jack White polished off the Australian tail-enders almost mechanically. Play had started late, owing to the conditions, and Hobbs and Sutcliffe had only a few minutes to struggle through before the luncheon interval.

Hobbs himself said he was afraid it would be all over by tea-time. I was invited to lunch with the President of the Victorian Cricket Association. All the cricket nabobs were there—the Trumbles and Nobles and Hills—and they received me with a genial blend of undisguised elation and jocular sympathy. I was with the Assistant Secretary of the Association when the officer in charge of the police arrangements came to consult him about how many of his men would be wanted at the ground next day. Next day? The Assistant Secretary laughed him to scorn. As if the match would still be alive next day. The police officer couldn't know much about cricket. I don't think the police officer did know very much; but this was an Australian insult and called for an Australian measure of retaliation. I myself witnessed the bet.

At the close of play that evening Douglas Jardine took me out on to the field to have a look at what Hobbs, Sutcliffe and Jardine himself had been batting on. The wicket had been pitted and furrowed into horrid corrugated patches which the sun had by this time baked as hard as concrete. Throughout this baking process, all the afternoon, Hobbs and Sutcliffe had been giving an extraordinary show of skill and concentration. Every ball, of whatever pace or length, was a fresh unpredictable menace—neither batsman nor bowler could foretell what last split-second antic it might perform. As in his other partnership with Sutcliffe, at the Oval in 1926, also on a ruined wicket, though not nearly so vindictive in its ruin as this one, Hobbs took charge at what appeared to be the worst end; but perhaps it was Sutcliffe's dexterity and unruffled temperament which made the other end seem less vicious. Hobbs was eventually out for 49 again; but Sutcliffe was still there with Jardine when play ended and he went on next day to make 135. Perhaps the best proof of what the batsmen had to contend with was that there were 29 extras in the innings, nearly all of them byes; and this with Oldfield keeping wicket. The slow bowlers made the mistake of pitching the ball short of a length and it was apt to leap up almost vertically and to go clean over Oldfield's head and out of his reach to the boundary.

There was some fresh moisture in the turf next morning; the spite was rolled out of the wicket and after a hectic anticlimatic last half-hour England won by three wickets. This was the last match I was to see in Australia but what more could I want? It had everything.

I got more enjoyment from watching Alan Kippax than from watching other contemporary Australians who batted twice as long and made double as many runs. He had a neat, almost prim and perfectly finished style. In this match he was at his best.

In this match Hammond played an innings of 200. In this match Bradman made his first Test century. In this match J. C. White bowled fifty maidens out of eighty-five eight-ball overs. In this match, above all, occurred the Hobbs-Sutcliffe miracle.

Above all? Well, there was one other episode, or short sequence of episodes, which contributed no little to England's success. Maesmore Morris and I were sitting with the twelfth man, Maurice Leyland, in the dressing-room on that gloomy evening half-way through Australia's second innings. For hours the atmosphere had been less like that of Melbourne than that of a Malayan jungle, a steam oven or Washington, D.C. in July; and now the thunderclouds were gathering, heavy with foreboding. The England eleven trooped in and sank down, utterly exhausted, dripping with sweat and, for once, dispirited and inclined to be acrimonious. Somebody had to restore things to their normal state. There was only one man there who could. And he did.

In the course of the stripping and cooling-off stage Pat Hendren began to imitate a monkey searching the more promising portions of its anatomy for fleas. Within a couple of minutes he had everybody in the room roaring with laughter. Half an hour later he somehow discovered and secured for hire a large and antiquated horse-drawn van, which had, no doubt, just finished unloading an immense cargo of beer. Into this van Pat Hendren ushered most of the England side and himself gave an imitation of a bus-conductor which was almost as meritorious as his monkey. It must have startled and perhaps shocked the Melbourne public to witness the English team returning to their hotel in this outrageous vehicle and singing as they went; with the odds now at something like ten to one against them and with the rain already beginning to descend in great preliminary individual drops of doom.

Of the English cricketers on that tour there were two whom the Australian crowds seemed to single out for particular approval—Jack White and Hendren. Their partiality for White was a sign of respect; for Hendren of affection. So the Australian barrackers were not bad judges after all.

The Australians toured England in 1930, when Bradman, now in top gear and full of confidence, established himself as the greatest fair-weather run-getter in history; though on all types of wicket neither he nor anyone else ever rivalled Jack Hobbs. At Trent Bridge I first struck up a friendship with Tom Webster. We watched all this series of Test Matches together and, as a result, he formed the pleasant habit of taking me along with him to football cup-ties and prize-fights. But of all the sporting events I enjoyed in his company the occasion I remember best was at a country-house party on the Sunday afternoon of the Manchester Test when Tom Webster and I, in shirtsleeves and socks, defeated Mailey and Grimmett 6–0 in a set of lawn tennis, to the quite serious dismay of the Australian team.

Tom Webster has always had a special gift of being able not only to detect the funny features of the immensely serious business of sport, but also to express the joke in a way which the public can seize upon and appreciate. I found him utterly self-reliant. He was continuously being pestered by chuckling contributors of "good ideas" for his cartoons and suffered them gladly; but even I, after sitting with him all through a day's cricket, never knew in the least what to expect to see in the *Daily Mail* next morning. Only once or twice did it turn out to be the result of our conversations. One of these exceptions was when he depicted Duleepsinhji going in to play his great innings of 173 in the second Test at Lord's seated on an Indian elephant, with Uncle Ranji leading the elephant and using its trunk as a speaking-tube in order to issue his instructions.

That 1930 tour served as a sort of sequel to my Australian jaunt, and during the next few years my English and Australian cricket associates began to drop, one by one, out of the game. But I still see some of them, middle-aged now and in some cases surprisingly corpulent, in occasional encounters of reminiscent reunion at Lord's or the Oval. Whenever I meet Jack Hobbs now we recall the evening in March, 1932, when he and his wife came to the first night of a new Aldwych farce. First-night audiences were inured to the often somewhat spectacular appearances of social and theatrical and screen celebrities in their midst, but the attendance of Hobbs appealed to this audience as a novelty and to the press as news. He was almost mobbed in the vestibule and headlined and reported by many of the morning papers, as being the chief attraction of the occasion; and although I have always accused him of having come and stolen my show, it was by no means the most successful of the Aldwych farces, and I dare say he did me a very good turn. Six years later, when Bradman was Australia's touring captain and still rampaging to the tune of an average of 108 in Test Matches, he and Stanley McCabe came along one night to see my farce, *Banana Ridge*, at the Strand. Bradman by then had become, thanks to his own most admirable strength of purpose, a strikingly exalted and colourful individual compared with that abashed boy from Bowral in 1928. This time the audience restrained itself from demonstration, but Bradman received what must have been, even to him, an original specimen of compliment after the show. I took the two of them to meet the performers back-stage, and here we were greeted by the management's representative, a remarkable character named Wallett Waller but universally addressed as Wally. Wally, beneath the veneer of the time-honoured professional, evening-dressed and carnation-buttonholed, courteous "front-of-the-house" man, was a convivial and singularly outspoken old spark. I duly presented Bradman.

"Ho-ho!" Wally said. He stepped forward with an air of great affability and lightly flicked Bradman's lapel with the backs of his fingers. "So *you're* he? Public enemy number bloody one."

Bradman managed to retain his smile but slightly recoiled. He looked puzzled. A rare sight.

It was during this same tour that Arthur Mailey managed to take a week-end off and came to spend it with us at Burnham. I invited him to play for the local side in a Saturday afternoon village match. He was only too pleased to play but said he wanted to remain incognito, so I impressed this special request on our home side. The result was that, when Burnham, having won the toss went in to bat, the visitors eyed each batsman in turn suspiciously, informed by rumour that one of them would prove to be a celebrated Australian player, though as yet they had no idea which one.

The game had been in progress some five or ten minutes and Burnham had therefore only lost two wickets when Arthur joined me at the crease. He, for one, aroused little suspicion. He looked rather more like one of the typical resident yokels than they did themselves, especially when he was clean out l.b.w. second ball. The bowler turned to our home umpire with a self-satisfied grin. His "'Ow's-aart" was almost casual in its assurance. Fortunately, the home umpire was none other than that splendid postman, well qualified by long experience to deal with this sort of situation. He looked the bowler up and down with a challenging contempt. "'Ow's thaat?" he repeated scornfully. "Why, you darned fool, this is *him*."

Charterhouse, after my time, continued to produce good cricketers and even better golfers. Among the former was R. C. Robertson-Glasgow, who, like myself, has always loved cricket almost fanatically but has loved laughter even more. He has an individual sense of humour which finds expression in sometimes almost Chestertonian samples of imagery and instance, which, as they occur, he pauses to reward with a moment of thigh-slapping glee. I have always cherished his company since that luncheon interval early in his cricketing career when he had spent an exhausting and unprofitable morning (good bowler as he was) against Hobbs and Sandham at the Oval. On the way up the pavilion steps he lingered a moment to issue a brief confidential report. He said, "It's like bowling to God on concrete."

The golfers, too, among my Old Carthusian friends, subscribe readily to the theory that fun is an important asset to success. One of these most notable subscribers is John S. F. Morrison, whom I first knew when we were both training at Hendon Air Station in 1914. We put him up when he came to compete in the English Amateur Championship on the Burnham-and-Berrow links in 1927. He brought his half-brother, Dale Bourne, along with him. Bourne was a brilliant golfer but his zest for enjoyment was above the average, even in an Old Carthusian, and was sometimes criticised by elderly dignitaries who frowned upon any association between golf and gaiety. The mixture worked well enough in this case and Dale Bourne won the championship. I look back on him with great affection. He was the perfect model for what Tom Walls must have meant when he wanted to play the part of a young man about town.

As the result of that championship I was enlisted as trainer (a somewhat loose term in more senses than one, I fear) to the Old Carthusian side which competed annually at Deal for the Halford Hewitt Cup. Halford Hewitt, himself an Old Carthusian, used to preside over the meeting in general and our team in particular with indulgent benevolence. But he was elderly and rotund and assertive and deaf (though nobody could ever be certain what he heard and what he didn't) and rigorous in his strictures concerning the limits of indecorum. Nature had devised in him an ideal butt for affectionate badinage, though his indignant reaction was as often as not assumed. But the whole spirit of rejuvenated, tom-boy jocularity of those Old Carthusian parties often, I think, sadly puzzled the representatives of other schools, particularly since Charterhouse enjoyed such a long run of success in the tournament itself. The annals of the meeting have been admirably chronicled by Henry Longhurst, who was soon a playing member of the Old Carthusian side. Among our players when I first joined them were such people as C. V. L. Hooman, J. B. Beck, Dale Bourne, Victor Longstaffe and John Morrison. So the trainer's duties were never very arduous except when the day's play was over. And, in some cases, before it began. I remember having to serve one illustrious golfer with his breakfast on the first fairway.

But apart from my unceasing attachment to the O.C. Golfing Society (they have made me President of it now) golf is to me a very secondary form of sport in a world which contains cricket. Since Mackenzie endowed me with a handicap of four at Malacca my abilities have steadily declined and since the last war I have given the accursed game up altogether.

I don't even want to watch golf—I was never much good at this either. The Halford Hewitt meeting always produces some exciting finishes and possesses, in any case, delights and memories of its own. But on any other occasion I have not the smallest incentive to plod around in a flock of big-match golf-watchers. They proceed self-consciously, so desperately intent on doing the right thing that they only communicate with each other in surreptitious gesticulations. Any one of them who dared to laugh would be shrivelled back into silence by the glare of a ferret-faced committee-man with a flag: a smile is suspect. They have come to pay earnest tribute to the awful seriousness of sport.

And apart from that, some characteristic lack of ability to do most things as well as anybody else has resulted in my never having been able, by any chance, to see where anybody hits his ball to. Above all, to set out and watch a round of golf means going for a long walk. You can have it.

But I would rather watch golfers than race-horses. Since that commissioned visit to Flemington I have seldom attended a meeting. I can never see which horses are which and I hate all that hanging-about business between the races. I didn't even see April the Fifth win the Derby. I had ten pounds each way on the horse and saw the result on the tape in a London club. Apart from cricket I am not a happy watcher of any sport. When I watch cricket I have a sense of tranquillity which brings me delight in anticipating excitement. When I watch rugger or soccer I am infected by a sense of impatience which brings me irritation tending to dwarf excitement. I don't think I can adapt my powers of pleasurable endurance to the appreciation of games with whistles in them.

Indeed if I take stock of my sporting interests and activities with candour I cut a poor figure. I cannot skate or ski and would hate to try to; for one thing I detest ice and snow. I have always been terrified of guns. If I tried to shoot it wouldn't do any good because I would instinctively shut both eyes in fearful avoidance of the bang. Even if anyone threatens to loose off a firearm in a play or film I squirm in my seat and screw my face into a petrified grimace. A dear old

Burnham preparatory schoolmaster once infected me with some preparatory enthusiasm for fly-fishing and I invested in a very extensive and expensive angler's trousseau. But I always caught my line in the branches of a tree or hooked myself in the seat of my trousers, and much as I enjoy eating fish I would have felt a compassionate remorse if I'd ever caught one.

I simply cannot understand how, in my younger days, I became such a competent and reliable pilot of aeroplanes; because I was always an indifferent and nervous car-driver; and once when I tried to ride a motor-cycle I left it in the road and sailed clean through a hedge into a ploughed field.

My wife and daughter used to do a good deal of horse-riding at Burnham and, anxious to join in the fun, I was measured for a becoming pair of breeches and bought an expensive steed which I named Pompey and started hacking for a season every afternoon. But I was always secretly terrified of Pompey, who was no doubt quick to sense this. After lulling me into a half-incredulous feeling of confidence he suddenly bolted with me on the sands and shot me off on to my becoming breeches, which, however, continued to look very decent on the old gardener's assistant.

But I have always loved watching cricket.

BANANA RIDGE

Alfred Drayton, Robertson Hare, Constance Lorne, Ben Travers, Kathleen O'Regan and Carla Lehmann

THE AUSTRALIAN CRICKET TEAM AT BURNHAM AND BERROW GOLF CLUB, 1930

Author sitting in the middle, Mailey sitting on right and Bradman standing left

CHAPTER IX

The Goldfish

By the time Aldwych farce had run its course nearly all the old actor-managers had taken their final curtain call. The control of theatres and production of plays had passed into the hands of syndicates large or small. Golding Bright, astute and imperturbable as ever, if at times a trifle sardonic, accepted and catered for changed conditions. The little office above the Leicester Galleries became a sort of matrimonial agency for managers who could not act and actors who could not manage.

There were still a few survivors of the old régime. Seymour Hicks, for instance, would occasionally dash into the West End with some creation of self-devised and self-governed effervescence. Gerald du Maurier was still going strong at Wyndham's. The all-star cast of the *Grand Giggle* play which he asked me to write for one of the Theatrical Garden Parties of this period contained the names of several of the new generation of London's leading actors. Du Maurier himself played the hero, a promising prize-fighter; Noel Coward was his fiancée. The hero's mother, Edmund Gwenn, was, it is true, a distinguished old-timer, but two more recent and high-ranking stage celebrities also participated—Cedric Hardwicke, as the Chinese villain, and Charles Laughton, as his Chinese mistress. Several others at or near the top of the profession were in the party, but du Maurier was the only one of them who had ever been an actor-manager. It meant that if I wrote any more plays Golding Bright would have to find me not an actor with a backer but a management with an actor.

I went to one or two rehearsals of this *Grand Giggle* play and watched these worthies in their mood of willing but artificial playfulness; but when the day came for the actual performance, never having been to a Theatrical Garden Party before or since, and being alone in London at the time, I was overcome by one of those peculiar fits of shyness which I have always suffered from since my schooldays and I couldn't bring myself to go. I wanted to be there but I couldn't take the plunge of going there. For one thing I wasn't certain what to wear.

Although my memories of that concentrated chunk of my lifetime, the Aldwych period, seem to belong mainly to the Aldwych itself—so far as any work was concerned—the Bodley Head and its founder still claim a portion. At last John Lane really did give up; but his successors published a volume of short stories and sketches I had written from time to time. These included two series which had been rather well received when they appeared in *The Passing Show*: some modern versions of old familiar fairy-tales re-told for the benefit of up-to-date children ("There was once a certain king. He died. That'll teach him to be so dashed certain"—that sort of thing) and *Misguided Lives*, being some studies of eminent mugs, such as Antonio, the Merchant of Venice, the Excelsior Hero and others. I also edited a Stephen Leacock anthology, a delightful job. I included some of my favourite bits and pieces which seemed to have been overlooked; such as his gem of an Ibsen play *The Sub-Contractor*. Here is the song which bursts from the lips of the heroine "in a moment of peculiar access of gaiety":

> "Was ik en Bütterflog
> Flog ik dein Broost enswog,
> Adjo, mein Hertzenhog,
> Adjë, Adjö."

I also recalled this neglected gem of Scandinavian lampoonery:

THE FRAM. August 20th 1896
(Fridtjof Nansen's ship, *The Fram*, returns safely to Skejervoe.)

What a glorious day
For old Norway,
When *The Fram* came sailing into the Bay
To the dear old fjord,
With its crew on bjord
All safely restjord
By the hand of the Ljord;
And they shouted "Whoe
Is this Skejervoe?"
And they rent the ajer with a loud Hulljoe;
While the crowd on skiis
As thick as biis
Slid down to the town on their hands and kniis.
And oh, what cries
When they recognise
A man with a pair of sealskin pants on
And thjere, I decljare, is Fridtjof Nansen.

I had an appreciative and grateful letter from Leacock but, although I had taken care to quote several of his most popular articles in full, *The Leacock Book* had little success even at that time. The present-day public is missing a great treat if I am right in thinking that now Leacock is seldom read or quoted except by his few old devotees surviving from the grandfather generation. But in his own day I was glad to have been given the chance to pay him a personal tribute; and, whether other people liked it or not, I liked it. And so did he.

John Lane lived for only a few years after the giving up. He and his old American wife used occasionally to come and spend a few days pottering about in a fumigated hotel at some West-country spa, and we would go and pay them an afternoon visit. He would sit and smile at me, with eyes grown very watery now; pleased that I, his pupil, had won my way to success. "A near man", H. B. Irving once designated John Lane to me in conversation some years before this; and by now I had been given ample cause to agree. But as Leacock said of O. Henry, "I don't care." If I remember his weaknesses it is to laugh at them—a true sign of affection. But memory of him finds far more genuine pleasure in the mild sunshine of his gentle smile.

Before he retired the old man had brought his nephew, Allen Lane, to London and had installed him as one of his successors at the Bodley Head. He specially requested me to make friends with Allen, which was as easy a job as I've ever been asked to do. I have always been glad to have been a rather mature friend of his youth, particularly on one memorable occasion a few years later. He had conceived an original, enterprising and hazardous project. He came to ask me what I thought of it. He showed me a list of ten well-known novels. We discussed them and their chances of successfully launching this huge, hypothetical scheme. They were the first Penguin Books.[1]

[1] The first ten Penguin Books, published on Friday, July 30th, 1935, at sixpence each, were as follows:

Andre Maurois: *Ariel*
Ernest Hemingway: *A Farewell to Arms*
Eric Linklater: *Poet's Pub*
Susan Ertz: *Madame Claire*
Dorothy L. Sayers: *The Unpleasantness at the Bellona Club*
Agatha Christie: *The Murder on the Links*
Beverley Nichols: *Twenty Five*
E. H. Young: *William*
Mary Webb: *Gone to Earth*
Compton Mackenzie: *Carnival.*

He had made a judicious selection, beyond any criticism I could make. And as for the project in general, nobody could have been less qualified than I to advise on any business proposition. But perhaps I, beyond almost anybody else, was entitled to encourage. For in whatever guise it appeared I knew the Lane flair when I saw it. And here it was.

Golding Bright philosophically concealed his disgust at the rapidly degenerating trend of popular taste in entertainment and read me—with that half of his mouth unoccupied by his cigarette—the terms of the voluminous three-party film contract to which he had agreed on my behalf. For Tom Walls, after making the film versions of three of the Aldwych farces at Elstree, had decided to part with Herbert Wilcox or perhaps Herbert Wilcox had decided to part with Tom Walls —I don't know the circumstances. I was sorry to leave Elstree, where I had the greatest fun making, in all, four Ralph Lynn and Winifred Shotter pictures, under the auspices of Wilcox himself and the direction of a real kindred spirit, a shrewd poker-faced humorist named Jack Raymond. And although I was always very well and generously treated by Michael Balcon, who was boss at the studios to which we now moved, there was precious little fun in the atmosphere in which I spent my next few working years, the most lucrative and least enjoyable years I ever knew as an author.

I suppose Tom Walls thought he could introduce his autocratic, overriding, "I'll-do-what-I-damn-well-choose" methods into a Film Industry which already seemed to have become controlled by a conglomeration of intricate and cosmopolitan Corporations, sub-Corporations, Distributors, Exhibitors and the rest of it—and get away with it? I suppose that's what he thought he could do, because that is precisely what he did.

I suppose, moreover, that Mr. Walls thought he could turn

up at the studios to direct a day's shooting (for which his fellow artists and the extras had been summoned to be ready made-up on the set at eight or nine a.m.) only just in time to proceed to his dressing-room and have a bracer, walk on to the floor and survey the general arrangements, return to his dressing-room to be made up, learn his lines and be prepared to have a preliminary run through a scene, before it was time for lunch and to go and see yesterday's rushes—and get away with that too? Yes, because he did. And suppose that he could cast a young lady whose ability he believed in, but in which the whole corporate production unit and the over-corporate assistant producer and others did *not* believe, for a leading part in a film; and when they threatened to go to law about it, tell them where they could go when they'd finished going to law?

The fact is that Tom Walls stalked into the film business, conscious of his own lack of technical knowledge and experience but armed with complete self-assurance; expecting opposition from the start, scenting it behind every bush; and spoiling for a fight in anticipation. Nobody hated him or regarded him as an enemy; the film trade appreciated his ability and strength of personality; and its members were quite ready to massage the palms of their hands at him, especially now that he had won the Derby. But he was so keenly on the alert to challenge opposition that if no opposition existed he had to create some himself so as to have some to challenge. He was soon causing the hosts of Midian to prowl and prowl around Wardour Street in gesticulating huddles of dismay at his independence, his methods, his delays, his dropsical time-schedule—time is money. But what could you do, when each film as it came along made an even bigger hit than the last and from all over the country came evidence of the great and growing popularity of Tom Walls himself?

So when five more of my Aldwych farces had been filmed I

202

had to devise scripts from original stories of my own for yet another five Walls and Lynn films, a Walls and Yvonne Arnaud film and three Walls and nobody-much-else films. No other authors participated; in each case I wrote the whole picture, down to the last word in the shooting-script. But my functions didn't finish there. I was at the studio all the time while each picture was being made. When in due course Tom arrived of a morning I was there to meet him and give him a résumé of the scenes scheduled for the day's shooting, telling him what they were about and their significance in relation to the rest of the film. I would re-read him the dialogue and teach him his lines. So when he proceeded to take charge on the floor he was always well briefed in what he had to direct and act and could be trusted to make the most of it. It was an anomalous sort of position but it ensured my getting the picture made more or less as I had intended; and I was always paid a good fee for my attendance in the studio in addition to my author's fees. These were extravagant. Golding Bright saw to it that if they were going to take his playwrights and use them for hack film-writers they must pay a becoming indemnity. He would hand me a new agreement for my signature with some serene pleasantry about the misguided course of my career. Then, when this demoralising document had been signed and witnessed, Golding, with both eyes behind his glasses screwed up in order to avoid the smoke from the everlasting cigarette between his lips, would turn to studying the things that really mattered—the promising script of a new real-stage play; or that morning's list of probable runners.

Yes, they were remunerative years. But fun? I can't recall a single day of them that brought me any special amusement or enjoyment. My recollections of them are concerned chiefly with hanging about for long, physically fatiguing, unspeakably boring intervals, during which the art-director and the camera-man and the sound-man and the men who had to stick up or tear down great wads of set and the men who fixed the lights and the effects-man and the prop-man and the make-up and hair-do experts and the continuity girl performed their various maddening duties; while an occasional group of privileged visitors, shepherded by some minor studio executive, stood discreetly in the background and garped at the wonders of film-land.

And Hollywood? Any offers? One heard perpetually at that time of British playwrights making highly-paid excursions to Hollywood. What about me?

Mr. Samuel Goldwyn came to London and stayed at the Ritz Hotel. Mr. Arthur Hornblow junior, who was accompanying him and whose job it was to arrange and supervise interviews with Mr. Goldwyn, kindly gave me an unsolicited invitation to come along. Arthur Hornblow was an enthusiastic and encouraging fellow and, willingly enough, along I went and was duly ushered into a private suite at the Ritz and the presence of Mr. Goldwyn.

Mr. Goldwyn was discovered reclining on a richly upholstered gilt settee or divan. He remained in this attitude throughout. Turning, without raising, his head, he looked doubtfully first at me and then at Arthur Hornblow, of whom he inquired bluntly, "Is this for Eddie Cantor?" as though I were some questionable-looking form of diet. Hornblow invited me to tell Mr. Goldwyn what I had done and could do, which was not, after all, asking much. I did myself brief but ample justice, while Mr. Goldwyn lay in abstracted silence. When I had spoken for about two minutes I paused, hopefully awaiting one of those comments for which he was famous. But, alas; he merely slightly shifted his reclining posture on the divan and his comment, though quite audible, was not verbal. And, although the kind and assiduous Arthur Hornblow continued occasionally to write and encourage me, that interview with Mr. Samuel Goldwyn may be said to have been the nearest I got to working in Hollywood. It was near enough for me.

But I should be grateful to the films. Apart from Golding Bright's handsome remittances of the wages of error they brought me another great satisfaction. They gave me the chance of writing for some actors and actresses whom I admired and who otherwise would have been lost to me. That favourite of my playgoing adolescence, Charles V. France, gave a perfect sketch of a genial old master-crook in one of the Walls–Lynn farces. Marie Löhr, whom I had first loved as an enchanting, juvenile Lady Teazle in an all-star production by Beerbohm Tree, I loved again now that she was less juvenile but just as enchanting as an aunt of Ralph Lynn or the prospective mother-in-law of Tom Walls, and even more enchanting as herself off the set. Of the younger generation, Diana Churchill stepped in to play in some of my films on her way to the top rank of contemporary actresses where she now belongs. Personally, I think she heads it, but perhaps I am prejudiced because I am so fond of her. Even at that time no one could have rivalled her in one character of mine—a complacent wife with a chronic cold in the head. Cecil Parker was giving evidence of his intention shortly to become a leading West End actor, and I am glad to think that I supplied him with one small piece of the evidence, when as counsel for the plaintiff in a divorce case he engaged in verbal conflict with Tom Walls who, needless to say, played the co-respondent. In another of my films the support part of a picturesque knave was played with exactly the right touch of casual, insidious charm by a little-known but obviously accomplished young actor named George Sanders.

We went one evening from Burnham to see *A Cup of Kindness* done by the Bristol Rep. and met Mervyn Johns.

He told me he had been at Bristol for ten years and had played about five hundred leads. Anybody could see that he was just about as good an all-round actor as could be found, and the performance he gave of Sir John Brute in Vanbrugh's *The Perplexed Wife* at the Embassy Theatre a year or so later drove James Agate to a state of ecstasy. When Mervyn Johns came back to London from Bristol I was influential in getting him included in a sequence of a farcical film called *Foreign Affairs*. (It was typical of British film mentality that, without my being consulted, it was renamed *Foreign Affaires*.) He acted quietly and sincerely and was so funny that he put the leading comedians' noses out of joint; and he was rewarded by the great compliment of having his part almost completely cut out of the finally edited version of the picture. I am always pleased at having given him his first job on the films.

And although the old spirit of Aldwych fun was missing from the studios, it was lucky for me that both Tom Walls and Ralph Lynn were able so readily to adapt themselves to the screen. I especially recall Ralph in two of his most Ralphish moments in my films. The first was when, as an egregious student of a school of dramatic art, he elected to recite a poem entitled *The Leper*, with its recurrent lament "Unclean— unclean—unclean"; which Ralph delivered like the baying of a forlorn hound. The second was at the beginning of a film called *For Valour*, when he was seen leading a bayonet charge as a subaltern in the Boer War:

Ralph: Forward—go on—charge. Give them the cold steel. (*He pauses and surveys an ill-equipped private*)*:* Here— you—where's your cold steel?

Private: I left it be'ind.

Ralph: Then go back and get it. That's the worst of recruiting plumbers.

I had two plays produced at about this time; and when I say that the first ran for two weeks and the second for three it might seem that however little I liked the film studios I was well advised to lump them. But the first play was put on for a prearranged limit of a fortnight at the Embassy Theatre at Swiss Cottage. I discovered the story in the Apocrypha of the New Testament and began writing the play for my own enjoyment without much hope or prospect of ever seeing it acted. It was the story of Thekla.

Thekla was, as many people no doubt are aware, a young patrician native of Iconium during the Roman occupation. When St. Paul visited Iconium she was one of his most ardent converts, and, as the Apocrypha clearly intimates, became infatuated with the apostle. She bribed the gaoler to allow her to visit St. Paul in prison and kissed his chains when she got there. Then, flouting her mother, her betrothed and the Roman authorities, she ran away from home and pursued him through various hazards and adventures. Finally, catching up with St. Paul at a later stage of his missionary journey, she was firmly and rather disappointingly counselled to cool off and apply herself to strictly celestial devotions.

Those who took part in the play will bear me out in saying that it was written without the smallest suggestion of irreverence or flippancy. I had written two acts when Laurence Irving and his wife came to pay us a visit at Burnham. He took a great delight in the theme and treatment, particularly as, in order to emphasise Thekla's rhapsodical approach, I had suggested that she created among St. Paul's other prominent local adherents some of the petty suspicions and minor dissentions which have always been liable to assail a parish council ancient or modern. Laurence Irving's enthusiasms have always been infectious and perhaps I stressed this idea unduly. This would seem to be borne out by the fact that at his suggestion I named the play *Certain of the Brethren*, though later the title was changed to *Chastity, My Brother*, a Miltonic phrase. But I must absolve Laurence Irving from any blame, for I had already portrayed, from between the lines of the Apocrypha, the character of Onesipheros, St. Paul's Iconian host and patron, as a somewhat venal old opportunist, who was to give early scope for the trenchant talent of Max Adrian.

Golding Bright was greatly intrigued by the play but said that to reveal that it was written by the author of the Aldwych farces would prejudice its chances with the critics and public. He sent the script to Ronald Adam, who was running the Embassy, and asked him (a) did he like it? and (b) could he guess the author? Ronald Adam replied (a) yes and (b) no. After some discussion he agreed to put it on for a fortnight, the author's name to remain undisclosed.

From the outset I had visualised Margaretta Scott as the ideal Thekla she proved to be. She had now blossomed into an actress of grace and dignity—the Labrador puppy no longer disported; though it is true that while we were discussing a scene during a meal together she did obliterate a wineglass with a fine sweeping gesture. St. Paul was played by D. A. Clarke-Smith, that distinguished actor who, at that period, specialised in what may be termed toga parts. And Henry Hewitt gave a most fascinating reading of a conscientious but bewildered and querulous Roman proconsul. John Fernald produced with great discrimination and sympathy. On the morning of the first rehearsal he and I told the company why my name was being withheld and asked all concerned to keep my secret. They said they would and all but one of them did. I kept clear of the theatre after that first rehearsal and there was soon some mild speculation in the press as to the identity of the anonymous author. But at the week-end before production this was disclosed in a news item of rather flattering prominence in the *Sunday Despatch*. The result was that, as Golding Bright had foreseen, most of the Press,

including even the *Times*, accused me of allowing my Aldwych mentality to enjoy itself at the expense of a religious
subject. This in itself I didn't mind; but I did resent the
superior attitude of the critics for two reasons; firstly, I would
have laid odds that I was quite as religious as any of them and
in some cases a great deal more so; and secondly, that I would
have laid even longer odds that without foreknowledge not
one single one of them would have guessed who had written
the play.

The B.B.C. was by this time going strong, or, at any rate,
going. I myself had broadcast a couple of talks from Savoy
Hill. When Radio Luxembourg started operations Tom
Walls and I were invited to go over and inaugurate its opening
programme by holding a conversation on the air. This may
appear a singular choice; but Tom Walls had, as I have
mentioned, become a universally recognised and popular
figure, and I suppose it was thought that I could aid the
conversation in the dual capacities of author of it and stooge
of it. While I was in Luxembourg I was told some story,
true or legendary, about the royal family of that country
which gave me an idea for a play.

As the ultimate result, on the 11th December, 1936, Yvonne
Printemps and Pierre Fresnay opened at the St. James's
Theatre in *O Mistress Mine*. This play, the reproduced
version of which is now known as *Nun's Veiling*, had already
been turned into a very presentable film for Tom Walls and
Yvonne Arnaud. I had written the stage comedy in the hope
that these two would act it in the theatre and I wish they had.
It was not the right material for Yvonne Printemps and
Fresnay and they were not the right artists for the material.
Pierre Fresnay is a fine, sensitive actor: anybody who saw his
Monsieur Vincent on the films will think that is an understate-
ment. But he hadn't the stature or the right sense of comedy

for my play—he admitted this to me with frank and charming contrition when it was too late. Yvonne Printemps spoke only French and had to be taught—by Fresnay—to speak her long broken-English part phonetically like a parrot—but what a lovely parrot. It was a wonderfully brave and patient undertaking on her part but it obviously did not help conviction. For some reason the play had to open cold at the St. James's without the benefit of even one week's preliminary hobble in the provinces; and although William Mollison directed it with great skill the production was heading for disaster when, at the last moment, Fate gave it a final, conclusive and unnecessary kick in its poor ill-fitting pants.

The story concerned a queen fleeing from a revolution in some minor mid-European realm. In Act 3 of the St. James's version she proceeded to join her husband, the king, in Paris. Her husband, the king, in Paris, kept firmly reiterating his decision to abdicate.

What was the date I mentioned? The date of the first night? The 11th December, 1936, did I say? Yes, on that very day King Edward VIII abdicated the throne of England. Every line of that accursed last scene might have formed part of a satirical commentary written by some scurrilous republican poison pen. The play was doomed before that happened, but when it did happen the audience sat silent and aghast. Some of the more sensitive of its members crept away. I was one of the more sensitive.

Golding Bright said nothing; he didn't believe in inquests. When I had taken him the original version of the comedy (in its present *Nun's Veiling* form) he told me it was the best play I had ever written. He resented handing it over to be turned into a film. He saw it now lying in untidy wreckage by the theatrical wayside; stirred by the toes of the critics as they briefly assessed the damage and passed on; nosed at by a few of the playgoing fraternity who find a fascination in the street accidents of the stage. It had been Golding who, in his enthusiasm for the play, had brought off, with habitual nonchalence, what had seemed a triumphant coup in securing Yvonne Printemps. But now he never said it had been a good idea which had been mishandled or a bad idea for which he apologised. He said nothing. He wasn't resentful; he wasn't even sympathetic. But he wasn't discouraged and above all he wasn't discouraging. He was a treasure.

There were three others, besides Golding and, I think, William Mollison, to whom that little play made a particular appeal. My wife was one. She had, on this first night, been sitting with my daughter in the stalls, while I wandered in disconsolate funk into the various lobbies and bars and lavatories of the St. James's Theatre or had gone forth to welcome pneumonia on excursions into the callous December streets hard by. She had faced the catastrophe throughout with a calm and practical imperturbability, and when I joined her afterwards she said she had enjoyed the play very much and where should we go for supper? But she did not underrate or seek to ignore the calamity. She did not pretend to be cheerful and unabashed about it. She did not avoid talking about it and she did not try to interfere with my feelings about it. But she did not lament or condole or analyse or explain away. She always thought the play was good and she loved good people and good things (or bad ones for that matter) for themselves and not for what they gained or lost. She was just herself. She ate a good supper and slept like a top. Of all the plays I wrote this always remained her favourite.

Pierre Fresnay loved it too. All through rehearsals he so delighted in the play and I in his delight that neither of us could admit, even to ourselves, that he was so miscast. And I have never known an actor more honest and more generous in a moment of failure.

The third individual who express a particular partiality for this play was a dear old dilettante and amateur critic named Ernest Walls Stephens. I would in any case want to salute his memory and the recollection of his opinionated but affable championship, but he also crops up at a convenient moment chronologically. For in 1931 a sudden unexpected circumstance had brought me into contact with Stephens and with several others who, like him, were to become from then onwards a set of new and most convivial acquaintances.

Really I am an incongruous character. It was difficult enough for people in the theatre and film world to picture me initiating the dropping of torpedoes from enormous single-seater aeroplanes, without their being asked to imagine my surely inappropriate figure arrayed in the fur-trimmed gown of the Prime Warden of a great City Livery Company, or even in the carefully self-respectful outfit of a worthy governor of a Public School. And yet in 1931 I was elected to serve on the Court of the Fishmongers' Company and, a few years later, to become a governor of Gresham's School, whose endowment is administered by the Fishmongers.

Not that I was unworthy. Travers has been a name associated with the Fishmongers' Company for centuries. Even during the last hundred years I have been the fourth member of the family to have held the office of Prime Warden to which I succeeded in 1946-47. Nobody, except perhaps myself, seemed to think that a farce-writer was miscast in that capacity. Fishmongers' Hall is the home of a noble and valuable tradition, and while there is always due observance of the formalities in its charitable and other duties this does not prevent the Court from being composed of the most impartial, diversified and entertaining companions in good humour that one could hope to meet.

The Clerk of the Company when I was its Prime Warden was Cyril Hooper, who distinguished himself greatly in his office and was made a C.B.E. on the strength of it. He was of the utmost value to me, but I treasured him even more for his personality than for his acumen. He was a contemporary of mine and we used to delight in recalling some of the scenes and experiences of our boyhood in the spacious Edwardian days. Once when we were competing in the luxury of reminiscence I was dwelling on what is always a favourite subject of such discussions—the good old Empire Theatre and Robert Hale, Binnie's father, who was its reigning comedian and whom I was destined to appreciate even more off the stage than on. Hooper capped this by reminding me of the establishment opposite the Empire which in those days boasted a strange and fascinating feature. This was the public lavatory for gentlemen. It still stands—if "stands" is the right term for an underground sanctum of this nature—on the same site, but in the years before the first war its appointment was in keeping with the arcadian spirit of the age. The water used for flushing purposes was contained in large glass tanks and in these tanks were goldfish. The flushing system was operated automatically at regular periods. Ever so often there would arise an ear-splitting "whooshing" noise and all but about a couple of inches of water would be drained from the tank. In the restricted space available to them the goldfish swarmed and jockeyed for position, their faces seeming to wear expressions of extreme indignation, antagonism and apprehension. But in the nick of time a torrent of salvation bubbled into the tank and within a few moments the goldfish were disporting themselves once more in carefree abandon and confidence. Then—"whoosh"— another crisis to be faced; another brief term of terror, tribulation and conflict.

Cyril Hooper was a man who could perform his official duties in administrating a great tradition with complete sincerity and unrivalled competence; yet his sense of humour was always predominant and infectious. I well remembered his goldfish when he reminded me of them and they proved very useful on one occasion when I had to make an after-dinner speech about cricket. This was when the Cricket Writers were entertaining a newly-arrived touring team from New Zealand. For it is, of course, obvious, in the ups-and-downs of fortune, not only in the cricket field but in the wider field of life in general, how like we all are to those poor wretched goldfish. And the application comes in handy when I review my own fortunes as a playwright at the time of the St. James's débâcle. If ever I found myself struggling for survival in two inches of water with a swarm of fellow goldfish-dramatists, that was the time.

Robertson Hare is not a boastful man; and indeed if anyone were to ask "Why should he be?" he himself would be the first to do so. But at this time he could fairly have boasted that he had won an unchallenged position as the public's favourite stage victim. In a moment of inspiration someone or other had visualised Alfred Drayton as his ideal partner. If it were decreed that Robertson Hare be victimised no better appointment could have been conceived. As a friend once shrewdly remarked to me, "You've only to see Alfred Drayton's name in the programme and Bunny Hare has begun to get bullied before the curtain goes up."

Hare and Drayton had, by the beginning of 1938, established themselves as a recognised stage partnership and were on the look-out for a new farce. Robertson Hare suggested to their management, O'Bryen, Linnit and Dunfee, that I might be able to oblige. I was able. I had a play under construction and was easily and confidently able to turn it into a farcical comedy with good leading parts for the lion and the mouse respectively. And as for obliging—I may have obliged Hare, Drayton, O'Bryen, Linnit, Dunfee and many others, including, I am glad to say, a large number of the general public. But I obliged nobody half as much as I obliged myself.

Banana Ridge remains my favourite play not only that I myself have ever written but that anybody has ever written. It began as straight comedy—broad if you like, but breadth is not inconsistent with straightness, which is only another and rather pompous way of stating the old Aldwych formula for farce. *Banana Ridge* did not tumble from comedy into the farce of its last act; the comedy quickened and gave birth to farce. It was a notable achievement in the technique of play-writing. One of my fellow dramatists recently told me that the work of a farce-writer could be enjoyed; it could not possibly be admired. He *is* an ass.

Nineteen-thirty-eight: exactly twenty years since the end of the first world war, in which Mr. Pound and Mr. Pink had been brother officers. On the strength of this Mr. Pound gave Mr. Pink a post-war job as manager of one of the rubber estates belonging to the company of which Mr. Pound was, by this time, the massive and formidable chairman. Mr. Pink, a cockily efficient but easily dominated employee, happened to be home on leave with his Scottish wife. One morning there arrived at Mr. Pound's London house a lady in the middle forties and her modest but prepossessing son. Mr. Pound could not fail to recognise her even after all those years—well, I'm blest; Sue Long. Yes, still Sue Long—she'd never married. The son, she revealed, was the offspring of one of the five subalterns who had dug with Mother at an early stage of the war. Dug with Mother? Had diggings with Mother. Were billeted on Mother. Oh, I see—yes, well? But which subaltern was the father Sue would never tell. Three of the gentlemen had already shown their appreciation of her reticence, and the successive stages of the boy's upbringing and education had been financed by Mr. Butcher, Mr. Corker and Mr. Tope. Now it was the turn of Mr.

Pound and Mr. Pink. Mr. *Pink*? Mr. Pound showed incredulous disdain. "You mean to tell me that Pink—qualifies?"

The upshot was that, after he had spent three weeks in Mr. Pound's employ, the boy was shipped off to serve as assistant on the rubber estate, Bukit Pisang (Banana Ridge) of which Mr. Pink was manager. It was high time. Every woman he had come across, including Mr. Pound's second wife, Mr. Pound's partner's wife and, worse, Mr. Pound's pretty daughter, had become the willing, potential victims of the lad's guileless charm. Mr. Pink found him neither guileless nor charming. He protested vigorously.

"All through the war I was beside you and, I make bold to state, occasionally in front of you. Since then I've not only served you loyally but I've organised and methodised and revolutionised and reclaimed and generally tinkered up a couple of particularly indifferent estates into tip-top number one order. And what's my reward? To be ensnared and tricked and ambushed and bamboozled into having to saddle myself with the unbearable burden of this loathsome youth."

Mr. Pound sought to justify himself:

"I couldn't help it, Pink. . . . He's only been with us three weeks, and what? My wife, my daughter, Bingley's wife and, if Bingley had had a daughter, Bingley's daughter. I had to take this chance to get rid of him."

He further inspirited Mr. Pink:

"You're a pretty good authority on the Malay States. How many women are there in that country?"—"Good heavens, sir, I've no idea. At a round guess I should say about three-quarters of a million."—"Ah. Well, you needn't worry. He'll be dead in a year."

A year later the Pounds and the boy's mother coincided on a visit to Banana Ridge and the parentage problem was solved when the mother was pursued and forgiven for blackmail by the genuine father. He was now a distinguished personage who had been an airman in the war and a forced landing had enabled him to spend a night in successful rivalry to Messrs. Butcher, Corker, Tope, Pound and Pink.

It all sounds fairly improper. But it was written in ingenuous vein and one of them, Bill Linnit, I think, had a brainwave in casting Olga Lindo for the boy's mother. She carried it off with an air of practical, undesigning good humour which was beautifully disarming. I dare say it was chiefly due to her that the critics decided to be broad-minded; for the play got an excellent press and jolly well deserved it.

Years before, I had seen Kathleen O'Regan in *Young Woodley*. I asked for her as Mrs. Pound and got her. So there was no lack of talent and, now, a guarantee of happiness and gaiety in the company. I had also seen Constance Lorne in that production of *The Perplexed Wife* which had caused James Agate to hail Mervyn Johns as the modern Garrick. Constance Lorne was to be in three of the four plays I wrote after *Banana Ridge*, which, for her sake, was a pity perhaps; for, as in the case of Winifred Shotter, she became stereotyped. She played lead in one West End comedy and made quite a hit, but her acting was more successful than the play and she lapsed again into Scottish support. She is much too accomplished and versatile for that. She, like Binnie Hale and Yvonne Arnaud and Ethel Coleridge and Dorothy Batley, became one of the actresses who were the close and particular friends of my wife, and she will always remain one of our family favourites.

Luckily Robert Flemyng had just reached that comparatively early stage of his prosperous career when he could be recruited for the part of the boy; and they got an actor to play the small part of the genuine father who looked so like him that when in the third act the two faced each other the audience audibly gasped. But this was just an instance of the care taken in the production. I got them to let Laurence Irving design the sets and he enthusiastically dived into obscure museums and places and made a minute study of what a planter's bungalow in Malaya really looked like. I have never in my life seen a better stage setting than Mr. Pink's veranda of the bungalow at Bukit Pisang.

Obviously a splendid cast then—but there was one problem. On this same veranda of Mr. Pink's bungalow there had to be a boy—in this case a "boy" in the local domestic sense, a Chinese servant. His part had been written and had to be spoken in colloquial Malay—none of your "two piecee missie come homeside makee tea no can do" stuff. That might have passed muster in a farce set in Hong Kong or even Malaya of to-day; but not in this conscientious production in 1938. And to-day, of course, one could have found dozens of genuine native actors capable of filling the part. But at that time not even an actors' agency could supply an artist qualified to sustain the role of Wun.

Rehearsals were almost due to start. Bill Linnit was my guest one night at a Livery Dinner in Fishmongers' Hall. I can't remember whether he said "You'd better play the part yourself" or whether I volunteered to. Anyhow, I told him that if he'd get a good man from the film studios to teach me my make-up I'd play Wun for the run. He asked me how much I'd want each Friday night. I told him—what the part was worth. We signed an agreement on the back of the menu card. I don't know what happened to it. Very likely we left it on the table.

Alfred Drayton was as downright a character off the stage as on. Exceptional, too—there has been no one to play Alfred Drayton parts since he died. He scoffed at my decision, not in scorn but in friendly raillery. "You amateurs —I know what it'll be. In a month's time you'll be sick of it and find someone else to take it on."

I said, "I'll play the part for the run and number-one tours and I won't miss a show unless I have a doctor's certificate."

He said, "I'll bet yer a fiver." This was a strong measure for Alfred Drayton, whose favourite hobby was collecting and preserving currency.

On the last night of the London run, as I made my final exit, Alfred Drayton was waiting for me in the wings. He said bluntly "Here y'are" and handed me a five-pound note. I should have had it framed.

If my former first nights had intimidated me into lurking with commissionaires and smiling wanly at refurbishing bar-maids, this first night should surely have reduced me to a state of knock-kneed panic. But no. There was not the same ordeal to face this time. I was on the job, in the thick of it and I felt only a novel, stimulating exhilaration as I sat and made up (it was always a three-quarters-of-an-hour job) with the first act going on down below. Dear Kathleen O'Regan came to my little dressing-room in the Strand Theatre towards the end of the first act and told me all was going well. I had to open Act 2 and I went sliding in my Chinese slippers down to the wings in the middle of the first interval.

There was chaos on the stage. Mr. Pink's bungalow veranda was up but there was a dreadful hitch in getting its roof to fit. The minutes slipped by. I stood and watched the stage hands arguing and bungling. A little devil sneaked up to me and began to taunt me—a paradoxical little devil, for his pitchfork with which he prodded me had prongs which were icicles and he whispered to me that I was awakening to a nightmare. He reminded me that my two schoolboy sons were in front, sitting with my wife and my daughter, who was an understudy in the show. They were waiting, waiting for the second act to begin. What had happened? Was the delay due to me? Had I suddenly been stricken with a palsy of stage-fright or something? Think of all the others out in front there, he said. Think of Golding Bright sitting with his chin on the knob of his stick propped up in his white wash-leather gloves, waiting, waiting without a trace of perturbation on his face but inwardly restive and cynical—he had always been sceptical about your decision to be an actor, you know, said the little devil. Then Laurence Irving and his wife—so closely involved in this crisis—and Binnie Hale and other friends and partisans, anxious to be indulgent but unable to help feeling that this was going to be a silly and shame-making experiment. And not merely friends and supporters—what of the critics? What of the horde of superior, captious first-nighters, hanging about in little groups and exhausting their bored gossip in bars and vestibules as this interminable interval dragged its weary length along?

This was one of the "whoosh" moments if you like. I was in my two inches of water, with that flustered gang of stage hands jostling around me, and oh, the water was cold. Then my eyes turned from the blasted, lop-sided, wouldn't-fit roof to the unruffled figure of the producer standing and giving quiet, decisive directions from the footlights.

Gardner Davies was a young man from the Coventry Rep. Tom Walls, with his usual discernment, had spotted his work there and had brought him down to lend a hand in the film studios. *Banana Ridge* was his first West End production. He made a great success of it and afterwards of *Gaslight* for the same management. He was preparing to produce my next farce when he was killed in an accident in the summer of

1939. I admired his work and liked him greatly. I don't think there was anybody who didn't.

A glance at him restored my confidence. I dismissed the little devil; Gardner Davies soon had the roof shipshape and I discovered that the interval hadn't been unduly prolonged at all. Up went the curtain on the empty stage. Laurence Irving's set got a big hand; then on I waddled with a teapot. I was almost knocked over backwards by the round of applause; it was most disconcerting and unexpected. I had anticipated—and hoped—that they wouldn't recognise me in my make-up; but I suppose they must have looked at their programmes. I planted my teapot on the table and beat the audience into silence with a gong-stick. Constance Lorne entered and spoke her line:

"*Tuan—dia t'ada sini?*"

I braced myself stiffly to attention and made reply:

"*B'lum lagi, mem; dia dalam padang. Mem mau sia panghil?*"

There was a sort of surprised laugh from the audience. I think most of them thought I had invented some sort of specious gibberish. But a Malayan-born *Daily Express* representative who was standing with Bill Linnit turned to him in astonishment.

"Good Lord," he said. "That bloke's talking the genuine stuff."

Bill Linnit coolly asked him what else he expected in one of *his* productions.

I deserved Alfred Drayton's fiver. I acted Wun over four hundred times, including a few weeks in the provinces, and never missed a performance. It entailed some sacrifices—I had to leave Vincent Square at half-time when my elder son was playing for Charterhouse against Westminster at soccer. I watched Hutton and Leyland batting at the Oval in the Test Match in which Hutton made his record score, and had to dash off and play in a matinée, to dash back again directly I had finished with Wun and find Hutton and Leyland still hard at it. It didn't mean parting with Burnham, for my wife and daughter and I used to go down there on Sunday mornings and get back in time for the Monday evening show. My daughter is a first-class actress and would have made a name for herself, but she got married during the war and settled for domesticity—a very sensible and desirable pity. Once, when she was playing as understudy in *Banana Ridge*, Gladys Cooper, who was in front, sent her a little message of praise and encouragement. None of us had the pleasure of knowing Miss Cooper, so it was one of those gracious acts of gratuitous kindness which one always remembers.

It was, I think, the happiest year I had ever known. I revelled in a very full tank of enjoyment and success. The only "whoosh" was when Mr. Neville Chamberlain had to fly to Munich; but the good man came back waving his bit of paper and the tank soon filled up again.

Following *Banana Ridge* my next Hare–Drayton farce, also at the Strand, had a very satisfactory reception and ran for nine performances. For it will be remembered that nearly all the West End theatres closed automatically at the outbreak of war. *Spotted Dick*, as it was called (Robertson Hare was a Mr. Dick and got the fair name of Dick spotted), returned to the Strand later in the year when the initial scare had subsided and played for a few months in the melancholy hand-to-mouth conditions of the time. Joyce Barbour was fortunately in the leading-lady part. In the circumstances it might seem difficult for any company to be jolly, but with her at hand it was difficult for any company not to be.

How lucky I had been about laughter—and still am. It was always in my home—it was always in my work. Tom Walls was a great laughter-lover; for even if Tom were in one of his troublesome moods he was still laughing and, anyhow, Ralph Lynn was there too. My other friends have all been lovers of laughter—Laurence Irving, Binnie Hale, Arthur Mailey, Robertson-Glasgow and the Old Carthusian golfing brigade and many others. Joyce Barbour is as good a laughter-lover as any.

We wanted laughter at that time pretty badly; and it did not fail us. Laurence Irving and I spent Christmas night of 1939 as pilot officers in fleabags on the draughty floor of a little room in the Air Ministry. We wrapped our martial cloaks around us and laughed ourselves to sleep.

CHAPTER X

Remainder Biscuit

OH, if only I had steered clear of that second wartime job at the start. But I couldn't do that for two reasons. If —I argued to myself—an old ex-Service volunteer of fifty-three was going to get taken on at all he must go and do what he's told to go and do without any quibbling. Secondly, I hadn't at the time the slightest notion what it was I was being told to go and do.

Moreover my confounded conscientiousness flung me blindly into acceptance of the first offer that came along. The Director of Intelligence of the Royal Air Force was, at that time, a man I had once taught to fly; so I told him he should arrange for me to be commissioned as a pilot officer and given suitable employment. He told me he had already accommodated Laurence Irving in the same way, so I had better go and join him. Thus I found myself in A.I.2C sub-section B. I spent the first week trying to memorise where I belonged.

I soon lost Laurence Irving whose services were wanted in some more active field of operations. A.I.2C sub-section B was then mercifully abbreviated into A.I.6. It grew rapidly in size and importance. It was the section responsible for Security.

Security, in this sense, meant seeing to it that the enemy didn't find out anything about the R.A.F. that he didn't know already. I don't think that up to the outbreak of war anybody had bothered his head much about Security. Then

Lionel Heald took it in hand. I have never known a man of such judgment and intuition. His perspicacity would light upon the one small detail which really mattered like the beam of a policeman's lantern upon a keyhole. He is an Old Carthusian and this may have been partly why he was so patient with my early flounderings. He was a most interesting person to have as one's tutelary genius and he is still a great friend of mine. But I always felt that working with him was rather like panting after an indulgent running coach who had shot ahead and was waiting at the next corner for me to catch up.

I feel prompted to try to recall some of the duties of the Security Section, if only to give some idea of what poor old Addlepate had to face up to. They were:

To impose secrecy covering operations past, present and projected.

To get to know every detail of what had been published and what hadn't about types and performances of aircraft, about equipment, personnel, establishments, casualties, armament, bombs, secret weapons, weather and goodness knows what.

To stop the Germans from knowing what they had done themselves when there was any chance they hadn't found out.

To stop the Germans thinking we knew anything about anything we knew about them if we didn't already know they knew we knew.

To draft in unemotional terms of prescribed restraint the Air Ministry Official Communiqué about what we had done to the enemy during the day or during the night and what he had done to us.

To get such communiqués written, approved and issued in time for the B.B.C. news at 8 hours or 13 hours or 18 hours or zero hours and at the same time to avoid incurring a flaming row with the Press by letting the B.B.C. have it before the Press did.

To advise the censors at the Ministry of Information as to whether there was any security objection to the publication of some news item cooked up by some enterprising pressman which they couldn't make their own minds up about.

To spend ghastly night duties in a torture of expectation that the telephone bell would startle one into the ordeal of having to cope with some such problem in a snap decision.

To engage in frantic arguments with indignant special air correspondents and disgruntled scooping journalists because, they said, we had stopped something we ought to have passed.

To suffer (in my case at any rate) agonies of apprehension because I thought I might have passed something I ought to have stopped.

Worst of all—to arrive, after an occasional week-end glimpse of the comparative Paradise of home, back into the bleak black-out of Paddington Station and hurry away to begin another haunting spell of duty.

I seem to have been influenced by some special and extra-ordinary predisposition for landing myself with unsuitable jobs in times of war. When I first started this one I found I could no more do it than I could fly in 1914. But eventually I seem to have made quite commendable progress at it, so I suppose I must have overcome my nature. Which is also surprising, because in other respects I have always found this a very difficult thing to do.

About two years of A.I.6. were enough. I had risen to the rank of squadron-leader but I felt I couldn't stay the course. I sought asylum. The Ministry of Information seemed an appropriate spot for this.

The duties here were similar (I was one of the Air Advisers to the censorship) but they were less arduous. With me from

A.I.6 came a companion of my own choice, Philip Sykes, whose name will be held in familiar respect by all connected with Company Law, whatever that may mean. He shared my new responsibilities and any fun that might be extracted from them. We managed to extract a surprising and refreshing amount. Another kindred spirit (another Old Carthusian too), Philip Hope-Wallace, was attached to our section. He was something to do with "Public Relations"—one of those dreadful examples of inflated modern terminology which, like "Press Conference", came into general use with the war. Hope-Wallace and one or two others associated with us were always ready to support any fun-extraction efforts and things began to seem a little brighter. I started to think out a story for a wartime comedy. And I dare say there are some who can still recall the spate of indecorous doggerel limericks which emanated at one period from the Air Advisers' quarters. They dealt with some of the notable personalities of the time, with particular reference to Russian generals. One of them began:

> "The sweetheart of bold Timoschenko
> Is a girl in the Swan Fountain Pen Co——"

but must not, even in these days, be quoted in full. The same stricture applies to the one which started:

> "The winter finds Marshal Budhenny
> Incessantly spending a penny——"

and to the occasion when

> "The Bishop of Upper Benghazi
> Lent his aid to a fugitive Nazi——".

When the United States went to war they instituted a Security Section of the Army Air Force Intelligence Branch.

Its conscientious interpretation of Security differed somewhat from ours. Before long we were between us—to state the matter bluntly—getting progressively into the very hell of a muddle. According to our views they stopped those things which they ought to have released and they had left unstopped those things they ought not to have released and there was no health in us. Someone had to be sent to act as liaison officer in this section of the Army Air Force and to get the whole thing tidied up.

"This can't really be true—— This can't really be me." I had always remembered saying that to myself the first time I found myself flying around alone in an aeroplane. And now, twenty-seven years later, I felt like saying it again, as I entered the towering, tumultuous warren which had been requisitioned for the temporary accommodation of the Army Air Force executive in Washington. The war brought most of us odd freaks of experience and this was a very minor one; but to a person of my age and nature the whole situation seemed to be the outcome of an inapt improbability.

But anyhow, there I was. I stood in a crowded lift, sardined into the sudorific bodies of female clerks who were carrying mountains of files full of didactic American official verbosity in triplicate. I got out at the right floor (the tenth I think) and wandered through a labyrinth of enormous rooms full of desks. From each and every desk resounded in strident competition the clangour of male American voices raised in desperate decision or momentous argument, on which apparently depended the whole conduct and outcome of the war. But here and there someone would settle this and sit back for a moment of brow-wiping recovery from his controversial violence, which enabled me to ask my timid way; and I eventually found myself confronting and being confronted by the small group of officers with whom I had been detailed to engage in the mutual tidying-up.

I don't know whom they had been expecting. I only know they hadn't been expecting me. And no doubt the spectacle of an elderly little man in Royal Air Force uniform, trying to square his bent shoulders against his chronic and perhaps obvious self-consciousness and smiling his best in preliminary conciliation must have been a trifle ludicrous. "Never mind," I said to myself. "Within a week I'll have you laughing at me to my face." And I did. Then I knew I had got them where I wanted them.

But even then it would have been fatal to sail in and try to teach them how to do their job. I sat and listened placidly while they made a series of extraordinary decisions and awaited the time when they should turn to me for advice. They didn't do this until I had been there nearly a month but from then onwards they became wildly co-operative. So, to my surprise and relief, were the American pressmen. Their prototypes of fiction and the films had filled me with horrified forebodings, but compared with some of our more contentious home-bred press representatives they turned out to be almost disappointingly tame and submissive. Often at the mere suggestion that what they wanted to publish was legitimate enough from the security angle but was calculated to cause contention or ill-feeling between ourselves and the States, they would fling it into the waste-paper basket with a flourish of high-principled abandon. And if, as I soon discovered, this chivalrous attitude was principally due to their prevailing fear of being labelled as unpatriotic, at any rate it did me a very good turn. I was, I believe, supposed to have achieved success in Washington; but if I did this was because success was handed to me on a plate.

Everyone I came across in the Army Air Force headquarters, from the generals downwards, struck me as being overwhelmingly energetic, exhaustingly enthusiastic and intensely juvenile. They delighted in the opportunities which service on the home front appeared to provide for adding to their collections of medal ribbons. Their system of holding departmental dinners at which, in the course of inexhaustibly hearty speech-making, every member of the party (already the bosom companion of everybody else) was traditionally bound to be mentioned by name and had to get up and take a bow, would have been considered puerile at any English junior school house. On one occasion the whole section of the Intelligence Branch to which I was attached was summoned to hear some vital announcement by its colonel. We assembled, outwardly stoical but agog with speculation. The Colonel entered. He was a bristling little man with a snappy, impressive manner. He took his seat; he compressed his lips; he narrowed his eyes. A tense, portentous pause as he looked keenly at each of us in turn—and at last he spoke.

"Gennelmen," he said. "Maybe some of you have already guessed why I've sent for you. Yes, sir; this is it. The big decision has been made. Gennelmen—we're going to town."

That was all. But apparently it sufficed. All his men looked at each other with a wild surmise. Some of the younger and more impressionable ventured to indulge in whispers of triumphant satisfaction—"Gosh, feller—you hear that? We're going to town." But none of them had the slightest idea what the Colonel meant and this, I rather fancy, applied to the Colonel himself. I did not, of course, display my ignorance by asking him what he meant. I even resisted the momentary temptation to quote Ralph Lynn and ask him what part of town. And it didn't really matter in the least because nothing ever happened. I returned from the States with the firm opinion, which I still hold, that in his own country and in the midst of his own species the oldest male American is eighteen.

Washington was still a beautiful and delectable city even

when it was trying to cater for at least four times its peace-
time population in its sub-tropical summertime. Its housing
problems were formidable but I was told I was lucky, because
one of the officers I was working with knew an old lady who
was willing to let me a small furnished room in her apartment
house; though from its size and appearance I judged that the
small furnished room was normally a closet—in the American
application of that forbidding term or even, perhaps, in our
own. But I was happy enough and was treated with kindness
and consideration by everybody except the old lady, who
seemed unceasingly suspicious of what I was doing to her
closet. All I was doing to it was sitting contentedly in it,
stripped against its glutinous stuffiness at nights, and going
ahead with my wartime comedy.

Towards the end of my visit the Colonel decided to make
amends for his unfulfilled pledge that I should go with him to
town. He had a single-engined two-seater Harvard trainer
allocated to him for his personal use and, as he found it necessary to proceed to Los Angeles for some reason or other, he
bade me considerately but briskly to get into the back seat.
It was, of course, an interesting experience to fly in a dual-
control two-seater across the whole breadth of the vast and
variegated American continent and back. But I would have
enjoyed it more if my rather peppery Colonel had been less
virulently contemptuous of my capabilities as co-pilot. When
he first handed me over the controls he immediately flew into
a paroxysm and accused me of trying to crash the machine
into a tract of country which, he alleged, almost with tears of
rage, was infested by rattlesnakes.

But in his less bristling moments he was a hearty and matey
little colonel and at least his indulgence gave me the chance of
spending a week in Hollywood and of pursuing all the
customary routine of the specially privileged visitor—touring
the studios and being introduced to various bemused film

stars ("Hallo there") and all that. My memory of this pleasant excursion fastens particularly on one individual. Walt Disney kindly sent me under escort to inspect his interesting premises, one department of which is a minor museum containing various gadgets for the production of every conceivable sound-effect. In the midst of this stood a little man looking like a modest senior bank-clerk who seemed to be one of the permanent exhibits. He was, I was told, indeed one of the most notable of these and one whom I would surely be glad to have myself get to know. He was the voice of Donald Duck.

On the return flight we were grounded by mist for four days at Greensboro, North Carolina. I should in any case mention this in grateful recollection of the hospitality of the Deep South, including that special favour reserved for honoured guests, a bottle of the genuine ten-years-matured corn liquor. But Greensboro had a particular interest for me, being the birthplace of O. Henry. I was given the chance to look at some of his manuscripts—page after page written in that faultless copperplate style which, in my experience, has been achieved only by lawyers' scriveners, Robertson Hare and some of those monks. I think Leacock's friend must have been rather hard on poor O. Henry. It is hard to believe that such perfect calligraphy could result from incessant intoxication. It is certainly not so in the case of Robertson Hare. I cannot, of course, answer for the lawyers' scriveners or the monks.

I went back to England soon after this, and concerning my six months with the Army Air Force I would add only a post-script of appreciation of the Colonel. Our acquaintance ripened during our flight together and at the end of it, mellowed perhaps by the corn liquor and no longer haunted by rattlesnakes, he wrote a letter of warm appro-bation of my services to the Air Ministry at home. So let me record a grateful and affectionate tribute to him in return.

When I had finished my job in Washington and had put in a few more months of intensified air-advising in London I felt it was about time that I finished that job too. An old man in uniform may think he cuts an exemplary and patriotic figure, but if he goes on thinking so for too long he is apt to become a nuisance.

Both my sons had left school and were in the Services. My son-in-law was in the army overseas. Earlier in the war my house had, reasonably enough, shared the lot of other available houses in the country and had been carved up into sections in which the local authorities had deposited war-working or evacuated visitors of their own choice. My brief periods of leave had been shared with strange figures lurking in the shadows of my staircase. That study, which so often had echoed with experimental snatches of Lynn-Walls argument, resounded with the screams of an infant billetee in its ill-timed moments of petulance. Intimidating smells issued from a temporary cooking-stove in a spare bedroom.

My wife had shown unfailing good humour in the midst of these domestic dislocations and her cheerful patience had been rewarded. A suitable compromise was effected between herself, the authorities and the screamer and I soon regained my study. And while I was still in Washington the temporary cooking-stove and its inexpert engineer had already been disposed of to make room for my daughter. So my eldest grandchild, Andrew Morgan, had been enabled to be born into a bedroom scoured clean of the last lingering hint of Woolton pie. By the time I got back there for good, home was itself again.

So now, what about that wartime comedy? I had written it for Robertson Hare, as a country vicar at loggerheads with his parishioners. Hare always was—and is—a very likely parson. My ambitions for him in this instance had been inspired by the pathetic figure of the notorious Rector of Stiffkey. Indeed, I named my fictitious parish Tufflock though nobody ever twigged the significance. The Rector of Stiffkey, I seem to remember, ended his enterprising career in a lion's den, which would, of course, be an ideal setting for any Robertson Hare last act. But apart from giving me the original idea for Hare's character the ill-starred Rector did not contribute to my story. The person who really contributed was one of my nieces.

On a beach in Cornwall she and a girl friend had seen a little parson emerge from behind a rock in his little bathing costume and deposit his little camera on a ledge of the rock while he went for his little bathe. Obviously the girls seized the chance of borrowing the camera and a couple of the parson's films to photograph each other in the nude; after which they carefully replaced the camera and went their way. The sequel was never known. My comedy sought to supply it.

Linnit and Dunfee agreed to present the play; Laurence Irving contributed a picturesque stretch of rocky Cornish coast for the first set and I produced the thing myself. In addition to Robertson Hare, Basil Radford, Catherine Lacey and Joyce Heron were in the cast. All seemed to be going well and then suddenly, in the middle of rehearsals, we ran into trouble with the Lord Chamberlain. The management got a letter saying that the play would only be licensed on condition that fourteen of my most promising lines were omitted.

At that time the Lord Chamberlain's office was in Windsor Castle. Bill Linnit and I journeyed thither by appointment and, after being conducted past long ranks of an intimidating guard of honour consisting of unoccupied sets of armour, we were shown into the handsome sunlit suite which contained the two gentlemen who had drawn up the catalogue of my fourteen mortal offences.

The spokesman was a small but virile, emphatic and mobile personage. I was dismayed—though with respect and admiration—to discover that he had studied and memorised every detail of the contested passages, their context and their meanings, both simple and double. His enthusiasm and efficiency were most impressive, but so was his determination.

He thoroughly agreed with the accepted principle that affliction and menace must be visited upon Mr. Robertson Hare. His objection was to their being visited upon him as a member of the cloth. "I will *not*," he cried and clouted his table, "I will *not* have Mr. Robertson Hare suspected of what he calls hi-tiddly-i-ti in a clerical collar."

At one point of the discussion I ventured to charge him with inconsistency. "Here," I said, "I have wrapped up a vulgar expression neatly, in order to avoid any crudity, and you rule it out. What do you want? Do you want me to say straight out 'He slapped my bottom'?"

"Yes," he replied immediately, and his eyes lit up. "Yes, I pass bottom." He relapsed and gazed past me in the manner of one indulging a momentary, rhapsodical lapse from his customary modesty, and he added proudly, "I was the first censor to pass bottom."

A little later—"I can't understand," I said, "why you want *that* word out. What's the matter with it?"

"*That* word? Oh, but it can be put to an utterly unspeakable meaning."

"Really?" I said. "I'm surprised I've never heard it." I turned to Bill Linnit. "Have you?" Bill Linnit shook his head. Even the rather dumb second inquisitor had to admit, on being challenged, that he had never heard it either.

"Well, come on then," I said. "What is it? Let's have it.

What is the horrifying hidden significance of this poor word?"

The spokesman bit his lip. He half raised himself with his hands on the arms of his chair and surveyed the room anxiously, as though fearful that it might harbour some sneaking eavesdropper. Then he sat back, drew a deep breath and eyed me guiltily. His voice dropped to an almost inaudible whisper. "Cock," he said.

We patched up our differences somehow and they didn't affect the issue because, in any case, the play received a general castigation from the critics, whom it seemed to catch in a severely sanctimonious mood which kept several of them in the bar for most of the evening. And, although I had run up against a punctilious and slightly ridiculous representative of the Lord Chamberlain, this personal encounter confirmed what I had always thought—that the censorship of plays is valuable and expedient. It safeguards managements and dramatists by lulling the public into an obtuse sense of assurance that any play they go to see has been officially declared to be moral. Abolition of the censorship would expose the play to the mercies of the local legislators and pietistic fanatics of every city in the land. And the censors carry out their task with good sense and equity. Besides, they know the meanings of words that we don't.

My comedy was called *She Follows Me About*; "she" being the spirit of deliberate persecution which catches the poor little vicar out at every turn—"Misfortune's practical sister", as he describes her. It withstood the critics' onslaught to be played for six months at the Garrick Theatre—not bad in the uncertain wartime conditions. I have affectionate memories of it, if only for the vicar's wife. Catherine Lacey created a study in eccentric, scatter-brained loyalty which remains my favourite performance in any of my plays. It has always been my habit to visualise beforehand my ideal conception of how each of my characters should be played—I expect all play-wrights do this. Only four times has the player surpassed my ideal. Tom Walls did it twice—in *A Cuckoo in the Nest* and *A Cup of Kindness*—Henry Hewitt did it in *Chastity My Brother*, and Catherine Lacey's Mona Cuffe simply wiped the floor with mine. She is a most accomplished actress, not underrated but never duly acclaimed. I think this is chiefly because she suffers from a handicap, rare in the profession, of possessing an extremely modest nature. That can't be helped I suppose; and, anyhow, it is a very sweet nature as well.

Ralph Lynn came back to join Robertson Hare again after the war and I wrote a couple of farces for them. The first of these, *Outrageous Fortune*, was so successful that it managed to achieve quite a long run at the Winter Garden, which at that time had become about as fashionable a resort of the play-going public as what still remained of the Crystal Palace. Ralph was as agile and inventive as ever, but at this period my most prized recollection of him and of his gift for the impromptu had nothing to do with the theatre.

I was visiting him at his house in Surrey and he proposed to drive me several miles to call on his daughter whose husband kept an hotel at Reigate. I had not until then had any experience of Ralph as chauffeur and, though I ought to be the last car-driver to criticise another, I soon had enough. But after several incidents on the road, including, I remember, an ugly tussle and altercation with a funeral, we duly pulled up outside the daughter's husband's hotel. When I say we pulled up we didn't pull up quite in time. The road in front of the hotel was on a slope and at the foot of this slope stood another car of imposing bulk and aspect. Ralph, I think, forgot which of his feet was doing what and accelerated. "Look out, Ralph," I cried, "you'll hit that car." "All right, all right," he replied anxiously; but he nevertheless caught the rear bumper of the big car a telling blow and came to rest.

"Don't say anything," he said.

"No. All the same, I think it's just as well there's nobody in that car."

"Yes; that's what I said—it's all right. Don't say anything."

At that moment the front door of the big car was flung open and a gigantic man prized himself from the driver's seat into the road. He was towering and florid and dressed in a check suit of startling design. He looked like an outsize bookmaker, as indeed he may well have been. He strode towards Ralph, exclaiming as he came, "What the hell do you think you're doing?"—only there was an adjective before the "hell".

Ralph looked up at him with a pitiable smile.

"*I'm* sorry," he said, and then, with a quaver of pathos in his voice, "It's my brakes. *Look* at them. They've been like that for years."

The bookmaker's face swelled into a large crimson balloon. It looked as if it were going to burst. Then it did burst. It burst into laughter. A Lynn answer turneth away wrath.

Charles Hickman, an astute and practical producer, had made a splendid job of *Outrageous Fortune*, and he also dealt with my other Lynn-Hare farce, *Wild Horses*. In preparing this I had unaccountably given Robertson Hare too much to say and too little to suffer. Hickman cut a lot of the Hare cackle during rehearsals, by the end of which the play was twenty minutes too short, which was perhaps just as well, because it was sadly lacking in incident. We took it and tried it out on the Army of Occupation in Germany. A distinguished and dressy audience at military headquarters chortled its approval of the first performance, but, after a fevered consultation with Bill Linnit and Charles Hickman, I had to double back home in order to reconstruct the whole story and rewrite most of the play, plus the docked twenty minutes, in time for its scheduled production in England. I averaged two hours per night in bed for over a fortnight. Eventually, after a good deal of tribulation, we opened at the Aldwych; so the last of my farces was safely delivered at the old maternity home.

It lasted for about six months but never really recovered from an early disaster. When it had been running for three weeks Ralph Lynn had a serious and painful accident. He slipped on a sheet of ice in his garden and dislocated his spine, when he was playing with his dog or some such folly. Personally, I am a stern and uncompromising anti-dog man. I think dogs should be licensed purely for utilitarian purposes, such as leading the blind and conveying flasks of brandy to people who are big enough damned fools to get stranded in Alpine avalanches.

We sold the house at Burnham soon after the war. My daughter had a new home of her own; my sons were away at work and got married before long, so my wife and I moved a couple of miles down the coast to a cottage beside the golf-links at Berrow. We had lived in the Burnham house for thirty years. How settled and contented a home it had been is shown by the fact that my memory takes the outstanding events in its history for granted. But a few odd, trivial incidents and occasions seem to flicker in my mind like stray sunbeams playing in a large deserted room.

Thus, I think—for no particular reason—of a night during our early years there, when a small party of visiting golfers autographed my downstairs lavatory wall. A scandalised cook scrubbed the wall clean in the morning, but I cottoned on to the idea and in course of time that wall became quite a noteworthy exhibition of the autographs of actors, of a limited but engaging selection of actresses, of visiting cricketers who came over from Taunton for a round of golf on Sundays, of Australian cricketers, golfing experts and many other less conspicuous but no less wanted and often far more permanent associates. It was pleasant to feel that even though we quitted the house we at least left behind us a catalogue of its familiar friends and its cheerful guests.

Again I remember and again for no particular reason one of the nights when Robertson-Glasgow was staying with us. We had spent the evening with the boys, playing that delightful game in which you fill a sheet of squared paper with numbers from one to six and with the various ways of getting out at cricket (the bowleds and caughts must always be enclustered with 4's and 6's) and play test matches by stabbing with a pin. When the boys had been bribed to go to bed Robertson-Glasgow and I had the splendid idea of playing a match between Australia and an eleven composed of notable figures in the world's history whom we would particularly relish watching at Lord's or the Oval. I recall that one of my opening batsmen was Beethoven. By judicious stabbing he was run out and returned furiously to the pavilion for nought, being too deaf to hear a call from his partner. It was a remarkable side, including Landru, the French Bluebeard, Sir Redvers Buller, of Boer War fame, and, as wicket-keeper, Mrs. Hemans. I would dearly have loved to have seen that team in action.

One of my sunbeam flickers of recollection lights upon that hardy perennial, our tricycling old gardener, Stacey. I remember him as he stood on the garden path outside my window, having slain a poor old doe-rat bulging with progeny, holding her up by the tail for me to inspect and saying, "Ah, a good catch, she be. Thurr's more'n one rat inside of he."

Another random memory of old Stacey is when he was requested by my wife to uproot and transplant some specimens of botanical growth which were rambling too profusely in her herbaceous border. Stacey did not conceal his contempt for this type of flora but he consented and duly made his report. "I done 'un," he said. "I put 'n back in down along-side'n the bottom fence down behind the rubbish heap. An thurr they can wrangle so furr'n they please."

The cottage at Berrow is a genuine five- or six-hundred-year-old cottage, with a layer of thatch beneath the tiles and with outer walls a yard thick and inner walls made of mud or dung or something—you can't drive a nail into them anyhow. It has horsehair inside its ceilings—this, I have been told, is very beneficial for some reason which I have forgotten; and is nice to have. It has rough-hewn beams and one of those big open fireplaces; and yet it can be furnished with the modern essentials without losing any of its character. From one window upstairs you can see the Quantocks and from another there is a view of the long range of Mendips, with a funny grove of trees shaped like a battleship on one of the ridges. There is honeysuckle over the front porch and withy-trees dotted about in the little garden and some cherry-trees and a very old and distorted apple-tree that spreads its gnarled limbs in several directions, so that when it blossoms in the late Spring it looks like the soul of some old twisted martyr who has at last gained Paradise and has been rather extravagantly garlanded by the angels.

It is altogether too blissful a place to be associated with dismay or anxiety or sorrow. But when we had been there for very few years they came upon us. Even then, in the midst of distress, the little cottage seemed always to enfold us in the compassionate spirit of its wise and enduring tranquillity.

A happy nature, if one is blest with it, does not try to challenge sadness or to try to ignore it. Affection can blend it into becoming a gentle accepted part of happiness itself. One's memory then turns only to those things which were glad, and especially to the glad moments of laughter.

Now, five years later, the cottage is still my home, but when

I leave it for long visits to London and elsewhere I find friendship and welcome wherever I go. At the end of 1952 I returned to Singapore for the first time since 1908. The friends who invited me there have encouraged me to form a habit of returning. Such kindness has been a great boon to one of advancing years and inadequate circulation. My recent Januaries and Februaries have been spent sitting in an open shirt, slacks, comfort and felicity, reading the reports of the coldest night in England for seventy-five years, as issued by that band of hardy experts who seem to endure permanent refrigeration on the Air Ministry roof in London.

So, though my movements can be of interest to very few, I have become like a plump and contented old bird whom I sometimes watch in my cottage garden. He alights on a tree and sits in rumination for a while; then, for some reason of his own, takes wing rather heavily, comes to rest on another tree and sits ruminating there instead. He has his favourite selected perches and goes back to each in turn. But what does he keep ruminating about?

A lot of old men seem to suffer, poor old chaps, from chronic nostalgic dyspepsia or from an odious nagging irritation of comparison. And I don't pretend that I am not sometimes goaded into a sudden passing resentment of some condition or trend or taste of the present time and into giving vent to an expostulation about the triumph of mediocrity or some such acrimonious platitude. But I don't suffer from this so often nowadays. For though it is only fair to recall the richness of past enjoyment the present isn't really so barren as some of those old boys in clubs have decided.

One of their favourite subjects for animadversion and teeth-grinding is the present state of the world of entertainment. Well, they may have some justification, but isn't it rather silly to draw comparisons in an era when entertainment has become the concern of an enormously increased public with new values of its own which are often derived from additional new-fangled sources? Moreover the old growlers are mistaken in assuming that the best must lie always in the past. Did any of them see Emlyn Williams in *Dylan Thomas Growing Up*?

I don't say that I am a judge of the theatre or of entertainment in general; I only say I ought to be. I have been a fairly consistent playgoer for over sixty years, from the time when I saw Coquelin aîné and Sarah Bernhardt in their prime to the present day and have witnessed productions varying in quality and interest from Granville Barker's *Twelfth Night*, with Ainley as Malvolio, to a performance by a Malayan company of *The Merchant of Venice*, in which Shylock, in a sarong and tennis shoes, came before the curtain at the end of Act I and sang "Oh, listen to the band". To recall the theatre of the past is like touring, in imagination, some expansive aquarium and pausing to admire its varied exhibits in turn—rare and beautiful fish, old slow fish, little nippy fish, funny fish; but there are still some splendid specimens in the sea. There is, for instance, one, rather of the porpoise type, named Peter Ustinov, who rises at regular intervals to the surface and disports for my delight.

When I was young, boys and girls, especially girls, used to take a delight in possessing little volumes entitled *Confessions*—they may still do so for all I know. In these volumes ponderous uncles and frivolous chums obligingly stated their favourite actor, actress, book, motto, fruit, painter, poet, dog, play, novelist, sport, composer, vegetable and quotation. Perhaps an autobiography ought to provide the reader with some such catalogue of the author's particular attachments. I hope not. My partiality for *Fortune*, an ignored and long forgotten masterpiece of humour by J. C. Snaith, and for Arthur Sullivan and Cox's Orange Pippins and Damon Runyon can surely be of little concern to anybody except myself. But one item I must in duty bound extract from the "confessions" list. Poet.

I said something at the beginning about Robert Browning —the supreme and constant delight and comfort of my latter years. In one of his poems, *By the Fireside*, he wrote of

> "—an age so blest that by its side
> Youth seems the waste instead."

I know what he meant.

INDEX

Abbey School, Beckenham, 1-3, 8-9
Abel, R., 173
Abercrombie, Lascelles, 59
Adam, Ronald, 208
Adelaide, 176
Adelphi Theatre, 43
Adrian, Max, 208
A. E., 59
Agate, James, 150, 206, 217
Ainley, Henry, 157-8, 243
Air Ministry, 223-6
Aldwych Theatre, 108, 123-33, 135, 138-42, 145, 148-71, 197, 239
Alexander, Sir George, 43
Alice-sit-by-the-Fire, 69
Ambrose Applejohn's Adventure, 100-1
Ames, L. E. G., 174
April the Fifth (*racehorse*), 195
Aquarium, The London, 47
Armstrong, W. W., 173
Arnaud, Yvonne, 131-2, 159, 203, 217
Asche, Oscar, 43
Asquith, Countess of Oxford and, 57
Attwill, Lionel, 165
Australia, 159-60, 169, 172-90
Ayer, Nat. D., 116

Badminton Club, 123
Baird, Dorothea, 58, 90-1, 96
Baker, Frank, 56-7, 65
Balcon, Sir Michael, 201
Banana Ridge, 191, 215-22

Barbour, Joyce, 222-3
Bardsley, W., 178
Barker, H. Granville, 45, 243
Barnes:
    Flight-Lieut. Douglas, 75-8
    Winifred, 114
Barrie, Sir James, 69, 98
Bates, Thorpe, 114
Batley, Dorothy, 217
Batty, Archibald, 169
Beardsley, Aubrey, 53
Beatty, Earl, 79, 84
Beck, J. B., 194
Bells, The, 91
Bennett, Arnold, 52-3
Berrow, 239, 241-2
Berry, W. H., 116
Bigsworth, Flight-Lieut., 79
Bit of a Test, A, 127, 169
Blast, 70-1
Blondin, 18
Blow, Sydney, 109-11, 156
Bodley Head, The, 47, 50-72, 80, 88-94, 193, 200
Bourchier, Arthur, 43, 82
Bourne, Dale, 193-4
Bradbeer, Elizabeth, 118
Bradman, Sir Donald, 174, 178, 180, 187, 190-2
Branston, G. T., 12
Bright, R. Golding, 96-8, 100-1, 110, 113-14, 118-22, 126, 144, 157, 165, 197, 201, 203, 208, 210-11, 220

245

Brisbane, 175–8, 186
Bristol Rep., 205–6
B.B.C., 209
Brockwell, W., 5
Brough, Mary, 132–3, 138, 145, 152, 154, 161, 169–71
Browning, Robert, 9, 123, 244
Brunner, Sir Felix and Lady, 91
Burges, Dan, 151
Burnham-on-Sea, 89–100, 118–9, 129, 135–7, 143–4, 146–7, 192–3, 195–6, 207, 222, 232, 239
By the Fireside, 244
Bywaters, F., 111, 156

Campbell, Herbert, 16–7
Cantor, Eddie, 204
Carlton Theatre, 167–8
Castle, Irene and Vernon, 92–4, 105
Censorship, 132, 234–6
Chamberlain, Neville, 222
Chance of a Night-time, The, 167
Chappell and Co., 48
Chaplin, Charles, 16, 20
Chapman:
    A. P. F., 174, 176–8, 186
    Frederic, 51, 63–4
Charterhouse, 3, 9–12, 193–4, 221, 223
Chastity, My Brother, 206–7
Chesterton, G. K., 49–51, 55, 193
Chingford Air Station, 76, 82–5, 88
Churchill:
    Diana, 205
    Sir Winston, 48, 74–6, 78
Cinquevalli, 48
Clarke-Smith, D. A., 208
Cochrane, Sir Charles B., 168
Coleridge, Ethel, 138, 141, 161, 217
Collier, Hon. John, 48
Cooper, Gladys, 222
Coward, Noel, 104–5, 197

Criterion Theatre, 100, 102, 105, 110–11
Crippen, H. H., 18
Crystal Palace, 17–8
Cuckoo in the Nest, A, 118, 120–33
Cup of Kindness, A, 127, 138, 161–2, 205

Dagnall, T. C., 100–2, 110–11, 118
Dance, George Co., 115
Davidson, John, 59
Davies, A. Gardner, 220–1
Deslys, Gaby, 48
Dippers, The, 94–112, 114, 118–20, 125, 143, 167
Dirty Work, 127, 169
Disney, Walt, 95, 232
Dowson, Ernest, 59
Dramatists' Club, 36
Drayton, Alfred, 214, 219, 221–2
Dresden, 22–4
Dreyfus, 47
Drury Lane Theatre, 16–7
Duckworth, George, 174, 179
Duleepsinhji, K. S., 191
du Maurier:
    Daphne, 122–3
    Sir Gerald, 44–5, 91, 93, 122–4, 173, 197
Dunn, Robert, 128, 152
Dunfee, Jack, 214, 234
Dylan Thomas Growing Up, 243

Ellis, J. C. R., 3
Elstree Film Studios, 201
Embassy Theatre, 207–9
Empire Theatre, 113–6, 120, 213
Esmond, H. V., 19

Fane, F. L., 12
Fernald, John, 208
First Mrs. Fraser, The, 157

Firth, E. L., 12
Fishmongers' Company, 212, 218
Flag Lieutenant, The, 104
Flanagan, Bud, 16
Flemyng, Robert, 218
Follies, The, 46
For Valour, 206
Forbes-Robertson, Sir J., 44
Foreign Affairs, 216
Fortune, 243
Fortune Theatre, 158-9
Fram, The, 197
France:
  Anatole, 63-7, 91
  Charles V., 48, 124, 205
Freeman, A. P., 174
Fresnay, Pierre, 209-11

Galsworthy, John, 45
Garrick Club, 142, 157
Garrick Theatre, 43, 236
Geary, George, 174-5, 179
Gerald, 122-3
Gibbons, Carroll, 163-4
Gieves' Ltd., 81
Giffen, G., 173
Gilbert:
  H. A., 12
  Sir W. S., 50, 134
Gilderdale, Miss, 27-8
Gillette, William, 20
Gingold, Hermione, 107
Goldwyn, Samuel, 205-6
Grace, W. G., 5, 18, 173
Graham, Harry, 117
Greensboro, 232
Gregory, J. M., 177
Gresham's School, 212
Grimmett, C. V., 190
Grossmith, Lawrence, 121-7
  Weedon, 121
Gulliver, G. J., 1-3, 5-10

Gwenn, Edmund, 197

Hackett, Walter, 126
Hale:
  Binnie, 106-7, 111, 113, 148, 217,
    220, 223
  Robert, 213
Hamley's Ltd., 85
Hammond, W. R., 174, 180, 187,
  189
Hardwicke, Sir Cedric, 197
Hardy, Thomas, 56, 72,
Hare, J. Robertson, 133, 138-40,
  145, 155, 161, 169-71, 214, 222,
  232-7
Harris, C. A., 49-50, 55, 119
Harrowing, R., 3
Harvey, Morris, 114-6
Hawtrey, Sir Charles, 15, 19, 44,
  91-6, 98-107, 110-11, 143, 173
Hayes (*Kent*), 95-6, 143
Haymarket Theatre, 43
Hayward, T., 13, 173
Heald, Sir Lionel, 225
Hendon Air Station, 64, 79-80, 193
Hendren, E., 174, 177, 179, 189-90
Henry, O., 62, 200, 232
Henson, Leslie, 137
Her Majesty's Theatre, 43, 58
Hewitt, Halford, 194
  Henry, 169, 208, 237
Hickman, Charles, 238
Hicks, Sir Seymour, 43-4, **197**
Hill, Clem, 82, 183, 187
Hippodrome, The London, 47
Hoare, Douglas, 109-11, 125
Hobbs, Sir J. B., 5, 174, 177-8, **185,**
  187-91, 193
Hood Seck, 34-5, 41
Hooman, C. V. L., 12, **194**
Hooper, C. H., 212-4
Hope-Wallace, Philip, 227

Hornblow, Arthur, junr., 204-5
How We Recovered the Ashes, 172
Hutton, Sir L., 13, 221-2
Huxley, Leonard, 10

Ipoh, 38-9
Irving-
  Elizabeth (*Lady Brunner*), 91
  Sir Henry, 14, 18
  H. B., 43-4, 83, 91-2, 200
  Mrs. H. B., 58, 90-1, 96
  Laurence, 44
  Laurence, H., 83-4, 89-92, 94, 96,
    163, 207, 218, 220, 223-4
  Mrs. Laurence H., 92, 163, 207
It Pays to Advertise, 123, 125-6, 153

Jackson:
  A., 178-80
  Hon. F. S., 173
Jacobs, W. W., 48
James, Gordon, 133, 138, 150-1, 161
Jardine, D. R., 174, 187-8
Jessop, G. L., 5, 173
Johns, Mervyn, 205-6, 217
Johnson, Jack, 75
Jones and Evans, Messrs., 43
Justice, 45

Kemp-Welch, M., 12
Kern, Jerome D., 107-8
King, 73, 88
Kippax, A. F., 179, 186-7, 189
Kingsway Theatre, 104
Kove, Kenneth, 153, 161-2
Kuala Lumpur, 38-9

Lacey, Catherine, 234, 236-7
Lane:
  Sir Allen, 200-1
  John, 47, 51-72, 80-1, 88, 94,
    118, 198-200
  Mrs. John, 53, 200

Larwood, H., 174, 177, 186-7
Laughton, Charles, 197
Leacock, Stephen, 60-3, 198-9, 201
Leacock Book, The, 198-9
le Gallienne, Richard, 59
Léhar, Franz, 113-6
Leno, Dan, 16-7
Lewis, Wyndham, 70
Leyland, M., 174, 189, 221-2
Lindo, Olga, 217
Line upon Line, 7-8
Linnit, S. E., 214, 217-18, 221,
    234-5
Literary Lapses, 60
Livesey, Roger, 133
Locke, William, J., 55-6
Logan, Stanley, 165
Löhr, Marie, 205
Longhurst, Henry, 194
Longstaffe, V. C., 194
Lonsdale, Frederick, 158
Lord Chamberlain's Office, 132,
    234-5
Lord's, 172, 191
Lorne, Constance, 217, 236-7
Lucifer in Starlight, 72
Luker, Annie, 47
Lyceum Theatre, 19
Lynn, Ralph, 124, 129-31, 133-9,
    142, 150-6, 161-2, 164-71, 182,
    201, 203, 205-6, 223, 237-9
Lynn Sydney, 133, 138, 150-1,
    161

McCabe, S. J., 191
Macartney, C. G., 172-3, 184
McFee, William, 108
Mackenzie, J., 37, 194
Madras House, The, 45
Mailey, A. A., 184-6, 190, 192-3,
    223
Malacca, 34-9, 42, 194

Marconi, 5
Martin, Mary, 106
Mary, H.M. Queen, 165
Matthews, A. E., 69
May:
  P. B. H., 12
  Phil, 48
Maude, Cyril, 15, 43, 91, 101–4
Mead, C. P., 174
Melbourne, 172–3, 176, 178–9, 186–90, 195
Merchant of Venice, The, 82, 243
Meredith, George, 72
Merriam, F. S., 82
Meynell, Alice, 59
Middlesex C. C. C., 172
Miller:
  Gilbert, 165–6
  K. L., 13
Ministry of Information, 226–7
Misalliance, 45
Mischief, 159, 167–8
Mollison, William, 210–11
Monckton, Lionel, 24
Monsieur Vincent, 209
Montero, 35
Moore, Decima, 17, 19
  Eva, 19
Morgan, Andrew, 233
  Josephine, 159, 220, 222
Morris, C. Maesmore, 176–7, 189
Morrison, J. S. F., 193–4
Morton, Clive, 169
Mouncey:
  D. B. W., 89, 95, 107, 220
  Mrs. D. B. W., 89, 95, 107
Munro, H. H., 72
My Financial Career, 60

Nero, 58
New Gallery Cinema, 164
Night Like This, A., 127, 164–5

Noble, M. A., 183, 187
Nonsense Novels, 60
Noon, Jas, 10
Novello, Ivor, 83–4, 104–5
Nun's Veiling, 209–10

O Chye Lah, 39–40
O Mistress Mine, 209–11
O'Bryen, W. J., 214
Ode in May, 57
Odell, O. F., 46
Oldfield, W. A., 188
On Approval, 158
One Summer's Day, 19
O'Regan, Kathleen, 217, 219
Orleans Club, 100, 103
Oval, The, 5, 188, 191, 193

Pacey, 157, 170
Paris, 134–5
Parker, Cecil, 205
Passing Show, The, 198
Payne, C. A. L., 12
Pelissier, Harry, 46
Pellatt, Thomas, 159
Penguin Books, 200–1
Perplexed Wife, The, 206, 217
Peter Pan, 98
Peter the Painter, 48
Petilleau, M., 10
Phillips, Stephen, 57–9
Pinero, Sir Arthur W., 19, 35–6, 43, 45, 72, 92–3, 96, 120
Plunder, 127, 153–60, 165
Pouishnoff, 99
Printemps, Yvonne, 209–11
Public Schools' Club, 67, 81
Pulford, Conway, 85

Radford, Basil, 243
Radio Luxembourg, 209
Ranjitsinhji, K. S. (*The Jam Sahib*), 5, 191

Redmond, John, 62
Raymond, Jack, 201
Reynolds, Thomas, 113–4
Roberts:
  John, 18
  Margaret, 66–7
Robertson-Glasgow, R. C., 193, 223, 240
Rogers, J. Innes, 30–2
Rookery Nook, 108, 118–20, 126–7, 135–40, 148–9, 152, 158, 164
Rothamstead, 143
Royal College of Surgeons, 25
Royal Court Theatre, Liverpool, 108
Royal Flying Corps, 79
Royal Naval Air Service, 73, 81
Ruff's Guide to the Turf, 98
Runyon, Damon, 243
Ryder, J., 187

Sacks, J. L., 112–7, 119
St. James's Theatre, 43, 209–11
"Saki," 70
Salome, 53
Sanders, George, 205
Sandham, A., 48, 193
Sandow, 47
Savoy Hotel, 66–7
Schüch von, 23
Scotland Yard, 94, 153–6
Scott, Margaretta, 169, 208
Sea View Hotel, Singapore, 13
Second in Command, The, 104
Second, Mrs. Tanqueray, The, 92
Secret Life of Walter Mitty, The, 14
Shaw, G. B., 45, 98
She Follows Me About, 234–7
Sherlock Holmes (play), 20–1
Shore, W. Teignmouth, 46–7, 72
Shotter, Winifred, 27, 137–8, 145, 150, 161, 164, 167–8, 201, 217

Silver Box, The, 45
Sims, George R., 48
Singapore, 32–5, 42, 48, 85, 242
Slater, O., 10
Smith:
  Sir C. Aubrey, 69
  Sir F. E. (*Lord Birkenhead*), 48
  Thorne, 108
Smith-Bingham, Mr. and Mrs., 78–9
Snaith, J. C., 243
South Pacific, 106
Sousa, J. P., 48
Spotted Dick, 222
Stableforth, W. H., 30–1
Stacey, W., 240–1
Staples, S., 174
Stephens, E. Walls, 212
Strand Theatre, 191–2, 222
Strauss, Richard, 24
Strife, 45
Sub-Contractor, The, 196
Sullivan, Sir Arthur, 243
Sunshine Sketches of a Little Town, 63
Surrey C. C. C., 172
Sutcliffe, H., 174, 187–9
Sydney, N.S.W., 173–6, 178–83, 186
Sykes, Philip J., 227

Tait, T., 43
Tate, M. W., 174
Tempest, Dame Marie, 157
Terry:
  Ellen, 69
  Fred, 43
Thark, 127, 149–53
Theatrical Garden Party, 197–8
Thompson, Edith, 111–2, 156
Three Graces, The, 113–6
Tichborne, Lord and Lady, 99, 103
Tons of Money, 125, 131–2, 137

Travers:
  Benjamin, P.R.C.S., 25-6
  Ben, junior (*son*), 96, 159, 220, 233
  Daniel Burton (*son*), 159, 220, 233
  Frank (*brother*), 30, 72, 80
  J. Linsday, 30
  J. Lindsay, junior, 75
  Joseph and Sons, Ltd., 22, 29-32, 41
  Margaret (*mother*), 5, 7, 22, 41
  Violet (*wife*), 88, 91, 96, 129, 143-4, 146-8, 211, 220, 233
  Walter Francis (*father*), 15, 22, 28, 30-1, 72, 109, 148-9
Tree, Sir H. Beerbohm, 43, 58, 205
Trelawney of the Wells, 45
Trent Bridge, 190
Trimmingham, Ernest, 112
Trott, G. F. S., 173
Trumble, H., 173, 183-4, 187
Trumper, V. T., 13, 175
Tucker, Betty, 136-7
Tuckey, C. O., 11
Turkey Time, 127, 139, 166-7
Twelfth Night, 243
Tyldesley, E., 174

Up in Mabel's Room, 99, 103
Ustinov, Peter, 243

Vanbrugh, Violet and Irene, 15
Vaudeville Theatre, 43
Victorian Cricket Association, 172-3, 188
Virgin, H., 23-4

Waller:
  Lewis, 43
  Wallett, 192

Walls, Tom, 26, 69, 123-42, 148-71, 193, 201-3, 205, 209, 220, 222-3, 237
Waring, Herbert, 156
Warneford, Flight-Sub-Lieut. 79-80
Warner, Sir P. F., 172, 177
Washington, D. C., 228-33
Watson, Sir William, 56-7, 59
Webb, Captain, 18
Webster, Tom, 190-1
Weekes, Rev. C., 10
Weld-Blundell, Frederic, 85
Wells, H. G., 52
Wensley, Chief Constable, 155-6
Weyman, Stanley, 42
Whistler, J. M., 50
White:
  J. C., 174, 187, 189-90
  W. Hyde, 169
Wilcox, Herbert, 163, 167, 201
Wild Horses, 163, 238-9
Wilde, Oscar, 50, 53
Wilkinson, E., 30-1
Williams, Emlyn, 243
Wilson, J. G., 43
Wimperis, Arthur, 116
Windsor, H.R.H. the Duke of, 167, 210
Winter Garden Theatre, 237
Wittich von, Frau, 23
Woodfull, W. M., 177-8, 187
Woods, Margaret L., 59
  S. M. J., 99, 172
Woolley, Frank, 82
Wright, Marie, 161
Wyndham's Theatre, 123, 197
Wynyard, E. G., 12

Yellow Book, The, 53